DECODING ROGER WILLIAMS

DECODING ROGER WILLIAMS

The Lost Essay of Rhode Island's Founding Father

Linford D. Fisher
J. Stanley Lemons
Lucas Mason-Brown

BAYLOR UNIVERSITY PRESS

Cover Design by Charles Brock, Faceout Studio
Cover Image is a sample of the Roger Williams shorthand, taken from the
"mystery book" at the John Carter Brown Library, which is subtitled
"An Essay Towards the Reconciling of Differences Among Christians."
Courtesy of the John Carter Brown Library at Brown University.
Book Design by Diane Smith

A slightly different version of "Roger Williams on Indian Conversion"
is reproduced with the permission of the *William and Mary Quarterly*,
where it first appeared as Linford D. Fisher and Lucas Mason-Brown,
" 'By Treachery and Seduction': Indian Baptism and Conversion in the
Roger Williams Code," *William and Mary Quarterly*, 3rd ser., 71, no. 2
(April 2014).

Library of Congress Cataloging-in-Publication Data

Fisher, Linford D.
  Decoding Roger Williams : the lost essay of Rhode Island's founding
father / Linford D. Fisher, J. Stanley Lemons, and Lucas Mason-Brown.
  212 pages cm
  Includes bibliographical references and index.
  ISBN 978-1-4813-0104-6 (hardback : alk. paper)
  1. Baptism—History of doctrines—17th century. 2. Williams, Roger,
1604?-1683. 3. Eliot, John, 1604–1690. 4. Norcott, John, –1676. 5.
Williams, Roger, 1604?–1683. Key into the language of America. I. Title.
  BV811.3.F57 2014
  234'.1612--dc23
                                    2013049571

CONTENTS

Figures and Maps
[vii]

Acknowledgments
[ix]

Foreword
Ted Widmer
[xi]

Part I
A Key into the Language of Roger Williams:
Cracking and Interpreting the Roger Williams Code
[1]

Part II
"A Brief Reply to a Small Book Written by John Eliot" (ca. 1680)
Roger Williams
[71]

Part III
Baptism Discovered Plainly and Faithfully,
According to the Word of God (London 1675 [1672])
John Norcott
[113]

Part IV
A Brief Answer to a Small Book Written by John Norcot
Against Infant-Baptisme (1679)
John Eliot

[153]

Suggestions for Further Reading and Research
[181]

Index
[191]

FIGURES AND MAPS

FIGURES

Figure 1	Sample of Roger Williams' shorthand	2
Figure 2	Portrait of Roger Williams	4
Figure 3	External view of *An Essay Towards the Reconciling of Differences Among Christians*	5
Figure 4	Title page of *An Essay Towards the Reconciling of Differences Among Christians*	6
Figure 5	Shorthand vowel example	8
Figure 6	Improvised shorthand example	9
Figure 7	Longhand flag example	9
Figure 8	Shorthand alphabet	12
Figure 9	Shorthand vowel system	12
Figure 10	Williams' shorthand sample transcribed from Heylyn's *Cosmographie*	13
Figure 11	Translation sample #1	14
Figure 12	Translation sample #2	14
Figure 13	Translation sample #3	15
Figure 14	Translation sample #4	15
Figure 15	Translation sample #5	16
Figure 16	Translation sample #6	16
Figure 17	Corresponding printed text in Heylyn's *Cosmographie*	17
Figure 18	*Mamusse Wunneetupanatamwe Up-Biblium God* title page	41
Figures 19–40	Pages from Williams, "A Brief Reply to a Small Book Written by John Eliot"	89–111

FIGURES (cont.)

Figure 41   John Norcott, *Baptism Discovered Plainly and
              Faithfully, According to the Word of God* title page   116
Figure 42   John Eliot, *A Brief Answer to a Small Book Written
              by John Norcot Against Infant-Baptisme* title page   156

MAPS

Map 1   Southern New England in 1650   18
Map 2   Southern New England in 1680   40

ACKNOWLEDGMENTS

It has been a singular opportunity to collaborate on a project like this. Many people graciously gave of their time and shared information with us along the way, including Ted Widmer and Kimberly Nusco at the John Carter Brown Library; Steven Lubar, Hal Cook, Tim Harris, Jeff Hoffstein, and Eugene Charniak at Brown University; Frances Henderson at Oxford University; and Curtis Freeman at Duke Divinity School. Special thanks to the original undergraduate decoding team at Brown University who first kicked off this project: Simon Liebling, Katherine Mead, and Christopher Norris-LeBlanc. Funding for various parts of the project was provided by a Humanities Initiative Teaching and Research Grant from Brown University, along with a Summer Research Grant from the John Carter Brown Library. Several people read through the book manuscript and offered valuable suggestions, including William Brackney, David D. Hall, Tim Harris, and Adrian Weimer, in addition to the anonymous readers for Baylor University Press. Several pieces of the introductory essay were presented at the John Carter Brown Library, Duke Divinity School, Roger Williams University, and the First Baptist Church in America (sponsored by the Roger Williams National Memorial and the National Parks Service), where attentive audiences asked probing questions. Jo Fisher helpfully copyedited the entire manuscript, and Lynn Carlson created the maps of New England. Images of the Roger Williams shorthand are reproduced courtesy of the John Carter Brown Library.

The authors thank the editors and staff at Baylor University Press, in particular Carey Newman, Diane Smith, and Jordan Rowan Fannin, who graciously guided this project from submission to publication.

FOREWORD

Ted Widmer

It is not the easiest thing in the world to surprise an institution that knows itself as well as the John Carter Brown Library. Each book is beautifully catalogued by devoted librarians. Detailed files are kept on the provenance of each item in the collection. Scholars then pore over the Library's treasures, adding to the store of bibliographic information. Knowledge is accumulated slowly and painstakingly, by well-trained professionals with deep experience in the field. The basic formula has been in place for over a century, when the holdings of a private collection were transferred to a building on the Brown campus, for the benefit of future research.

Yet all of these assumptions were thrown aside in the spring of 2012, when a team of undergraduates unveiled a breathtaking series of revelations about a document in the library that no previous scholar had been able to decipher.

For generations, the JCB staff had referred to this document as "The Mystery Book." That was a fitting description for an item that was book-like in many ways, a 234-page quarto, but defied easy categorization. The Mystery Book was several books in one—a printed book (albeit with the title page missing), and also a manuscript, written in a convoluted hand, around the printed words of the book. But there was a catch—the manuscript was in a complex code that had never been cracked.

The mystery deepened, with the strong supposition that the hand in question belonged to Roger Williams. That came from an unsigned note attached to the book and dated November 11, 1817. It read, in part, "The margin is filled with Short Hand Characters, Dates, Names of places &c. &c. by Roger Williams or it appears to be his hand Writing. . . . brot me from Widow Tweedy by Nicholas Brown Jr."

These were tantalizing clues. They also threw the question into a special sphere of local importance, touching upon the identity of both Brown University (named after a gift from the same Nicholas Brown Jr.) and Rhode Island (founded and forever stamped by Roger Williams). Arguably, no other state has as profound an identification with a single founding figure—Pennsylvania comes closest, but in that case the colony was founded by a gentleman living in England, whose influence came from his proximity to the king. In Rhode Island, the story is personal, and stems from the heroism of a founding figure who displayed both physical and intellectual courage in his flight from persecution, and his creation of a refuge for other free-thinkers.

For all of these reasons, the question of what Roger Williams (if it was he) meant to say (if his code could be broken) over the pages of this book (if we knew what it was) was meaningful. But for centuries, no one had been able to crack the code. Even Nicholas Brown Jr. had no idea what the book-manuscript said. It was written over a century before he acquired it, and for all he knew, it might have been written in Aramaic.

As director of the library, I had taken a personal interest in the book, and spoke about its mysteries to local audiences. But I had no plan for solving the mystery. That began to change in the fall of 2010, when a hard-headed diplomat, Bill Twaddell, heard one of my lectures. With a tenacity worthy of a seasoned ambassador, Bill began to probe the question deeply. At his urging, the library began to convene gatherings of scholars with related expertise—mathematicians who might help us with the code, and English and history professors with background in the seventeenth century. These were fascinating conversations. But the mystery remained a mystery.

That began to change, however, when a team of Brown University undergraduates caught the scent. One of them, Lucas Mason-Brown, a coauthor of this book, began to reveal to us, over the winter of 2011–2012, that they were cracking the code. In the spring he presented the team's findings in a dramatic lecture that had some of the qualities of a fast-breaking news conference. Indeed, the local press covered it prominently the next day. Our state founder was saying something new to us, for the first time since the seventeenth century. Roger Williams speaks! Stop the presses!

As director of the library, I was thrilled by this adventure. It represented everything I believe in—that the best history is collaborative, that young people should be invited into the conversation, and that an institution like the JCB is in the business of eternity—building bridges

between the centuries. That the public took such an interest in the revelations validated the work of all of the scholars and librarians who had
preserved The Mystery Book until its decipherment was finally possible.
It was as if we had brought some finality to a restless soul, eternally
questing—and a close reading of Williams confirms that the argument
was never entirely over.

After the hubbub died down, the team needed to return to the work
of due diligence and exacting scholarship, and that is why this publication
is so valuable. Linford D. Fisher, J. Stanley Lemons, and Lucas Mason-
Brown have presented the new writings of Roger Williams in their full
context. All scholars owe them a debt of gratitude for their patient work,
bringing The Mystery Book out of the shadows and into the light of day.
That it took more than three centuries does not diminish the reward.
The men and women who founded New England knew that they (and by
extension, we) were in it for the long haul. In the last long letter that he
wrote, to Simon Bradstreet, Williams signed off, "Eternitie (O Eternitie)
is our Busines."[1]

*Ted Widmer is the assistant to the president for special projects at Brown Univer-
sity. From 2006 to 2012 he was the Beatrice and Julio Mario Santo Domingo
Director and Librarian of the John Carter Brown Library.*

---

[1] "To Governor Simon Bradstreet, 6 May 1682," in Glenn W. LaFantasie, *The Correspondence of Roger Williams* (Lebanon, N.H.: University Press of New England, 1988), 2:778.

I

A KEY INTO THE LANGUAGE OF ROGER WILLIAMS

Cracking and Interpreting the Roger Williams Code

Around 1680, in the twilight of his life, Roger Williams picked up his polemical pen once again to sketch out his last major treatise.[1] Because paper was scarce, he selected a book from his library, flipped to a section with blank space in the margins, and began to write in a shorthand script that he had learned as a young boy.[2] The resulting marginalia essay never made it into print, however. Williams died in 1683, and the mysterious scrawl with its irregular strokes remained undeciphered and the essay's meaning hidden to the world.

In the past, various scholars have attempted to decipher this script, yet it remained an enigma until recently. In the fall of 2011, a team of undergraduate researchers at Brown University, supported and advised by an interdisciplinary group of scholars, came together to undertake the ambitious project of cracking the code and translating the marginalia.[3] In early 2012 one member of the team, using a combination of statistical attacks and paleographic clues, cracked the code.[4] Soon thereafter, historical evidence confirming Williams' authorship was uncovered.[5] The decoding revealed an entirely new essay by Williams, the contents of which were previously unknown.

Williams' shorthand essay was part of an ongoing early modern Protestant theological debate between those who believed the Bible supported the baptism of infants and those who opposed it on the grounds that believer's baptism was the only biblically defensible position. Jumping into a pamphlet war that was already underway,[6] the English Baptist minister John Norcott in 1672 wrote a defense of believer's baptism titled *Baptism Discovered Plainly and Faithfully, According to the Word of God.*[7] The book proved to be immensely popular; it was reprinted in 1675, 1694, 1700, and

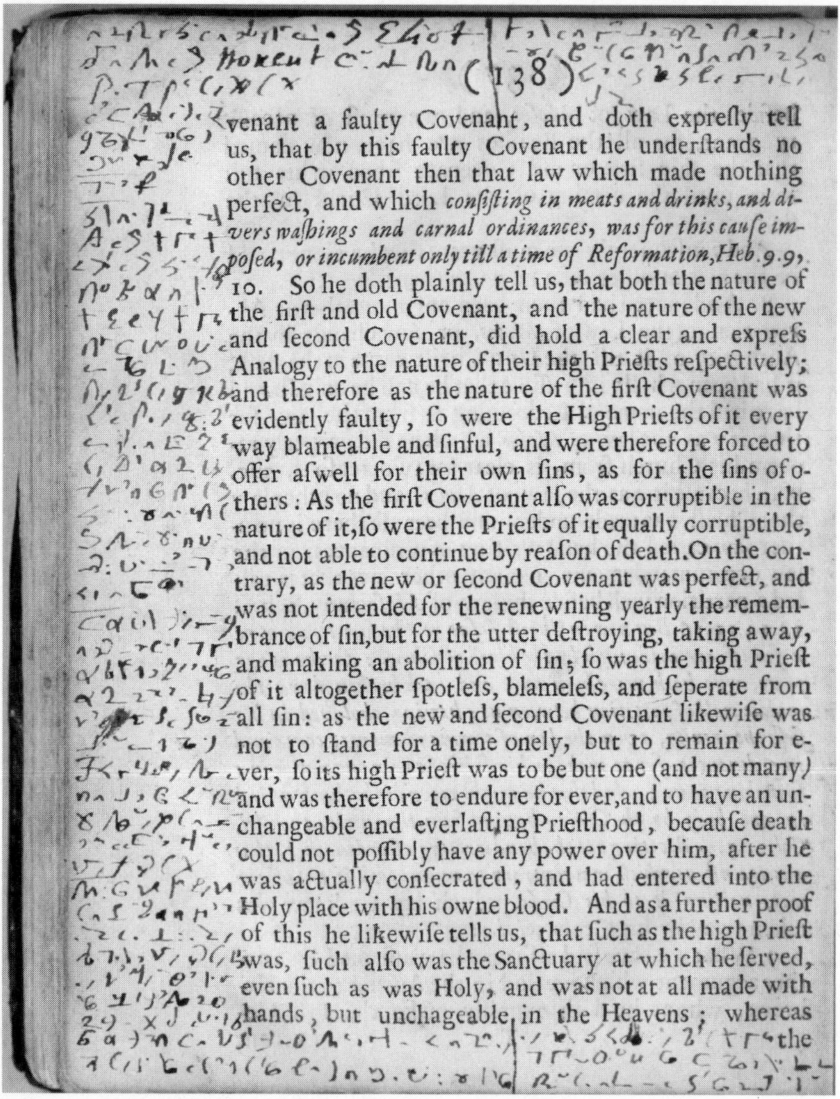

(138)

venant a faulty Covenant, and doth exprefly tell us, that by this faulty Covenant he underftands no other Covenant then that law which made nothing perfect, and which *confifting in meats and drinks, and divers wafhings and carnal ordinances, was for this caufe impofed, or incumbent only till a time of Reformation, Heb.9.9,* 10. So he doth plainly tell us, that both the nature of the firft and old Covenant, and the nature of the new and fecond Covenant, did hold a clear and exprefs Analogy to the nature of their high Priefts refpectively; and therefore as the nature of the firft Covenant was evidently faulty, fo were the High Priefts of it every way blameable and finful, and were therefore forced to offer afwell for their own fins, as for the fins of others: As the firft Covenant alfo was corruptible in the nature of it, fo were the Priefts of it equally corruptible, and not able to continue by reafon of death. On the contrary, as the new or fecond Covenant was perfect, and was not intended for the renewning yearly the remembrance of fin, but for the utter deftroying, taking away, and making an abolition of fin; fo was the high Prieft of it altogether fpotlefs, blamelefs, and feperate from all fin: as the new and fecond Covenant likewife was not to ftand for a time onely, but to remain for ever, fo its high Prieft was to be but one (and not many) and was therefore to endure for ever, and to have an unchangeable and everlafting Priefthood, becaufe death could not poffibly have any power over him, after he was actually confecrated, and had entered into the Holy place with his owne blood. And as a further proof of this he likewife tells us, that fuch as the high Prieft was, fuch alfo was the Sanctuary at which he ferved, even fuch as was Holy, and was not at all made with hands, but unchageable, in the Heavens ; whereas the

FIGURE 1
Sample of Roger Williams' shorthand. Taken from An Essay Towards the Reconciling of Differences Among Christians, *p. 138.*
Courtesy of the John Carter Brown Library at Brown University.

almost a dozen more times in the following century, with reprintings continuing into the twentieth century in several additional languages.[8] A copy of Norcott's treatise fell into the hands of John Eliot, the Roxbury, Massachusetts, minister and well-known missionary to New England Natives, who in 1679 published a pointed rebuttal of Norcott's views, titled *A Brief Answer to a Small Book Written by John Norcot Against Infant-Baptisme* (1679).[9] Eliot's book clearly provoked the elderly Roger Williams, for some time after reading Eliot's *A Brief Answer*, Williams sat down and produced a draft in his modified shorthand of a point-by-point refutation of Eliot's defense of infant baptism, titled "A Brief Reply to a Small Book Written by John Eliot."[10]

In many ways, it is unsurprising to find Williams inserting himself into yet another theological controversy, since he devoted his life to defending the principles he believed in, no matter how unpopular these were among his ministerial colleagues and government authorities. Williams (ca. 1603–1683) was born and raised in London, where in his teen years he came to the attention of England's great seventeenth-century jurist Sir Edward Coke. He became the amanuensis of Coke in his dealings with the king and the courts. Educated at Pembroke College, Cambridge, Williams increasingly sympathized with Puritans and Separatists who sought to reform more fully the Church of England. Under growing pressure to conform more completely to the religious practices of the Church of England (in particular, the use of the Prayer Book), in December 1631 Williams joined a growing stream of Puritan- and Separatist-minded ministers heading for New England. Upon arriving in Boston, Williams immediately clashed with local religious and civil authorities over the issue of separation from the Church of England. During the following four years, he challenged leaders about the propriety of civil magistrates exerting power over spiritual matters and the legitimacy of the king's land grants for Native lands. Williams' refusal to acquiesce culminated in October 1635 with his trial and banishment. He fled south to the Narragansett Bay in February 1636 and founded Providence that spring.

Williams' religious views and church affiliations evolved during his first decade in New England. In the years following his departure from Massachusetts, he was briefly a "Baptist," during which time he gathered the first Baptist church in the New World in 1638, in Providence, Rhode Island. In 1643 Williams traveled to London to secure a patent for "Providence Plantations in Narragansett Bay in New England," which scholars have often seen as the first completely secular government in modern history. While in England he published his most popular book, *A Key into*

· Roger Williams ·
a study from the Bust in the Hall of Fame, by McNeil

FIGURE 2
Portrait of Roger Williams. Drawn by C. Dodge in 1936 from a bust of Roger Williams in the Hall of Fame for Great Americans at Bronx Community College. Williams is presented accurately here as a Puritan, with plain clothes and a "Roundhead" haircut. Reproduced with permission from the First Baptist Church in America.

the Language of America (1643), a book about New England Natives for which he was widely known and admired in his lifetime. Before returning to New England, Williams published *The Bloudy Tenent of Persecution for Cause of Conscience* (1644), which provoked immediate outrage at the time but garnered the admiration of later generations. For the rest of his life, he was almost continually engaged in the governance of the colony and the town of Providence. Williams generally had good relations with local Native groups and worked hard to keep the peace with them for nearly forty years. Unlike John Eliot, the missionary-minister from Roxbury, Massachusetts, Williams did not encourage or pursue a comprehensive evangelization program among the Natives in his colony.

One of the greatest disappointments in Williams' life was King Philip's War (1675–1676), which saw the fiery end of his efforts to maintain peace with local Natives.[11] The United Colonies (Massachusetts Bay, Plymouth, and Connecticut) brought the war to Rhode Island by launching a bloody preemptive attack on the Narragansetts in their fortress in southern Rhode Island in December 1675.[12] The war then spread across the colony (except Aquidneck Island) and resulted in the destruction of all colonial settlements on the west side of Narragansett Bay. Native bands burned Providence on March 29, 1676, including Williams' home, resulting in the loss of unknown numbers of books, documents, letters, and sermons. The aged Williams found himself in a new role, serving as a cocaptain of the Providence town militia and, after the war, chairing a committee that assigned various lengths of servitude to captured Natives to compensate for damages.[13]

Williams published many significant tracts and treatises during his lifetime, many of them with a polemical purpose in mind. In addition to a lengthy series of printed exchanges with Boston minister John Cotton in the 1640s and 1650s, Williams also published a book against the Quakers (with whom he disagreed, even as he believed in their rights to full religious freedom) in 1676 titled *George Fox Digg'd out of his Burrowes*. Williams kept up a vibrant correspondence with a wide variety of people in New and Old England. "A Brief Reply" is the last substantial piece of writing we have from Roger Williams. It was written late in his life, sometime between 1679 and 1683, and symbolizes his role—even in its unpublished form—as a controversialist in the wider world of English Protestantism.

CRACKING THE CODE
Roger Williams' Shorthand System

The volume that contains the Roger Williams code is itself a mystery. It was donated to the Brown family in 1817 by an unknown "Widow Tweedy."[14] The book, now housed in the archives of the John Carter Brown Library, is without a title page. Its title, author, and year of

FIGURE 3
External view of An Essay Towards the Reconciling of Differences Among Christians. *A photograph of the book that holds the Roger Williams shorthand, housed at the John Carter Brown Library at Brown University. Photograph by Linford D. Fisher.*

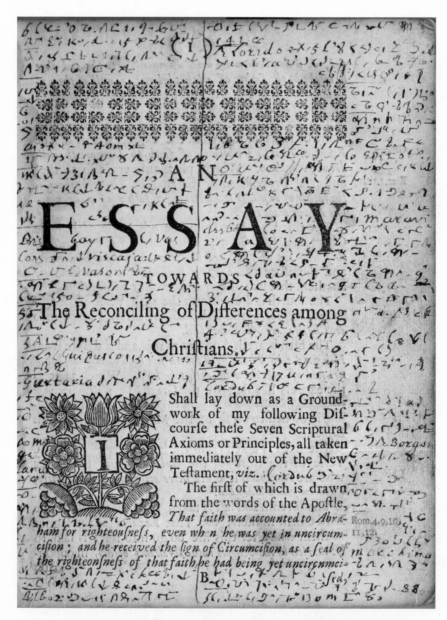

FIGURE 4

Title page of An Essay Towards the Reconciling of Differences Among Christians. *The shorthand is divided into two columns by a long vertical line. These columns are further subdivided into paragraphs by short horizontal lines. The shorthand on this particular page was transcribed from the chapter in Peter Heylyn's* Cosmographie *pertaining to the history, culture, and geography of Spain. A perceptive reader will notice over a dozen longhand terms interspersed throughout the marginalia, including "Biscay," "Vascons," "Bilbo," "Loredo," and others.*
Courtesy of the John Carter Brown Library at Brown University.

publication remain unknown. The first page of printed text (immediately following the front matter) bears the heading "An Essay Towards the Reconciling of Differences Among Christians," which scholars have occasionally cited as the title of the book itself; in reality, it was probably a subtitle.[15] Virtually every square inch of margin space on the book's 234 pages has been filled with cryptic shorthand writing, long presumed to be the work of Roger Williams.[16]

Cracking the Roger Williams code involved a combination of rudimentary cryptanalysis and historical detective work. The first attempts to decipher the shorthand began with a series of statistical analyses. For the kinds of simple substitution ciphers one would expect from the colonial era, a technique known as *frequency analysis* usually suffices. Frequency analysis looks at the relative frequency of cipher characters to establish a tentative key or correspondence. For example, one might reasonably conjecture that the most frequently occurring symbol in the Roger Williams shorthand corresponds to the English letter "e," since "e" is the most frequently occurring letter in the English alphabet. Similarly, one might conclude that the second most frequently occurring character in the Roger Williams shorthand corresponds to the English letter "t," since "t" is the second most frequently occurring English letter. Of course, frequency analysis only works for the simplest sorts of ciphers, since it presupposes a straightforward one-to-one correspondence between code symbols and English letters. If the cipher is any more nuanced than a direct substitution, frequency analysis is of little practical use. Such was the case with Roger Williams' shorthand.

Crucial insight was gained into the structure of Williams' shorthand by looking closely at the biography of Roger Williams and the history of seventeenth-century stenography. Williams learned shorthand at a young age, recording sermons and speeches at church, which brought him to the attention of Sir Edward Coke.[17] Coke hired Williams as an amanuensis and clerk in the Star Chamber (England's most powerful and highly secretive court), where he continued his use of shorthand before attending Charterhouse School and, later, Pembroke College, Cambridge University.[18] Though adapted and customized for his own personal use, Williams' shorthand system was based on a popular seventeenth-century shorthand system developed by John Willis in 1602.[19] Willis' system gained popularity in the early seventeenth century, quickly replacing Timothy Bright's 1588 system, which was the first English shorthand system of the early modern era.[20] Bright's shorthand system was *logographic*, assigning a unique shorthand character to over five hundred frequently occurring words, and thus was exceedingly difficult to master. Willis' system, by contrast, was highly flexible and relatively easy to learn.[21] That Roger Williams adapted an existing shorthand system for his own personal use was not particularly unusual. After all, the primary purpose of any shorthand system is efficiency. Seventeenth-century practitioners frequently improvised new symbols or shortcuts to conserve paper or improve writing speed. Indeed, many of the early shorthand manuals encouraged practitioners to do so.

Like Willis' *Stenographie*, Williams' shorthand system was *consonantary* in nature; only consonants were encoded explicitly. Except in rare cases, vowels were encoded through the physical arrangement of abutting consonant symbols. For example, placing a shorthand "t" to the bottom left of a shorthand "b" yields the word "bat." Moving the shorthand "t" upward slightly on the page produces the word "bet." Configuring these symbols differently, one can also encode the words "bit," "boot," and "but."

Bat Bet Bit Boat But

FIGURE 5
*Shorthand vowel example. Different spatial
arrangements of shorthand symbols correspond to
different intervening vowels.*

Thus, in Roger Williams' shorthand, as in most seventeenth-century shorthand systems, characters were not written out linearly, but organized into little constellations. The configuration of these clusters would convey important information about the vowels contained in the corresponding words, which leads to the first major interpretive challenge: even slight changes in the physical arrangement of characters can have enormous ramifications in the translated text. Written out in shorthand, the sentence "Her smile was appealing" is virtually indistinguishable from "Her smell was appalling." When deciphering shorthand, context is absolutely critical.

With these new insights into the structure of Williams' shorthand, the statistical techniques, unsuccessful at first, were altered and refined. Soon, a partial and tentative key was developed. The key was tentative, because no frequency analysis is completely error-free,[22] and partial because, as soon became apparent, the core alphabet of shorthand symbols was only a small component of the larger shorthand system. In addition to the core alphabet, Williams relied on a variety of pictographs, rebuses, puns, and arbitrary abbreviations, many of which appear to have been improvised.

FIGURE 6

Improvised shorthand example. In this bit of shorthand, which translates to "Testimony of the Father[,] Son," Williams incorporates wordplay. The symbol used to encode the word "Son," a small circle with a dot at its center, looks like a crude drawing of the sun.

Throughout, one feature of the marginalia proved particularly useful. The 234 pages of marginal notes were divided into three sections. Interspersed throughout the first and third sections were hundreds of longhand "flags." These were words, typically place-names or proper nouns, that had been written out, in part or in full, in standard longhand English. When these words were not written entirely in longhand, they were frequently completed in shorthand. Thus, each partial longhand flag supplied valuable information. If one could guess the word Williams was getting at from the longhand portion of a flag, one could infer the meaning of the shorthand characters in the remaining portion of the word.

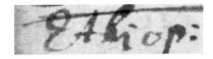

FIGURE 7

Longhand flag example. A longhand "flag" from the first section of shorthand notes. The colon that appears to the right of "Ethiop" denotes the "-ia" suffix.

By application of this strategy to each of the several hundred partial longhand terms, the key was gradually improved and refined. Moreover, examination of the longhand flags in the first section of notes ultimately yielded a list of more than a hundred proper nouns (Utrecht, Antwerp, Venetia, Neptune, Proteus, Borneo, and Java, just to name a few). The list spanned a variety of disciplines, from history and geography to alchemy and cosmology, and many of the terms were highly esoteric. It seemed reasonable to conjecture that the first section of notes had been transcribed from a published textbook or gazetteer. Further research and consultation confirmed this hypothesis. The shorthand in the first section had been transcribed from Peter Heylyn's *Cosmographie in Foure Bookes.*[23]

Originally published in 1652, Heylyn's *Cosmographie* was intended to provide a broad and comprehensive description of the world. The book, though organized geographically, was much more than a geography textbook. It contained detailed historical, sociological, and demographic information about nations and cultures all across the globe (including what appear to be the first in-print descriptions of Australia and California).

The discovery of a source text for the first section of notes was an enormous breakthrough. Not only did it offer compelling proof of process, it provided, in effect, a Rosetta Stone. Over the next several months, with Heylyn's *Cosmographie* as a guide, a dictionary of more than a thousand frequently occurring terms was compiled. Applying the insights gleaned from the first section to the third section of shorthand revealed a source text for that section as well. The shorthand in this section had been transcribed from Thomas Bartholin's *Bartholinus Anatomy*, a well-known medical encyclopedia, originally published in 1654.[24]

With a key in hand and source texts identified for the first and third sections, three questions remained. First, could Williams' authorship be confirmed beyond all reasonable doubt? Second, could the shorthand writing in the enigmatic middle section be deciphered? And finally, why was shorthand employed in the first place? The first question was settled in the affirmative by comparing the shorthand marginalia to shorthand samples found in Williams' private correspondence.[25] Close examination of these samples revealed a near-perfect match.

The focus then turned to the middle section of notes, which fill the margins of twenty-two pages of the book. Whereas the first and third sections were peppered with helpful longhand flags, the middle section was virtually devoid of longhand. The only two longhand words in the entire middle section were on the very first page. But these two words—"Eliot" and "Norcut"—were important clues as to its subject matter. After some analysis, the first sentence of the essay emerged: "[Here is a] brief reply to a small book written by John Eliot called, 'an Answer to John Norcut Against Infant Baptism,' a plea to the parents of the children of Christ. [Argued] from 'Acts' . . . and other scriptures, [written] with love."[26]

Puritans, like the vast majority of early modern Protestants, believed in infant baptism; Baptists, by contrast, believed that only adults professing faith in Christ should be baptized. In Massachusetts, citizens were required by law to baptize their infants. In 1679 John Eliot published a small book titled *A Brief Answer to a Small Book Written by John Norcot Against Infant-Baptisme.* Eliot's book was the Puritan rebuttal to John Norcott's *Baptism Discovered Plainly and Faithfully, According to the Word of God* (1672), which argued against the baptism of infants. The middle section of shorthand notes was Williams' reply to John Eliot—a rebuttal to a rebuttal to John Norcott's book, substantiated by fairly standard believer's baptism arguments from the Bible.

Soon, much of the essay in the middle section had been translated, yet certain obstacles remained. Given the many ambiguities built into Williams' shorthand, the abbreviated nature of the text, and the poor quality of the handwriting, a verbatim reconstruction proved difficult. There was little recourse, in the case of this essay, to a source text, since the middle section of notes was original, unpublished work.[27] Frequently, translating text into English meant deciphering a skeletal sequence of shorthand marks and filling in the gaps with educated contextual guesses. Although some of the text still remains undeciphered, a reasonably coherent essay, touching upon contentious theological issues including infant baptism and the conversion of Native Americans, has been pieced together.

The question still remained, however, as to why Williams employed shorthand at all. At first, it was tempting to surmise that the shorthand had been used to conceal something secret or illicit. Other well-known seventeenth-century individuals used shorthand for precisely this reason. English naval administrator and member of Parliament Samuel Pepys recorded diary entries in shorthand to keep aspects of his personal life private (including several extramarital affairs).[28] However, it is unlikely that secrecy was a concern for Williams. Although in this new essay he expresses controversial theological views, Williams articulated similar ideas and sentiments in earlier published writing, such as *Christenings Make Not Christians*, published in 1645. Moreover, there is evidence within the essay itself to suggest that Williams had plans to publish his rebuttal to John Eliot. For example, on the first page of his essay, Williams addresses "the Reader."[29] Williams died in 1783, at most four years after the middle section containing this new essay was filled with shorthand. If Williams had lived even a few years longer, there is a possibility this essay would survive today among his published writings.

There are other, more plausible explanations for Williams' use of shorthand. For one, writing in shorthand is extremely time-efficient for fluent writers such as Williams. His shorthand system removes the need to write out vowels explicitly, which improves writing speed. Frequent use of word abbreviations and the simplicity of most shorthand characters also saves time, as can be seen in other shorthand samples from this era.[30]

Additionally, shorthand writing is a skill that needs to be maintained; perhaps Williams took notes or made transcriptions of other books in shorthand to practice his stenography. For reasons that are not entirely clear, throughout his life Williams occasionally interspersed lines and phrases of shorthand writing into his correspondence and—even more curiously—into letters addressed to the town of Providence; the last such instance dates from December 8, 1680.[31]

A	∧	I	α	P	/	W	)
B	∩	J	>	Q	‿	X	Ю
D	⌐	K	Γ	R	—	Y	ర
E	<	L	Ɔ	S	|	Z	Z
F	L	M	U	T	C	Ch	X
G	⌐	N	\	U	⌒	Th	6
H/Th	O	O	(	V	V	Cl	+

FIGURE 8

Shorthand alphabet. The twenty-eight core symbols used in Roger Williams' shorthand and their respective longhand correlates.

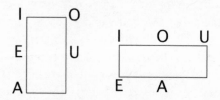

FIGURE 9

Shorthand vowel system. The system used for encoding vowels in Roger Williams' shorthand. When a small shorthand consonant is placed at the periphery of a larger shorthand consonant, there is an implied vowel between them. Which vowels correspond to which character placements is illustrated in the two diagrams above. Note that the rules depend on the orientation of the larger consonant symbol. This system for encoding vowels was one of the major innovations of John Willis' Stenographie, and was largely preserved, with some modifications, in subsequent shorthand systems.

Finally, writing in shorthand also saves space. In seventeenth-century New England, paper was an expensive commodity and difficult to obtain. There was not a single paper mill in the American colonies during Williams' lifetime; all paper in the colonies was imported from England. Even before the March 1676 Indian raid on Providence, which destroyed Williams' house and possessions, paper was scarce in Rhode Island. At least twice, Williams requested additional paper from correspondents in Massachusetts.[32] The dearth of paper in New England was, without a doubt, an important motivating factor for Williams' decision to use shorthand and to record his essay in the margins of a book.

Translation Exercise

To illustrate the process and challenges of decipherment, we will guide the reader through the translation of a few lines of shorthand marginalia. For this exercise, we have selected a passage from the first section of notes, since this section was transcribed from a source text (Peter Heylyn's *Cosmographie in Foure Bookes*). Thus, we have the advantage of being able to verify our work by referencing the corresponding passage in the source text. The passage we have selected (believe it or not) is more legible than most. In this passage, Williams was generous enough to give us more than two shorthand characters for most polysyllabic words, and his use of extra-alphabetical symbols and nonstandard constructions is minimal. This passage is drawn from a chapter of Heylyn's *Cosmographie* on the people and culture of Spain.[33]

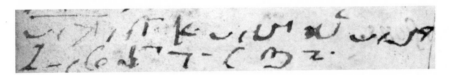

FIGURE 10
Williams' shorthand sample transcribed from Heylyn's Cosmographie. *A shorthand passage from the first section of marginal notes. This passage pertains to the ethnic decomposition of Spain. Courtesy of the John Carter Brown Library at Brown University.*

We have divided the shorthand passage into six sections, each consisting of three to five words, and we will analyze each of these sections separately. The reader is encouraged to try to decipher each section on her own before consulting the guides included in figures 8 and 9. However, the reader should be warned that some of the constructions employed in this passage, like any passage in Williams' shorthand, are unconventional and that figures 8 and 9 are not intended to express strict algorithmic rules, but rather loose guidelines that Williams followed when convenient.

FIGURE 11
Translation sample #1

At first glance, one might assume that the first two symbols stand for the letters "p" and "q," respectively (see figure 8). However, many shorthand symbols double as arbitrary substitutes for common words or phrases. The first two symbols in this section are being used in this latter capacity. The first symbol, which looks like a shallow "U," stands for the word "from." The second symbol, a forward slash, stands for the word "the." The meanings of these symbols have been deduced through context and comparisons with the source text. The cluster following these first two symbols consists of a shorthand "j" with a shorthand "s" in its "u" position. Hence, the word "Jews" (notice that Williams' shorthand is phonetic). [*Translation of sample #1:* "From the Jews"]

FIGURE 12
Translation sample #2

The first symbol in this section is a forward slash. However, this time the forward slash stands for the word "they," not, as it did in the first portion, "the."[34] Next comes a cluster consisting of a large shorthand "b" followed by a shorthand "r" in the "o" position. Hence, "bor." In fact, this is an abbreviation for the word "borrow." The final cluster in this portion consists of four elements. First is a large shorthand "s." In its "u" position is what looks like a longhand "c" or, perhaps, a shorthand "t."

But this is actually a shorthand "p" with a shorthand "r" attached to its base. Finally, hovering to the right is a small dot. Williams frequently used small dots or dashes to indicate that a cluster is an abbreviation for the word being encoded. In this case, the word is "superstition." [*Translation of sample #2*: "they borrow superstition"]

FIGURE 13
Translation sample #3

We have already encountered the first two symbols in this next series. They stand for the words "from" and "the," respectively. Next is a cluster consisting of a shorthand "m" with a shorthand "r" in the "o" position followed by a shorthand "s." Putting these pieces together, we obtain the word "Moors." The final cluster also contains a shorthand "m." In its "e" position is a shorthand character that is somewhat difficult to make out. If one looks closely, one sees the muddled outline of a shorthand "l." The mark at the top right is either an error or included to indicate that this is an abbreviation. In fact, "mel" is short for "melancholy." [*Translation of sample #3*: "from the Moors melancholy"]

FIGURE 14
Translation sample #4

Once again, in this section the first two characters stand for the words "from" and "the," respectively. The cluster that follows consists of a shorthand "g" with the shorthand symbol corresponding to "th" in its "o" position. Attached to the shorthand "th" is a shorthand "s." Hence, the word "Goths." [*Translation of sample #4*: "from the Goths"]

FIGURE 15
Translation sample #5

The first cluster in this portion features a shorthand "p" with a short-hand "r" at its base. In the "i" position is a shorthand "d," producing the word "pride." The next symbol looks like a shorthand "r." However, like the shorthand "q" and "p" in the first, third, and fourth portions, this symbol is being used in its alternate sense—as a special stand-in for a fre-quently used word. The shorthand "r" is often used as a special substitute for the word "and," which is how it functions here. The next character looks like a shorthand "p," but, as before, it is being used to represent the article "the."

The next cluster is a good example of what is almost certainly an error in Williams' shorthand. Although the symbol resembles a shorthand "th," in fact the word he intends to encode is "old" (this will become clear once we examine the source text). One can make some sense of this. Attaching a shorthand "l" to the base of a large shorthand "o" gets us partway there. But the mark at the base of Williams' shorthand "o" is a full circle, and it is unclear how a shorthand "l" and a shorthand "d" could combine to create that shape. Minor errors like this one are frequent. The final cluster in this portion consists of five elements. First, there is a shorthand "s." At its base is a shorthand "p." In the "a" position of the shorthand "s" is a shorthand "n." In the "o" position is a shorthand "r" connected to a shorthand "d." Putting these pieces together, we obtain "spanord." Clearly, given the context of the passage, "Spaniards" is the word Williams had in mind. [*Translation of sample #5:* "pride and the old Spaniards"]

FIGURE 16
Translation sample #6

The first cluster in this section consists of a shorthand "d" and a short-hand "r." This is a special recurring abbreviation for the word "desire" (one must disregard the fact that the "r" is in the "o" position of the "d"). Next is a solitary shorthand "o." In this particular context, "o" is short for the preposition "of." The final cluster consists of five elements. The largest character is a shorthand "l." In its "i" position is a shorthand "b." Placed in the "u" position of the shorthand "l" is a shorthand "r" connected to a shorthand "t." The small dot at the top right indicates an abbreviation. Thus, phonetically, we obtain "liburt," which must be short for "liberty." [*Translation of sample #6:* "desire of liberty"]

Putting all translation pieces together, we obtain the following:

From the Jews they borrow superstition, from the Moors melancholy, from the Goths pride, and [from] the old Spaniards [the] desire of liberty.[35]

Compare this to the corresponding passage in Heylyn's *Cosmographie*:

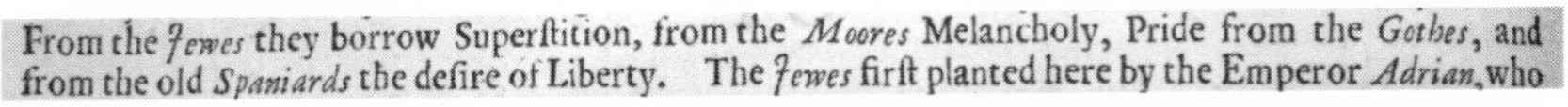

From the *Jewes* they borrow Superſtition, from the *Moores* Melancholy, Pride from the *Gothes*, and from the old *Spaniards* the deſire of Liberty. The *Jewes* firſt planted here by the Emperor *Adrian*.who

FIGURE 17
Corresponding printed text in Heylyn's Cosmographie. *Peter Heylyn,* Cosmographie
in Foure Bookes, 2nd ed. (London: Printed for Henry Seile, 1657), 242.

As this translation illustrates, even with a source text, Roger Williams' shorthand is often difficult to decipher. The transcription of Williams' "A Brief Reply" in this book is presented as a new and revealing addition to Williams' primary source record, but also as an open invitation to future scholars to refine and improve upon what is surely a provisional reconstruction.[36]

INTERPRETING ROGER WILLIAMS

From the beginning of this project, the question has been not just "What does the shorthand actually say?" but also "What does it mean?" That is, how does this new shorthand essay change, if at all, how we view Roger Williams on the topics contained in the shorthand? Roger Williams has long loomed large in the historiography of colonial America as well as in the popular imagination, sometimes viewed as the prescient promoter of full religious liberty in the early modern world with his "lively experiment" of Rhode Island.[37] This new essay significantly adds to our understanding of Williams' theology and belief, in part because it is a clear articulation of his views and comes so late in his life. The two most important areas of Roger

Williams' thought and theology that this new essay illuminates are, first, believer's versus infant baptism, and second, the propriety and necessity of Native American evangelization and conversion. In both cases, there are more continuities than disjunctions, as well as a surprising number of clarifications regarding his beliefs on these topics.

The Baptistic Roger Williams and Believer's Baptism

The first important aspect of Williams' essay is that it shows him joining an ongoing debate about believer's baptism in the religious world of England and New England during the seventeenth century.[38] It reveals that he held fast to ideas that he had adopted in the 1630s and 1640s, and that he took the same position and made the same arguments about believer's baptism that Baptists had advanced during that century. This new essay also shows that Williams felt that the proper mode was "dipping" or plunging the person into the water, not sprinkling, washing, or pouring. In this way, it confirms and reinforces most of the scholarship (often by Baptists) on Williams' views of baptism.[39] Finally, this discovery

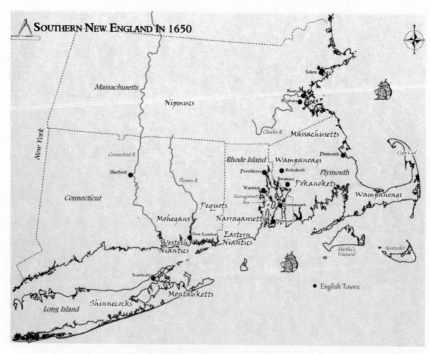

MAP 1
Southern New England in 1650. Map created by Lynn Carlson, GISP,
Brown University. Copyright Linford D. Fisher.

again demonstrates that Williams placed the biblical text above any effort to amend it by tradition or interpretation. Indeed, it particularly focuses on what Williams regarded as Eliot's distortion of the biblical text on the topic of believer's baptism.

Most scholars agree that in 1638 Williams gathered the first Baptist church in the New World in Providence, Rhode Island.[40] Everybody agrees that Williams did not remain with his little church more than a few months. One of the notable gaps in the manuscript record of Roger Williams is his time as a "Baptist."[41] Williams never wrote about his short time in the church he founded, and most of the surviving correspondence from 1638–1639 deals mainly with Indian matters.[42] Nevertheless, he professed baptistic beliefs long enough to be the founding pastor of what is now the First Baptist Church in America, gathered in 1638. Becoming a "Baptist" was the next-to-last step in his evolution from a minister in the Church of England, to Puritan, to Separatist, to Baptist, to "Witness beyond Christendom."[43] That Williams was baptistic, at least for a time, is found in the testimony of his enemies and critics. After Massachusetts governor John Winthrop learned that Williams had baptized his Providence congregation, he wrote in his journal on March 16, 1639: "At Providence things grew still worse; for a sister of Mrs. Hutchinson, the wife of one Scott, being infected with Anabaptistry, and going last year to live at Providence, Mr. Williams was taken (or rather emboldened) by her to make open profession thereof, and accordingly was rebaptized by one Holyman, a poor man, late of Salem. Then Mr. Williams rebaptized him and some ten more. They also denied the baptizing of infants, and would have no magistrates."[44]

Further evidence that this happened was the action taken by the Salem church where Williams and others of his congregation had been members before going into exile in Rhode Island. Hugh Peter, who succeeded Williams as minister at Salem, rooted out the "Williamsites" in the fall of 1638 by excommunicating them, mostly for being rebaptized in Providence.[45] In September 1638, an order of the Massachusetts General Court required individuals who had been excommunicated for six months or more without attempting reinstatement to be referred to the Court of Assistants for prosecution and fines. Subsequently, in 1639, Hugh Peter sent a letter to all the churches in Massachusetts with the names of ten people excommunicated from the Salem church, including Roger Williams and his wife, Mary.[46]

Williams did not remain long with his flock. In 1678 Richard Scott, one of the people baptized by Williams in 1638 and who later became a Quaker and critic, recalled: "I had walked with him in the *Baptists* way for about 3 or 4 months . . . in which time he brake off from his *Society*, and declared at large the ground and *Reason* for it: that their baptism could not be right, because it was not *Administered* by an Apostle."[47]

Williams left the Providence church in 1639 and never again affiliated himself with any church. Instead, he became a self-described "martyr" for Christianity for the rest of his life. He saw himself as a "Witness,"[48] but not a "Seeker," a label attached to him by enemies who sought to discredit him.[49] Today, "Seeker" carries a positive connotation, but in Williams' time it was almost completely negative.[50] In fact, some historians regard the "Seekers" to be an imaginary sect invented by the heresiologists to stigmatize people that did not fit the usual categories of heresy, such as Anabaptists, Familists, Armininans, Antinomians, Arians, Socinians, Pelagians, Brownists, Libertinists, Enthusiasts, and so on.[51] Most of the beliefs attributed to the Seekers were ideas that Williams himself abhorred.[52]

Despite that fact that Williams (in this newly deciphered essay) defended believer's baptism by immersion, it was highly unlikely that he was immersed in his 1638 rebaptism.[53] Nevertheless, by the late 1640s he came to accept that dipping was what the Scriptures required. When Williams saw John Clarke and Mark Lucar in Rehoboth and Swansea fully immersing baptismal candidates in Plymouth Colony in 1649, he informed John Winthrop Jr., "I believe their practice comes neerer the first practices of our great Founder Christ (Jesus) then other practices of Religion doe," even though he doubted that anyone actually had a valid warrant to baptize.[54]

It is notable that Williams had little to say about baptism in his writings. A major exception was his explanation in *Christenings Make Not Christians* as to why he did not baptize the Native Americans.[55] But, even in that essay, he defended believer's baptism. He explained why he had not converted the Indians, despite boasting that he could have "brought many thousands of these Natives, yea the whole country" to observe the Sabbath, be baptized, attend church services, and maintain "priests and formes of prayers, a whole forme of *Antichristian* worship in life and death."[56] He argued that the churches in the whole of Christendom were corrupted so that "converting" Indians would be to subvert their souls "from one false worship to another."[57] A true conversion was not possible in those circumstances. What is significant to note was his emphasis that one had to be a believer. A baptism that followed conversion would be believer's baptism. In the rest of his writings, baptism is mentioned only in passing, but in his "Brief Reply" to John Eliot, believer's baptism by immersion was *the* issue.

Believer's baptism was the one practice that most distinguished Baptists from their Christian contemporaries in England and America.[58] The John Smyth/Thomas Helwys group of English Separatists in exile in Amsterdam first adopted this baptistic practice around 1609, when they gathered the first "Baptist" church, which came from the Puritan-Separatist movement.[59] They rejected the rites and rituals of any church derived from the Roman Catholic Church, including the Church of England, so they began anew. Causing great scandal, John Smyth baptized himself (by pouring water), and then he baptized the others in the flock. These new "Baptists" held that a "true church" was composed only of believers, and baptism was valid only for those who had confessed and repented. The *Amsterdam Declaration of 1611*, drawn up by Thomas Helwys, defines the church in Article 10: "That the church off CHRIST is a company of faithful people seperated from the world by the word & Spirit of GOD being knit unto the LORD, & one to another, by Baptisme. Upon their owne confession of the faith and sinnes." Article 13 further states, "That everie Church is to receive in all their members by Baptisme upon the Confession off their faith and sinnes wrought by the preaching off the Gospel, according to the primitive Institucion Mat. 28.19 And practice Acts 2.41. And therefore Churches constituted after anie other manner, or off anie other persons are not according to CHRISTS Testament."[60] Of course, no infant could repent and profess belief; therefore, an infant could not be baptized.

Thomas Helwys returned to England with some of his followers in 1611 and founded the first Baptist church in England in Spitalfields, London. He wrote a plea for religious liberty, entitled *A Short Declaration of the Mistery of Iniquity*, sent it to King James I, and was imprisoned as a result. Their opponents immediately denounced the Baptists as "Anabaptists" and persecuted them.[61] Because they shared the concept of believer's baptism with the Anabaptists, their enemies always sought to merge the Baptist/Anabaptist identity. The name "Anabaptist" carried the weight of heresy, fanaticism, anarchy, and revolution. No one would forget or forgive the radical Anabaptist occupation of Münster in 1534–1535 (no matter how unrepresentative of the movement the episode had been), so for two hundred years afterwards one way to discredit someone was to call him or her an Anabaptist. Even John Adams, speaking in 1775 about Baptist opponents of the Massachusetts Standing Order, called them Anabaptists.[62]

While the Anabaptists on the Continent had arrived at believer's baptism by the 1520s (and were severely persecuted for their beliefs and practices), some historians today argue that the Anabaptists had little influence upon the development of the idea among the English, concurring with British historian Stephen Wright "that anabaptism left no mark on the puritan-separatists."[63]

For their part, the Baptists vehemently denied that they were Anabaptists. Edward Barber, writing the first published defense of "dipping" or immersion, noted that those who practiced dipping were "reproached with the name of Anabaptists, although our practice is none other than what was instituted by Christ himself."[64] The *London Confession* of the Particular Baptists in 1644 bore the title "THE CONFESSION OF FAITH, Of those CHURCHES which are commonly (though falsly) called ANABAPTISTS."[65] Likewise, the *Standard Confession* of the General Baptists in England (1660) opened with the line "Set forth by many of us, who are (falsely) called Ana-Baptists, to inform all Men (in these days of scandal and reproach) of our innocent Belief and Practise; for which we are not only resolved to suffer Persecution, to the loss of our Goods, but also to life it self, rather than to decline the same."[66]

One great objective of Reformation churches was to recover the original and true church, which they held had been corrupted and lost over the centuries. A common tenet of the Puritan-Separatist movement was that the Roman Catholic Church was the church of the Antichrist and the "whore of Babylon." What, then, did this mean with respect to the Church of England, which had branched off from the Catholic Church? That question caused divisions in the Puritan ranks that produced varying degrees of accommodation, leading some to complete separation.[67]

Andrew Ritor, the second Baptist to publish a defense of immersion, wrote that the baptisms of the Church of England were "counterfeit" because the English Church derived from the church of the Antichrist, the Roman Catholic Church.[68] John Spilsbury, the pastor of the first Calvinist Baptist church in London, denied the validity of the baptisms of the Roman Catholic Church and the doctrine of Apostolic Succession, which meant, of course, that the rites of the Church of England were invalid as well.[69] A stream of Baptist writers defended believer's baptism and attacked the scriptural basis of infant baptism. As William H. Brackney notes, "No less than a hundred books and tracts came off the English presses in the seventeen century to prove that infant baptism" was, in the words of Samuel Fisher, a Baptist polemicist, "mere babism."[70]

Most Baptists held that believer's baptism was fundamental to the establishment of a true and pure church.[71] Thomas Helwys went so far as to declare that anyone who believed "or even acquiesced, in infant baptism could expect eternal damnation."[72] However, most Baptists never went that far. They did not "deny that their fellow Puritans were true

Christians, only that they were deficient in their obedience to Christ's precepts."[73] Baptists held that paedobaptizing Puritan-Separatists had failed to cleanse themselves entirely of the effects of the "Great Apostasy" by not removing the last vestige of the church of the Antichrist—infant baptism.

Like the Puritan-Separatists, Baptists held that the mark of a true church was that the Word was rightly preached and the ordinances of the Lord properly administered.[74] Since infant baptism was the practice of nearly all of Christendom, the Baptist stance called into question the legitimacy of the others. In addition, by the 1640s Baptists concluded that the mode of baptism of the others was defective or illegitimate. It was not just *who* was baptized, but *how* they were baptized. Edward Barber refused to use the word "baptize" because it was only a transliteration, not a translation, of the Greek βαπτίζω. Instead, he used "dip" and "dippt" and "dipping" wherever it appeared in the Bible. For example, Barber's version had Jesus commanding, "Go and make disciples of all nations, *dipping* them in the name of the Father [Matthew 28:19]," and "Peter said upon them, Repent, and be *dipt* every one of you in the name if Jesus Christ [Acts 2:38]."[75] Andrew Ritor also made the point that the Greek word for "baptize" meant "to dip" and that the Greeks had an entirely different word for "sprinkle."[76] Believers had to be dipped under the water in order to experience symbolically the death, burial, and resurrection of Christ. Baptists concluded that the mode of baptism must be "dipping" (*immersion*) or else baptism was not properly administered.[77] No wonder that the seventeenth century was marked by vigorous attacks upon the Baptists and their doctrine of believer's baptism.[78]

One effect of the outbreak of the English Civil War was a new freedom to preach and publish because the censorship and licensing laws were no longer enforced. As a consequence, an unprecedented outpouring of printing and preaching erupted between 1641 and 1660; one London book collector accumulated twenty-two thousand books and tracts published during that time.[79] The uncontrolled nature of the process and the proliferation of ideas greatly alarmed those who regarded themselves as the guardians of social stability and religion. It was a "world turned upside down" as the "vulgar voices" and deeds of ordinary people clamored for change.[80] The avalanche of books, tracts, pamphlets, and papers and the ferment and clash of ideas was well underway when Roger Williams returned to England in 1643–1644.

With the dismantling of Church of England in the mid-1640s, various Calvinist parties struggled to create a new national church for England, but the divisions in their ranks provoked a bitter debate between the Presbyterians, Independents, and those who championed the "New

England Way" (the church-state model of Massachusetts). The goal was to create "a reformed, coercive, national church" and combat "political and religious radicalism."[81] Roger Williams plunged in and wrote *The Bloudy Tenent*, which rejected any idea of a national church and argued instead for religious liberty.[82] This so infuriated the Presbyterian-dominated Parliament that the book was ordered to be burned by the public hangman. William Prynne (1600–1669), a prolific pamphleteer, denounced "Master Williams in his late dangerous, *Licentious Booke*."[83] Likewise, Daniel Featley, D.D. (1582–1645), a Calvinist defender of the episcopal form of church government, raged against Williams:

> Witness the Book printed in 1644, called the "Bloudy Tenet,"[84] which the Author affirms he wrote in Milk, and if he did so, he hath put much Rat-bane into it, as Namely, That it is the will and command of God, that since the coming of his the Lord Jesus, a permission of the most Paganish, Jewish, Turkish, or Antichristian Consciences and worships be granted to all men of all nations.[85]

From the vantage point of the major players, the uncontrolled situation allowed heresy, heterodoxy, blasphemy, and dangerous social disorder to flourish. Most felt that the problem resulted from the government's toleration of sectarian groups and ideas and the lack of a national church to discipline heretics and sectarians. As the religious and ideological struggle between the Presbyterians and Independents intensified by 1644, Presbyterian polemicists began writing heresiographies—books which sought to identify all heretical ideas and their proponents so they could be combated and defeated.[86] In 1645 Ephraim Pagitt published the first one, entitled *Heresiography*, which gave the name to this genre.[87] He was followed by William Prynne, Robert Baillie, and Thomas Edwards.[88] The most notorious Presbyterian propagandist was Edwards, whose "*Gangraena* was the most famous printed book in a revolutionary era."[89]

Edwards and Baillie particularly feared and loathed the Baptists, always calling them "Anabaptists." They reacted to the fact that the Baptists had erupted into plain sight, were spreading across the land, and were gaining prominence in the New Model Army.[90] On the eve of the English Revolution, the Baptists were a small sect, having about ten congregations in London.[91] The General Baptists, who had been in London since 1611–1612, now became better organized and self-confident. Edwards was scandalized by the fact that most General Baptist preachers were an uneducated, unlicensed lot of soap boilers, smiths, tinkerers, "mechanics," tailors, shoemakers, peddlers, belt makers, weavers, heel makers, and worse, "she-preachers."[92] The Particular Baptists, who had emerged around 1638–1639, also became better organized in the 1640s, established more churches, and began publishing books and pamphlets that attacked infant baptism. Moreover, Baptists had been calling for freedom of conscience since at least 1612.[93]

Daniel Featley denounced the "Anabaptists" in his book *The Dippers Dipt* (1645). He declared, "Now of all Heretiques and Schismatiques the Anabaptists in three regards ought to be most carefully looked unto, and severely punished, if not utterly exterminated and banished out the Church and Kingdome." His reasons were threefold. First, they had an affinity for beliefs held by all sorts of heretics: Marcionites, Donatists, Apostolici, Adamites, Enthusiasts, Psychopannychists, Polygamists, Jesuits, Arminians, and Brownists. Second, they boldly published and preached their heresies and "defile our Rivers with their impure washings, and our Pulpits with their false prophesies." Third, they struck at authority itself, saying that the civil officers are "not Governors and defenders of the Spiritual and Christian state of worship," thereby undermining "the powers that are ordained of God and endeavor to wrest the sword out of the Magistrates hand, to whom God hath given it for cutting off of all heresie and impiety." Featley predicted that if the Baptists went unchecked, anarchy would result.[94]

In *Gangraena* (1646), the Reverend Thomas Edwards accused the Baptists of being social revolutionaries.[95] Edwards was a forthright opponent of "liberty of conscience," even writing a *Treatise against Toleration*.[96] He argued that such liberty led to heresy and must be "fervently opposed."[97] He described the New Model Army as "that mis-shaped Bastard-monster of a Toleration" which served as a "miscarrying womb" for sectarians, such as the Baptists, spreading their heresies across the nation.[98] The Scottish Presbyterian minister Robert Baillie, one of the most vigorous and vehement heresy hunters in the 1640s (and the person who first labeled Roger Williams as a "Seeker"), denounced the Baptists as the "fount of all heresy."[99]

Heresiographers were incensed at the reports of Baptists "depraving" infant baptism. An example was a case in Middlesex in June 1644 when an "Anabaptist" heel maker and his wife were indicted by a grand jury for degrading baptism by saying "that a Catt or a dogg may be as well baptized as any Child or Children in their Infancie."[100] They repeated tales of soldiers in the New Model Army baptizing horses and urinating into the baptismal fount to prevent infant baptism.[101] Worse were the lurid reports of Baptists dipping naked women. Heresy bred immorality. The principal heresiographer, Thomas Edwards, wrote that Anabaptism allowed the "dipping of naked women . . . to feed wanton eyes, by looking upon young women naked, to satisfie their unchaste touching, by handling young women naked."[102]

Baptist writers, preachers, and exhorters heatedly defended their views and experienced a degree of toleration during the rule of Oliver Cromwell in the 1650s, but persecution returned with the restoration of the monarchy in 1660. The Church of England was vigorously restored through the so-called Clarendon Code.[103] As a result, Baptists were jailed, pilloried, fined, executed, and their property confiscated.[104] Among the estimated 1,700 nonconforming pastors "ejected" from their pulpits were dozens of Baptists, including John Norcott from his parish in Hertford-shire in 1662.[105] King Charles II attempted to relax the suppression of dissenters on March 15, 1672, with his Declaration of Indulgence, which suspended the penal code against all religious nonconformists including Catholics and dissenters. As a result, the only remaining restrictions on religious freedom were that dissenting ministers and meetinghouses had to be licensed and Catholics should refrain from public worship.[106] Nor-cott published *Baptism Discovered Plainly* later that year.[107]

In John Eliot's New England, the defenders of the Standing Order faced increasing challenges in the 1660s and 1670s.[108] For one thing, in 1661 King Charles II forced greater toleration in Massachusetts by order-ing an end to the persecution of the Quakers. Between 1656 and 1660, four Quakers had been hanged and dozens arrested, whipped, fined, and mutilated. After 1661 the persecution lessened slightly, and by 1675 Quakers lived and worshipped openly in Massachusetts.[109] Secondly, the apparent and alarming decline in religious fervor among the general pub-lic had resulted in the "Half-Way Covenant" of 1662.[110] The dispute over the adoption of this innovation in membership practices caused a schism in the ranks of the Puritans.[111] Moreover, Baptists, Anglicans, and Quak-ers inundated the crown with petitions complaining about their treatment at the hands of the Puritan authorities, which caused their Puritan allies in England to apply pressure upon Massachusetts to become more tolerant.[112]

And then there were the pestiferous Baptists, who continued to spread their message and founded new churches. The Puritans had felt so threat-ened by the Baptists that the General Court enacted a law in 1644 against the "Anabaptists," making it illegal to openly oppose infant baptism. The preamble to the law explicitly invoked the specter of Münster: "Foras-much as experience hath plentifully and often proved that since the first rising of the Anabaptists, about one hundred years since, they have been incendiaries of the commonwealths."[113] In the late 1640s, Baptist ministers had been baptizing converts just over the boundary in Plymouth Colony, which threatened to spread the perceived infection into Massachusetts. In 1651 three Rhode Island Baptists from Newport—John Clarke, John Crandall, and Obadiah Holmes—were arrested in Lynn, Massachusetts, for their illegal baptistic activities, and Holmes, who refused to pay the fine levied on him, was brutally beaten.[114] Henry Dunster, the president of Harvard, was forced to resign in 1654 for his baptistic beliefs, and "Anabaptists" were identified in Billerica, Woburn, Charlestown, Boston, and Lynn. In Swansea in 1663, John Myles, a Baptist pastor who had fled from Wales because of the suppression of nonconformists under the Act of Uniformity, gathered a mixed-communion church, and in 1665 Baptists established a church in Boston despite all efforts to stifle it.[115] These events led to a two-day debate in April 1668, where the clergy and magistrates attempted to convince the Baptist leaders to repent of their erring ways.[116] The arrival of John Norcott's book in 1672 attacking infant baptism was another threat, and one that Eliot felt called to parry. In doing so, Eliot joined a line of New England Puritan clergymen who had written rebuttals and rejoinders to Baptist books flowing from England, including John Cotton,[117] Richard Mather,[118] Thomas Hooker,[119] Thomas Shepard,[120] George Phillips,[121] and Thomas Cobbett,[122] all of whom had written tracts attacking the Baptists in Old and New England.[123]

Eliot simply reiterated and built upon these prior refutations of believer's baptism in his answer to Norcott in 1679. Norcott argued that infant baptism had no scriptural basis, and (like all the Baptist tract writers before him) he cited chapter and verse to demonstrate that the multitude of baptisms were of adult believers only, beginning with Jesus himself.[124] Unconvinced, Eliot insisted that "[t]he Baptizing of Believers and their Infants was one of the first Gospel Apostolical Institutions commanded in the Gospel politie."[125] To overcome the fact that the New Testament never explicitly said that a child was baptized, Eliot concluded that "always, when the baptism of believers is mentioned, add in your mind (and their Infants)."[126] Williams most particularly pounced on the notion that one could add a gloss to the Bible's words. In his preface Williams declared, "But the words of the Great King enjoin [us] to *protect* the Gospel, whose written word *refutes* John Eliot . . . and whose Word must prevail over the book of John Eliot."[127] Again, he wrote, "To add in the mind 'and their Seed, the infants' [whenever Baptism of Believers is mentioned] is not to add only to Norcott's book, but to add to the book of Holy Scripture . . . contrary to the plain word of God."[128] Williams made light of Eliot's assertion that had baptism "been instituted when Jesus was an Infant, he would have submitted to it," writing "[there is] no doubt that he would [have submitted to baptism]."[129] The fact that an infant had no choice, no voice, no understanding, and no faith was the whole point that the Baptists (and Williams) made in denying the validity of infant baptism.[130]

Eliot admitted that an infant could not speak for him or herself, but a major part of his argument was to rebut Norcott's dismissal of a covenant that included children.[131] Eliot argued, "From the first Creation of man God hath transacted with man by a Covenant, and hath always comprehended the Parents and children together in his Covenant."[132] He maintained that the covenant "is our spiritual Patrimony, our Estate in Religion" which parents convey to their children.[133] As a result of the faith of the parents, "Now Infants of Believers are members of the Church of Christ, the Covenant comprehends them, the promise belongeth unto them, and therefore they ought in due order to be baptized."[134] Baptism was the seal of the Christian covenant, just as circumcision was the seal of the covenant "in the old Church."[135]

John Norcott had argued that the covenant that God made with Abraham did not apply to all of Abraham's offspring, but to Christ and the "children of promise."[136] Williams agreed, adding, "The men of the Holy Spirit are the true children of the Promise," and " 'For as many as are led by the spirit of God, they are the sons of God.' "[137] Williams declared that " 'faith cometh by hearing, and hearing by the Word of God' . . . not by patrimony."[138] No infant could hear or comprehend the Word of God.

Norcott emphasized that Jesus taught disciples and baptized them: "[T]hey are made Disciples, not born Disciples (that is) they are made Disciples by the preaching of God's Word, and then they were baptized."[139] Eliot rejoined with the argument that while this was true of the first believers, "their Infants had the privilege to be born Disciples."[140] Williams responded, "For if children are born Disciples, as Eliot says, then there is no difference between being born of the flesh and born of the Spirit."[141] Williams argued that this assertion was contrary to 1 Corinthians 15:46.[142] Then he references the words of Jesus: "That which is born of the flesh is flesh, and that which is born of the Spirit is spirit. . . . Ye must be born again."[143] Norcott and Williams both maintained that repentance preceded baptism, and repentance was the result of teaching and hearing. " 'He that believeth and is baptized, shall be saved' when you have taught them, then baptize them."[144]

Both Norcott and Williams rejected the argument that circumcision and baptism were initiation rites serving the same purposes. Indeed, Norcott said, "Once Circumcision was something. . . . Now in the Gospel it is nothing because abolished."[145] Circumcision was the seal of the covenant with Abraham, but as Norcott observed, "Circumcision concerned only Males, but Acts 8:12, 'When they believed, they were Baptized, Men and Women.' "[146] Williams repeated the point, "For though Circumcision was a Seal of Abraham's faith, yet it cannot become a Seal of the

Righteousness of the male's faith. . . . The covenant of Circumcision *shuts out* their female children: Circumcision was only for the males."[147] The old covenant, sealed by circumcision, was replaced by a new covenant sealed by the "blood of Jesus Christ." And "the children of the new Covenant, it is written, are the only born of the Spirit."[148] One entered that covenant only by faith—something impossible for an infant.[149]

The mode of baptism (sprinkling versus pouring versus dipping) was an integral part of the debate over infant versus adult baptism. Norcott insisted dipping was the correct mode, writing, "Baptism is *Dipping* or *Plunging.* Sprinkling is not Baptism, therefore Sprinkling will not serve."[150] Eliot dismissed Norcott's discussion of dipping as "digressing into another litigious point," but still spent several pages disputing the Baptist argument and providing an alternative interpretation of the Scriptures.[151] Eliot declared that "there is no proof that any in the times of Christ were baptized by dipping, nor that *John* nor *Phillip* baptized by dipping."[152] He argued, "Baptism is a signe, and a little of the signe is enough to signifie great matters." Therefore, sprinkling was a good as dipping: "The face is the most eminent and principal part of man, if therefore the face be a little washed, buryed, sprinkled, covered with water, it is enough to signifie unto our faith all that is signified by Baptisme."[153]

Baptists all through the seventeenth century used the examples of Jesus and Philip as proof that immersion was the scriptural model of baptism.[154] Williams responded to Eliot by saying that sprinkling was not good enough because "the word of God *Almighty* was dipping, for when Jesus was baptized 'he went straightaway out of the water.' "[155] Williams also referenced the story of Philip and the eunuch in the book of Acts, where they "went both down into the water, both Philip and the eunuch, and he baptized him . . . [and] they were come up out of the water."[156] Eliot interpreted those texts to suggest that no one was dipped. He said that John the Baptist baptized in the River Jordan because in the wilderness "there was no accommodation to do otherwise." Furthermore, at that place the river was broad, which meant that it was shallow near the bank, "so that people might come to him, standing in the water, and lifting up their faces to Heaven, he taking up water in his hands sprinkling and [pouring] it on their faces."[157] Likewise, Eliot said that Philip took the eunuch down in the water only because "they had as little accommodation to do otherwise, as *John* had in the Wilderness."[158] He also pointed to Acts 2:41, which told of the baptism of "three thousand souls" at Pentecost as a result of Peter's preaching. Eliot assumed that this occurred in the Temple in Jerusalem, where the water was kept in various vessels and containers from which water had to be dipped for sprinkling.[159] Williams responded by noting, "It doth not appear clear that the *Pentecost* was in the temple, when Peter spake to them."[160] In any case, Eliot maintained that the Bible was indifferent as to how baptism was administered.[161]

Eliot not only disputed the doctrines laid out by Norcott, he also harshly attacked the "Anabaptists." His outrage at them is shown by the only uses of the exclamation point in the text[162] and by his switching from speaking to his own flock to directly addressing the opponents of infant baptism.[163] Early in the seventeenth century, Thomas Helwys and other Baptists had challenged the validity of infant baptism; sixty years later, Eliot impatiently declared that the "all the Gospel Churches in the world" had administered infant baptism since Apostolic times. But the Anabaptists judged that infant baptism "is null, all the world are unbaptized persons, saving themselves, and they now call themselves Baptists, and all the rest of the christian world baptized in their Infancy are unbaptized persons[;] Churches, Ministry, Sacraments, all are nullified, &c. What an horrible degree of uncharitableness is this, to say no worse of it."[164]

Eliot made condescending references to the "Anabaptists" for their "uncharitable opinion" and "censoriousness of others, especially when better then themselves is exceeding contrary to the Spirit of the Gospel, and such doth their opinion expose them to be what their inward state is. I do not meddle with it, but if they follow their opinion, as this book of *John Norcot* doth thoroughly, it leadeth them to the highest excess of censorious uncharitableness, (to say no worse,) and that against men much better then themselves."[165] Later he said, "yet it seemeth great boldness to nullify Baptisme, and to affirm, that all the Churches and Saints from the Apostles to this day are unbaptized persons, except your inconsiderable selves. O what need have we of humility and charity!"[166]

Eliot also said that "Anabaptists" were devoid of any natural affection for their children.[167] He concluded that "the more I experience the charity of the Gospel, (which God knoweth is but a little) the more doth my Soul loath that uncharitable opinion of the Anabaptists."[168] To deny baptism to infants, Eliot asserted, was to

> rob the Lambs of their interest in the Church, in the communion of Saints, and in the Covenant of God, which is a wicked injury done against the Lambs of Christ, who are not able to help themselves, therefore Christ will help them, and wo to those that do them this injury. . . . What think you, he [Christ] will say to the Anabaptists, who teach and cause their very Parents themselves to put away their Children from Christ? . . . never since the world began was there more unnatural affection then this is.[169]

In essence, Eliot charged "Anabaptists" with the ultimate form of early modern child abuse by endangering an infant's eternal soul by refusing to baptize a child. Williams responded by saying that believer's baptism was the will and command of God. "For faith [in the Scripture] is not uncharitableness nor censoriousness"; rather, believers' baptism was the will of God. Williams dismissed the accusation that the "Anabaptists" lacked natural affection as being "without true [grounding]."[170]

Of course, the principal justification for infant baptism for hundreds of years had been the necessity of washing away the taint of original sin lest an infant's soul be lost. The doctrine of original sin held that all of humanity was corrupted by the sin of Adam, so that even infants were condemned by the fall. Baptists disagreed among themselves about original sin and salvation. Smyth and Helwys, the earliest General Baptist leaders, held that there was a difference between original sin and an actual sin. Helwys wrote that while all of humanity was affected by the sin of Adam, all of humanity was equally affected by the atoning grace of Christ. He said that "grace in Christ, hath freed Adam, and in him all mankind from that sin of Adam." No one was any longer condemned by the sin of Adam, but each person had willfully to commit his or her own sins. With this view of original sin, the General Baptists wiped away the chief reason for infant baptism.[171] The Particular Baptists did not agree that Christ's death atoned for everyone, holding, like all Calvinists, that infants were not automatically cleansed of original sin. They looked at the issue of infant death as a "dark and mysterious subject," but they came to the view that God would take care of everything. John Spilsbury wrote, "and so leave them [infants] to the grace and good pleasure of God of all grace, who only knows who are his and hath the disposing of them, and all his creatures to his own glory."[172] Testifying at his trial in 1664, Benjamin Keach declared, "Infants who die are members of the kingdom of glory, though they be not members of the visible church."[173] As Calvinists, it is likely that both Norcott and Williams accepted these conclusions. Original sin was not an issue addressed by Norcott, and Williams' response to Eliot returned to the point that salvation did not come by birth, but by faith (which only an adult believer could have).[174]

The issue of believer's baptism was central to the Baptist identity from the beginning, distinguishing the Baptists from nearly all other Christians. By rejecting infant baptism, the Baptists, like the Anabaptists before them, shook the Christian world by denying the belief and practice of nearly all other Christian churches for hundreds of years. The sprinkling of infants had been the sign of admission into the visible church, but the Baptists maintained that "baptism" meant *immersion* of a believer, of a person who understood and voluntarily consented to be dipped. The Baptist idea provoked a long-running debate over infant baptism versus believer's baptism. Beyond rejecting infant baptism, the Baptists by the 1640s had settled on immersion as the scriptural method. This was the debate joined by Norcott, Eliot, and Williams late in the seventeenth century. The newly deciphered essay in this volume shows that Williams agreed with the arguments and examples that John Norcott had advanced for believer's baptism and immersion. It is interesting to note that Williams defended baptistic principles more than he embraced actual Baptists themselves.[175] In this essay, he made only brief rejoinders to Eliot's assaults on the Baptists, but he took Eliot to task for having distorted "the written word of God."[176] He accused Eliot of "going beyond" and contradicting what is written in the Bible in order to try to defend infant baptism. To a thoroughgoing biblicist, this was a serious charge.

Williams on Indian Conversion

The second major insight afforded by this newly decoded Roger Williams essay is regarding his late-life views on Native American evangelization and conversion. Historians often point to Williams' relatively unusual interest in Native cultures as illustrated by his *A Key into the Language of America* (1643), which still stands as a rare early, even if flawed, quasi-ethnographic description of Native customs and rituals.[177] Earlier generations of scholars had a more optimistic view of Williams' missionary labors and evangelistic interests. Since the 1980s, the scholarship on Williams has tended to locate him more precisely within his own seventeenth-century context, highlighting his biblicism and ethnocentrism and the political, self-serving uses of his Indian language and knowledge.[178] Recent historians have eschewed older hagiographic descriptions of Williams' "missionary labors," instead granting that he displayed some missionary interest early in his time in New England but eventually turned to other things or gave up.[179]

Historiographical analyses of Williams' views of Indian conversion rarely extend beyond the early 1650s, in part because Williams had virtually nothing to say about these issues later in life in his extant writings and correspondence. Roger Williams' reply to John Eliot breaks that silence, for on one important page of the shorthand essay he takes head-on the topic of Native evangelization and conversion in a surprisingly direct manner. These late-life musings on the topic of Indian baptism and conversion reveal the deep, ongoing misgivings Williams harbored regarding the well-funded and carefully orchestrated attempts by Massachusetts Bay

Colony ministers and magistrates to bring Native peoples from across New England into the Christian fold.[180] Williams' critiques are even more important because they are directed at the very mastermind of the evangelization attempts: the "Apostle to the Indians," John Eliot, the long-time Roxbury, Massachusetts, minister and missionary employed by the New England Company (NEC), a London-based Puritan/Independent missionary society.[181] This short diatribe against Eliot and Indian conversion is important, then, because it comes so late in Williams' life; it was written in the precarious years after King Philip's War; it provides a new window into Williams' rare engagement with Eliot; and it reveals a basic continuity in Williams' thinking between the 1640s and the 1680s regarding his ongoing interest in, as well as the enormous difficulty of, producing "true" conversions among the Native peoples of seventeenth-century New England.

When Roger Williams arrived among the Narragansetts in the spring of 1636 after his banishment from the Massachusetts Bay Colony, Europeans were no strangers to the Natives. The Narragansetts first discovered European traders and explorers on their shores at least as early as 1524, when the Italian explorer Giovanni da Verrazzano reconnoitered the Narragansett Bay, staying for two weeks and trading with the Indians.[182] French, Spanish, Dutch, and English traders plied the shores of New England over the next century, taking furs and even Indians in exchange for European kettles, shirts, blankets, and guns. The Narragansetts and other local Native nations kept a close watch on Dutch trading posts and settlements on the shores of the Long Island Sound to their west and the new English settlements not far from the eastern edge of their lands, first at Plymouth in 1620, then at Wollaston (Quincy) in 1622, and finally in Shawmut, or present-day Boston, in 1630. At the time of the arrival of the English colonists, the Narragansetts were one of the largest of the Southern New England nations and were completing their bid for hegemony in that region.[183]

By 1636 Natives were no strangers to Williams, either. Soon after he arrived in Boston in February 1631, Williams moved first to Salem and then to Plymouth, where he began to study Native language and culture, lodging with the local Wampanoags in their comfortable but "Smoakie" wigwams to "gaine their Toung."[184] After moving back to Salem, Williams repeatedly incurred the wrath of the Massachusetts Bay Company magistrates for his rather unorthodox views, including the need for full separation from the Church of England, the impropriety of the civil government ruling over human conscience in spiritual matters, and the injustice of royal prerogative and presumption in giving Native lands to the colonists.[185] As a result, in October 1635, the Massachusetts Bay General Court ordered his banishment.[186] A note from Governor John Winthrop in January 1636 warned Williams that the General Court intended to ship him to England, so he immediately fled via well-worn trails to his Indian friend, Massasoit, near the Plymouth Colony. After a gentle but firm note to Williams from Plymouth governor Edward Winslow claimed that Williams had settled on Plymouth territory, he picked up and moved again, this time settling at a place the Natives called Moshassuck, on the edge of the Great Salt Cove near the head of the Narragansett Bay. Williams renamed the place "Providence" and from there positioned himself as an important arbiter of Native-European relations through trade, diplomacy, and political leadership in what later became the colony of Rhode Island and Providence Plantations.[187]

Williams professed an interest not just in Native communities but also in their conversion to Christianity, during the first decade of his residence in New England. Within a year of his arrival, Williams wrote to the governor of the Massachusetts Bay Company, John Winthrop, "I am no Elder in any church, no more nor so much as your worthy selfe, nor ever shall be if the Lord please to graunt [grant] my desires, that I may intend what I long after, the natives Soules."[188] During the Pequot War (1636–1638), Williams partially blamed the conflict on English hypocrisy, namely "the little sence" shown by the colonists of Natives' "soules Condicion and our large protestations [i.e., affirmations] that way."[189] Less than a year later, Williams was still optimistic: "Sir I hope shortly to send you good newes of great hopes the Lord hath sprung up in mine Eye of many a poore Indian soule enquiring after God. I have convinced hundreths at home and abroad that in point of Religion they are all wandring etc. . . . I hope the time is not long that Some shall truely blesse the God of Heaven that ever they saw the face of English men."[190]

Perhaps the fullest expression of Williams' evangelistic optimism came with his publication of *A Key into the Language of America* in 1643.[191] Part of the rhetorical force of *A Key* is the overwhelming impression it gives of Williams, the missionary and astute student of Indian culture, alone with the Indians in the desolate wilderness of the New England frontier. Williams observes, he discusses, he evangelizes; he dutifully abstains from participation in their rituals, which he calls "Sathans Inventions and Worships."[192] He praises the civility and religiosity he finds in Native culture and speaks well of Native intelligence. Although *A Key* covers a wide range of Native practices and customs, including marriage, eating, hunting, and childbirth, it is also a document infused with theological application.[193] The overall thrust of the work leaves the impression that Williams' intimate knowledge of Indian language and culture could easily be leveraged for securing their conversion to Christianity. And, in fact, even in the introduction addressed to the reader, Williams demonstrates this to be the case. Williams recounts that he heard that his "old friend" Wequash, the "*Pequot Captaine*," was dying, and so he paid him a visit. Wequash admitted to Williams that his prior words concerning the condition of Wequash's soul "*were never out of [his] heart to this present*" and that he "*much pray[ed] to Jesus Christ*."[194] Although Williams did not wish to "be so confident as others" about Wequash's spiritual state, he hints that Wequash's parting would not be their last meeting, thereby illustrating to his readers the supposed spiritual and evangelistic benefits of knowing the language of the Indians.[195]

As scholars have pointed out, however, Williams was using *A Key* for wider political purposes.[196] With hostile Massachusetts Bay magistrates threatening to invade and take over his colony, Williams desperately needed to get the upper hand and prove to English officials that his colony deserved a separate patent. Jonathan Beecher Field argues that *A Key* allowed Williams to define the parameters of the debate, in particular by showing that the Narragansetts had a notion of property rights, thereby legitimizing his purchases of and claims to the land around the Narragansett Bay. The goal of *A Key*, Field suggests, was "not so much to teach Londoners how to speak to Native Americans but rather to teach them how to think about America"—particularly in ways that benefited Roger Williams.[197] Similarly, the story of Wequash's conversion, Kristina Bross has argued, should be read as Williams' attempt to obtain "discursive control of Wequash's deathbed scene"—and by extension, Indian evangelization more broadly, particularly since the authors of *New England's First Fruits* (published while Williams was still finishing *A Key*) recounted the life and death of Wequash as an example of the evangelism undertaken by the English.[198] By showing his linguistic abilities, Williams also gave English officials great confidence that he was actually going to *do* the work of evangelizing the Natives, not just talk about it, putting himself at the forefront of missionary efforts and thereby remedying earlier accusations of evangelistic disinterest exhibited by New England's colonists.[199]

Williams was granted a Parliamentary patent for his colony in 1644, much to the chagrin of Massachusetts officials, but expectant evangelistically minded readers of *A Key* must have been disappointed to read *Christenings Make Not Christians* (1645) a year later.[200] In *Christenings*, Williams boasted that it was within his power to bring about the mass conversion of New England Indians: "I know it to have been easie for my selfe, long ere this, to have brought many thousands of these Natives, yea the whole country, to a far greater Antichristian conversion than ever was yet heard of in *America*. . . . [H]ow readily I could have brought the whole Country to have observed one day in seven . . . to have received a *Baptisme* (or washing) . . . to have come to a *stated Church meeting*, maintained priests and formes of prayer."[201] Given this boast, Williams anticipated a difficult and logical question: "Why then if . . . you have such a *Key* of *Language*, and such a dore of *opportunity*, in the knowledge of the Country and the inhabitants, why proceed you not to produce in *America* some patterns of such conversions as you speake of?"[202]

It was a fair question, and Williams had answers. The first reason given in *Christenings* was the difficulty of attempting to "proceed to such a further degree of the Language, as to be able in propriety of speech to open matters of salvation to them."[203] This was surely a strange excuse when one considers Williams' apparent proficiency in describing the essentials of English Christianity and the ability of the Natives to understand those concepts—at least as they are represented in *A Key into the Language of America*. On his deathbed, for example, Wequash remembered that Williams had previously "acquainted [Wequash] with the *Condition* of *all mankind,* & his *Own* in particular, how *God* created *Man* and *All things*: how *Man* fell from *God*, and of his present *Enmity* against *God*, and the *wrath of God* against *Him* untill *Repentance*."[204] Williams also asserted that his *Key* provided "proper expressions concerning the Creation of the World, and mans Estate, and in particular theirs also."[205] "[G]reat numbers" of Indians, Williams claimed, "many hundredths of times" had heard "with great delight, and great convictions" these spiritual truths.[206] Apparently, the Natives in *A Key into the Language of America* did not see linguistic difficulties as a barrier to effective communication and comprehension of Christian truths.

Williams, however, identified two other additional important obstacles to Indian conversion. The first was his growing belief that the church in the present age lacked the proper apostolic commission to evangelize the Natives.[207] Williams believed that "Gods great businesse between Christ Jesus the holy Son of God and Antichrist the man of sin and Sonne of perdition" must first come to pass, and *"Zion* and *Jerusalem* be rebuilt and reestablished, before the Law and word of life be sent forth to the rest of the Nations of the World, who have not heard of Christ."[208] It followed, then, that "there can be no preaching (according to the last Will and Testament of Christ Jesus) without a true sending."[209] But a second and even deeper barrier was a constant fear of false conversions, whether Indian or European. Williams spends two full pages in *Christenings* first defining what conversions are not, and then what they are. Taken all together,

Williams was fearful of simply converting Natives "from one false worship to another," but also of "a mixture of the manner or worship of the true God, the King of Israel, with false gods & their worships."[210] Instead, true conversions needed to be "by the free proclaiming or preaching of Repentance & forgivenesse of sins," but they also needed to be all-encompassing, "a turning of the whole man from the power of *Sathan* unto God," in ways that included proper "waies of his holy worship, appointed by his Son."[211]

This powerful presumption against false conversions completely ruled out evangelization by force. Conversion "must not be," Williams asserted, "a conversion of People to the woship of the Lord Jesus, by force of Armes and swords of steele."[212] This strong conviction of noncoercion in religious matters is partly what got him in trouble in the Massachusetts Bay in the first place; it continued to permeate his writings and civic leadership throughout his life, even as it related to Native conversions. In 1654 Williams wrote to the Massachusetts Bay General Court, imploring it to refrain from war with the Narragansetts and the Long Island Indians. In particular, he found it especially troublesome that such a war might simply be a pretext for subduing the Natives in order to force them to profess Christianity. Williams had been visited by some Narragansett sachems who asked him to petition "the high Sachims of England that they might not be forced from their Religion, and for not changing their Religion be invaded by War. For they said they were dayly visited with Threatnings by Indians that came from about the Massachusets, that if they would not pray they should be destroyed by War."[213] In keeping with his views of religious freedom and passivity with regard to Indian conversion, Williams pointedly protested that in pamphlets published in London the Narragansett sachems were "publikely branded for refusing to pray and be converted."[214]

After his 1654 letter, Williams barely mentioned Indian evangelization again until this unpublished shorthand essay, "A Brief Reply to a Small Book Written by John Eliot," written ca. 1680.[215] It was John Eliot who first raised the subject of Native Americans in the context of the debate over baptism in his 1679 treatise *A Brief Answer to a Small Book Written by John Norcot Against Infant-Baptisme*, but it was a minor—literally parenthetical—reference. Much of Eliot's defense of infant baptism stemmed from his belief in the spiritual benefits that extend to the children who receive it. Eliot argued children are "*the heritage of the Lord . . . by virtue of their parental Covenant*."[216] The benefit given to baptized infants by this parental covenant Eliot calls a "spiritual Patrimony, our Estate in Religion which our Parents conveigh unto us," a benefit that continues throughout the life of the believer, "especially at some difficult times."[217] As E. Brooks Holifield has pointed out, Calvinist ministers like Eliot walked a fine line; they argued that baptism "sealed the covenant of grace" and yet they had to "avoid the appearance of suggesting that every baptized soul had an automatic claim to God's mercy."[218] Therefore, according to Eliot, a baptized child was expected to move into an "acquired state in grace . . . by the good improvement of his Patrimony."[219] This spiritual inheritance was, in Eliot's mind, an essential starting point, a foundation upon which all of the Christian life rested.[220]

But Eliot, the famous (and, by 1679, infamous) missionary to the Indians, knew spiritual patrimony, if exclusively insisted upon, potentially undercut his Native evangelization efforts. After all, Eliot's entire missionary program was predicated on the idea that Indians could and had come to faith for the first time under his care and without the benefit of spiritual patrimony. Accordingly, Eliot wavered, just for a moment: "our spiritual Patrimony is a great & sanctified means of conversion, though not the only means, for strangers (as our Indians) are converted by the Gospel without that means, as far as we know."[221] Williams capitalized on this chink in Eliot's defenses by asserting that the more direct conversion by the gospel, which allowed for the inclusion of Native Americans, was actually the preferable and intended route for all people everywhere. As for those who lean on their spiritual inheritance through baptism, Williams simply states, "Surely we be *cautious* of such conversions to Christ. The Apostle Paul [in] Romans 10.17 speaks clearly against this: 'faith cometh by hearing and hearing by the word of God' . . . not by patrimony."[222]

But Williams goes beyond mere refutation of Eliot's stance regarding the benefits of spiritual patrimony. Instead, he questions the very idea that Native Americans themselves are truly being converted, whether directly by the gospel or through spiritual patrimony. Williams claimed that "it would be [a] cause of great joy" if such conversions of Native peoples were "true" (sincere), but, in fact, the very process by which Indians were being evangelized was problematic; the end result was false conversions. "They might speak [or] do *something* as they are taught," Williams acknowledged, but this is not conversion. To make his point, Williams levels the most devastating critique possible for early modern Protestants when it came to Indian evangelization: "*[T]his* conversion [of the] Indians appears as the French and Spanish [conversions]."[223] The near-universal seventeenth-century Protestant assessment of Catholic missionaries was that they produced patently false conversions among the Indians in two ways. First, many Protestants believed that Catholic missionaries (especially Jesuit and Franciscan ones) merely baptized their proselytes without requiring serious Christian knowledge and a genuine turning away from Native cultural practices. But second, even if Natives did fully and genuinely embrace Catholicism, their conversions would still be false, according to most Protestants, since they embraced a corrupted version of Christianity.[224]

Williams' critique of Eliot's evangelistic methods seems somewhat out of place within the larger flow of his "A Brief Reply." The rest of his essay more directly refutes the practice of infant baptism in English churches. Even in this short section on Indian conversion, Williams does not directly address the occurrence of the baptism of Indian infants, even though by 1680 the Indian children of Christianized parents were being brought forward for baptism, thereby enacting the practice of spiritual patrimony within Indian communities.[225] His critique of Indian infant baptism is implied in his criticisms of spiritual patrimony and infant baptism among the English, but his primary focus in this section is on the touted success of Eliot's overt evangelization of Indian adults.[226]

This short section concerning Natives in Williams' "A Brief Reply," then, gives a rare window into the serious disagreements regarding Indian evangelization that existed between Eliot and Williams. As Cesarini has argued, Williams' *A Key* "has almost always seemed antithetical, in its assumptions and in its purpose, to the writings of New English missionaries such as John Eliot."[227] If Eliot and most English men and women read the various elements of Native lifeways as "signs of Indian degeneracy" that needed to be civilized and Christianized, Williams argued that "in many respects Indian culture was superior to the ways of 'the civiliz'd World.'"[228] Although this may have been true in *A Key*, Glenn LaFantasie has argued that Williams seems to have over time adopted the "civilizing before Christianizing" framework of his Massachusetts Bay counterparts. More than a decade after the publication of *A Key*, Williams closed an address to the General Court of Massachusetts Bay by affirming the general practice of moving Natives from "Barbarisme to Civilitie, in forsaking their filthy nakednes, in keeping some kind of Cattell etc.," and acknowledging that "Civilitie may be a leading step to Christianitie."[229]

If Williams had accused the Massachusetts Bay Puritans in the early 1640s of pretending to evangelize the Indians (whereas Williams implied he was actually doing it), by the late 1640s the tables had been reversed and would remain that way for the rest of Williams' life. Williams had claimed in 1643 to have a key into the language of the Natives, and yet had nothing to show for it over time, while Eliot's labors starting in 1646 produced hundreds of "Praying Indians," at least fourteen Praying Towns (by 1675), the creation of a written version of the Massachusett language, and dozens of books, primers, and even the entire Bible, all in Indian languages emanating from the press in Cambridge, Massachusetts.[230] Even worse, these Native conversions—no matter how false in Williams' mind—were attracting lots of attention in the British Isles, something Williams witnessed in person. "[A]ll Engl. and other nations ring with the glorious Conversion of the Indians of New Engl.," reported Williams—who had just returned from London earlier that year—to the Massachusetts General Court in 1654. "[H]ow many bookes are dispersed throughout the nation of the subject . . . how have all the pulpits in Engl. bene commanded to sound of this Glorious Worck and that by the highest Command and Authoritie of Parliamt."[231]

Williams was referring to what historians have termed the "Eliot tracts," a series of promotional pamphlets and treatises published in London describing, as the subtitle of *The Clear Sun-shine of the Gospel* optimistically proclaimed, "An Historicall Narration of Gods Wonderfull Workings upon sundry of the Indians, both chief Governors and Common-people, in bringing them to a willing and desired submission to the Ordinances of the Gospel."[232] Six such treatises were published in

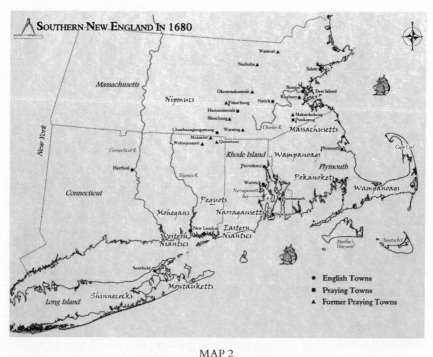

MAP 2

Southern New England in 1680. Map created by Lynn Carlson, GISP, Brown University. Copyright Linford D. Fisher.

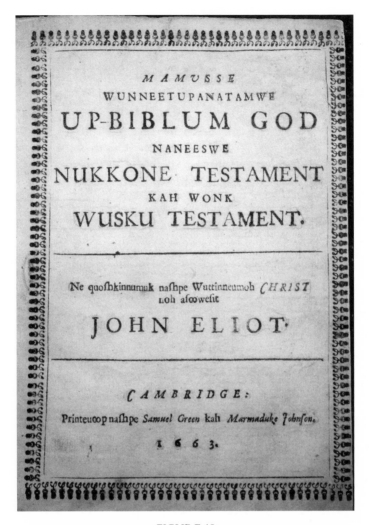

FIGURE 18
Mamusse Wunneetupanatamwe Up-Biblium God *title page.*
Photograph by Linford D. Fisher.
Courtesy of the John Carter Brown Library at Brown University.

London between 1647 and 1653, at least two of them while Williams was in England on colony business.[233] Williams could not—and likely did not want to—compete with this outburst of promotional materials that centered on John Eliot (whom he did not mention in this 1654 letter); instead, he merely commented dryly to the Massachusetts General Court, "Honored Sirs Whether I have bene and am a friend to the Natives turning to Civilitie and Christianitie, and whether I have bene instrumental and desire so to be (according to my Light) I will not trouble You with."[234] The main point of Williams' letter was to critique the increasingly untenable twin policies of warfare and evangelization pursued by the Massachusetts Bay.[235] Nonetheless, Williams demonstrated that he was aware—perhaps even painfully so—of the attention and funding Eliot was receiving.[236]

There is little evidence that Eliot and Williams were in active dialogue over the years, which seems peculiar given their mutual interest in Native communities. Not one letter between the two men has survived.[237] Williams only mentions Eliot twice in his correspondence, both times almost in passing, first in 1649, and again near the very end of his life, in a May 6, 1682, in a letter to Massachusetts Governor Simon Bradstreet.[238] Whatever shared interests they had were likely soured by Eliot's role in not only Williams' but also Anne Hutchinson's banishment from the Massachusetts Bay Colony.[239] Like most other Massachusetts Bay Puritans, Eliot never hesitated to use Williams as a negative foil in their Indian evangelization. In *The Clear Sun-shine of the Gospel Breaking Forth upon the Indians in New-England* (1648), Thomas Shepard reported Eliot's visitation with a Narragansett sachem who knew and understood "the means of salvation by Christ" but refused to say whether or not he believed them. Eliot then pointedly asked the sachem "why they did not learn of Mr. *Williams* who hath lived among them divers yeers?" The sachem's response— filtered through Eliot—was a thinly veiled jab at Williams: "because hee is no good man but goes out and workes upon the Sabbath day."[240] Similarly, John Cotton in *The Way of the Congregational Churches Cleared* (1648) asserted that not only had Williams been "too prodigally hyperbolicall" about the ease of Indian conversion in *Christenings* (Williams boasted he could have brought hundreds to be baptized), but that Williams' "sinne is so much the greater before the Lord" since he "did neglect to take the opportunitie of preaching to them the Word of the Lord."[241] Cotton juxtaposed Williams' nonaction with the slow but steady progress of "Mr. *Eliot*, the Teacher of the Church of *Rocksbury*," who preached to local Indians "in their own language weekly."[242]

Williams, rarely content to ignore public and printed attacks on his character, responded by directly attacking the linguistic competency of John Eliot. In *The Bloody Tenent Yet More Bloody* (1652), Williams continued his in-print debate with Boston minister John Cotton over the issue of religious freedom.[243] In a short section responding to Cotton's boasts regarding Massachusett ministers' progress in Indian evangelization, Williams responded by, first, challenging once again the possibility of a true apostolic commission for such activity, and second, questioning the ability of such missionaries to adequately communicate Christian ideas: "yet I believe that none of the *Ministers* of *New England*, nor any person in the whole *Countrey* is able to open the *Mysteries* of *Christ Jesus* in any proprietie of their *speech* or *Language*."[244] In case the target of his criticism was unclear, Williams made it plain by noting an episode in one of the Eliot tracts in which "Mr *Eliot* (the ablest amongst them in the *Indian Speech*) promising an old *Indian* a suit of Cloths, the man (sayth the relation) not well understanding Mr *Eliots* speech, asked another *Indian* what Mr *Eliot* said."[245] If Eliot was unable to adequately communicate about clothing, Williams implied, how much less so regarding salvation? Although Williams claimed he did not wish to "dampe Mr *Eliot*" or others from doing what they can, Williams insisted "how great that mistake is, that pretends such a true *preaching* of *Christ Jesus* to them in their owne *Language*."[246]

Whatever criticisms Williams leveled regarding Eliot's facility with Native languages were drowned out by Eliot's Indian-language publications rolling off of the Cambridge press at Harvard starting in the 1650s, the most impressive of which was the entire Christian Bible in the Massachusett language in 1663, titled *Mamusse Wunneetupanatamwe Up-Biblum God*.[247] Williams obtained a copy and proceeded to use the open spaces in the front and back of the thick volume as a place to take notes, remarkably, in the same shorthand he would later use to write out his critique of Eliot.[248] After the publication of the Indian Bible, Williams largely fell silent on the issue; his critiques no longer seemed credible, and indeed, he himself had been sidelined on the topic of Indian languages and the possibilities of Native conversion.

Williams' taking on of John Eliot in an entire essay after 1679, then, represents a surprisingly direct engagement with someone who had always lurked in the back of Williams' Native dealings. And Williams' essay shows that, late in life, he still remained profoundly skeptical of the entire evangelization project as conducted in Massachusetts and acutely resentful of Eliot himself, who Williams says sounds like a "grievous wolf."[249] In his response to Eliot, Williams also takes it upon himself to critique not just the *conversions* of Indians, but the *converter* of Indians. "[I]t would be [a] cause of great joy if they were feeling true," Williams acknowledged, referring to Native professions of Christianity, "But if the shepherd of their chiefs [uses] treachery and seduction, [it] is much a sore to the wisdom of the gospel of Christ."[250] Although the shorthand is a bit vague here, the most straightforward translation is "the shepherd of their chiefs," meaning John Eliot himself. With a misguided "shepherd" as their leader, and with such a dubious process of spiritual training in place, Williams fundamentally doubts genuine Christianity can ever be transmitted: "But if their leaders be prepared in error, how can their duties be considered true or according to the Gospel?"[251]

More surprisingly, perhaps, is that Williams charges Eliot not only with producing false conversions but also for using "treachery and seduction" to do so. Williams' use of the phrase "treachery and seduction" at first seems mismatched to the context and topic at hand; one might expect a more explicitly theological critique of Eliot regarding Indian conversion. It is possible Williams intended to evoke several connotations. The first and most obvious is a parallel to Protestant stereotypes of Catholic missionaries, who, as he described in *Christenings Make Not Christians*, effected conversions by "baptizing thousands, yea ten thousands of the poore Natives, sometimes by wiles and subtle devices, sometimes by force compelling them to submit to that which they understood not, neither before nor after such their monstrous Christning of them."[252] This connection is made explicit by Williams' reference in "A Brief Reply" to Native conversions under Eliot appearing "as the French and Spanish [conversions]."[253]

But perhaps the most important—and more immediate—context for Williams' comments was the devastation visited on the region through the lamentable events of King Philip's War just five short years prior to the writing of Williams' essay. Triggered largely by decades of increasing English encroachment on Native lands, losses of Native political sovereignty, and a decline in Native cultural autonomy, the war divided Native communities and mostly soured colonial views of Natives as a whole, particularly Christianized ones. But concentrated attempts to convert Natives was also part of the bundle of complaints leveled against the English. The main leader in the uprising, the Wampanoag sachem Metacom or King Philip, stated early in the war that he and his leaders, among other concerns, "had a great Fear to have ani of ther Indians should be caled or forced to be Christian Indians."[254] During the war, the general public consensus was that the "Praying Indians" so carefully cultivated by Eliot had largely abandoned their Christianization and instead turned directly on the English at their weakest moment. In reality, Christian Indian response to the war varied greatly. Although many Christianized Natives did serve with the English as translators, warriors, and spies, others tried to remain neutral; others still clearly used the opportunity to join in the general rebellion against the English.[255]

Nonetheless, given the public outcry against Eliot's "Praying Indians"—the greatest manifestation of which was the forced exile of five hundred of them to Deer Island in the Boston Harbor during the winter of 1675–1676—it is likely that Williams was pointing to the popular perception of Praying Indian perfidy during the war as an example of just how shallow he believed these Natives' conversions were in the first place and how misguided Eliot's evangelization efforts had been all along.[256] After all, Mary Rowlandson's captivity narrative *The Soveraignty & Goodness of God* (1682), published within the possible time frame of Williams' "A Brief Reply" (1679–1683), highlights precisely the kind of activity that Williams may have intended to invoke with the phrase "treachery and seduction."[257] Praying Indians, according to Rowlandson, joined King Philip's forces, fighting alongside of the other Indians; they went back on their former convictions (like not eating horse meat); they betrayed their family members to save their own lives; and they were rightly (in her mind) hanged for their treacherous rebellion. "There was another Praying *Indian*," Rowlandson recalled, "so wicked and cruel, as to wear a string about his neck, strung with *Christians* fingers."[258] Christian Indians, in the popular perception, were indistinguishable from non-Christian ones in terms of their actions. Scholars have argued that King Philip's War proved to be the decisive turning point during which English perceptions of New England Natives shifted to a point of no return.[259] Given the real and public setback the war had been to Eliot's evangelization efforts (fourteen praying towns reduced to four, for example), Williams' postwar critique was gratuitous at best, an indictment of a missionary movement that barely survived the war itself.[260]

King Philip's War surely must have intensified Williams' conviction of the relative impossibility of Indian conversions that conformed to his standards. Even before the war, in 1668, Williams confessed to the Massachusetts General Court, "I abhor most of their Customes. I know they are Barbarous," which was a far cry from the ethnographic admiration of *A Key* twenty-five years prior (although, to be fair, he said this even as he noted Natives' decorum in mourning practices).[261] And in December 1675, as united English and Indian forces from Massachusetts, Plymouth, and Connecticut gathered in Rhode Island to attack the Narragansett stronghold (largely against the wishes of the Rhode Island magistrates), Williams simultaneously lamented and tacitly accepted the possibility that "it is not possible at present to keepe peace with these barbarous men of Bloud who are as justly to be repelld and subdued as Wolves that assault the sheepe."[262] With Rhode Island dragged into the war, the aged Williams headed a local militia for the public defense of the colony, but even he could not prevent roving bands of Indians from burning most of Providence to the ground, including Williams' own house. At the war's end, he oversaw the public execution of at least one Indian rebel, Chuff, and chaired a committee in Providence that divvied up the human spoils of war in the form of limited-term enslavement of Natives as recompense to the colony's residents for damage done to them and their properties by the Indians (which Williams and others saw as a less-harsh punishment than shipping them to the Caribbean as lifelong slaves).[263]

The combination of Williams' lifelong nonbelief in the propriety of certain modes of Indian evangelization (at least after the early 1640s) along with the cultural vitality of the Narragansetts and their military prominence until King Philip's War spared the Narragansetts from intensive, Eliot-style proselytization into the early eighteenth century. Daniel Gookin noted in 1674 that the Rhode Island Indians were "more indisposed to embrace religion [i.e., Christianity], than any Indians in the country," and a 1698 NEC survey of Native Christian churches and schools in New England omitted Rhode Island entirely.[264] Although the opening decades of the eighteenth century brought about a "second wave" of Indian evangelistic and educational attempts among the Narragansetts that began to reshape their lifeways, it was not until fifty-nine years after Williams' death, in the years surrounding the First Great Awakening of the 1730s and 1740s, that significant numbers of Narragansetts professed Christian beliefs, adopted Christian practices, and even formed their own separate Indian Christian church.[265] And, ironically, the Narragansett Indian Church was led by a baptistic-minded Narragansett minister, Samuel Niles, who himself was rebaptized and would have likely embraced the arguments for adult baptism set forth by Williams in his "A Brief Reply," had Niles ever seen them.[266]

Undoubtedly, Williams would have felt equally ambivalent about such Native professions of faith, even during times of religious revival. Although previously it was not possible for scholars to know how, if at all, Williams' ideas about Native evangelization and conversion changed between the 1650s and the 1680s, this newly deciphered Roger Williams shorthand essay gives us important insight regarding these issues. As gauged from Williams' "A Brief Reply," he went to the grave profoundly skeptical of the larger Indian evangelization project, surprisingly resentful of John Eliot himself, ever cautious about producing false conversions among English and Indians alike, and confident that his vision for religious liberty and noncoercion as embodied in Rhode Island still stood as a necessary corrective to the Massachusetts Bay Colony.

CONCLUSION

Williams' "A Brief Reply" is important because it sheds new light on two issues that were central to the life and thinking of Roger Williams, namely, baptism and Indian conversion. In both cases, this new essay demonstrates an essential continuity in Williams' thinking. Late in his life, Williams still believed that the Massachusetts Bay Puritans had it wrong; baptism was to be reserved for believers who could make their own professions of faith. And with regard to Native Americans, Williams continued to believe that heavy-handed methods of conversion and proselytization were misguided. Ever fearful of false conversions, Williams far preferred his long-term friendship with and occasional sermons to Natives over Eliot's much-publicized, large-scale Native Christianization. One wonders what the ripple effect might have been if Williams had been able to publish this essay. Would Eliot have responded to such a direct attack on his lifelong Native evangelization efforts? And would the printing presses of the Massachusetts Bay have spun off refutations of Williams' views on baptism? One can only imagine. Instead, the essay lay hidden and unintelligible to readers and historians until now.

NOTES

[1] The essay is undated, but it was written between 1679 (when Eliot's book was published [see below], to which Williams was responding) and early 1683 (when Williams died).

[2] The book in which Williams wrote was subtitled *An Essay Towards the Reconciling of Differences Among Christians*; it is now housed at the John Carter Brown Library in Providence, Rhode Island.

[3] The members of the Brown undergraduate research team included Simon Liebling (Brown '12), Lucas Mason-Brown (Brown '13), Katherine Mead (Brown '12), and Christopher Norris-LeBlanc (Brown '13). The team received support and advice from a wide variety of scholars, including Kimberly Nusco (reference and manuscript librarian, the John Carter Brown Library), Ted Widmer (former director, the John Carter Brown Library), Steven Lubar (professor of American studies, Brown University), Jeffrey Hoffstein (professor of mathematics, Brown University), Eugene Charniak (professor of computer science, Brown University), Linford Fisher (assistant professor of history, Brown University), J. Stanley Lemons (professor emeritus, Rhode Island College), Tim Harris (professor of history, Brown University), and Hal Cook (professor of history, Brown University). For early press coverage on the start of the process, see Alexa Pugh, "At the JCB, Cracking the Williams Code," *Brown Daily Herald*, November 7, 2011, http://www.browndaily herald.com/2011/11/07/at-the-jcb-cracking-the-williams-code. For a detailed account of the code-cracking process, see Ben Schreckinger, "The Roger Williams Code: How a team of scholars decrypted a secret language—and discovered the last known work of the American theologian," *Slate*, December 12, 2012, http://www.slate.com/articles/life/ history/2012/12/the_roger_williams_code_how_a_team_of_scholars_discovered_the _theologian.html.

[4] A mathematics concentrator, Lucas Mason-Brown, cracked the code, developed a key, and, over a period of one year with grant support from Brown University and the John Carter Brown Library, translated much of the marginalia.

[5] The two main pieces of Williams' shorthand outside of this essay are contained, first, in a letter at the Rhode Island Historical Society, and second, in Williams' copy of the Eliot

Indian Bible (1663) at the John Hay Library, Brown University. Shorthand fragments occasionally appear in his correspondence as well.

[6] A small sample of pamphlets and treatises that appeared between 1640 and 1675 includes Christopher Blackwood, *The Storming of Antichrist, in His Two Last and Strongest Garrisons, of Compulsion of Conscience and Infants Baptisme* (London, 1644); Thomas Blake, *Infants Baptisme, Freed from Antichristianisme in a Full Repulse Given to Mr. Ch. Blackwood* (London: Printed by R.W. for Thomas Underhill, 1645); Thomas Lambe, *Truth Prevailing Against the Fiercest Opposition, or, An Answer to Mr. John Goodwins Water-dipping No Firm Footing for Church Communion* (London: Printed by G. Dawson, 1655); Richard Baxter, *Plain Scripture Proof of Infants Church-membership and Baptism* (London: T.V.F.T., 1656); William Parker, *Infant-Baptisme Justified by a New Discovery: And Also Several Scripture Allegories Adjusted Upon the Like Account* (London: Printed for the author, 1668); Thomas Grantham and Jeremy Taylor, *The Pædo-baptists Apology for the Baptized Churches Shewing the Invalidity of the Strongest Grounds for Infant Baptism Out of the Works of the Learned Assertors of That Tenent* (London, 1671). Thanks to Curtis Freeman, who graciously provided many of these references.

[7] John Norcott, *Baptism Discovered Plainly and Faithfully, According to the Word of God* (London, 1672). The original publication date of the treatise is somewhat unclear, since copies of the original printing are rare, and at least one surviving original copy at the Angus Library, Regent's Park College, Oxford, is missing the title page. But other sources place the original publication in 1672. Personal correspondence by the authors with archivist Julian Lock, Angus Library. More common—but still rare—are copies of the second edition, printed in London in 1675. See William Thomas Whitley, *A Baptist Bibliography* (Hildesheim: Georg Olms Verlag, 1916), 96. At least one nineteenth-century Baptist historian dated it no earlier than 1670. Henry Martyn Dexter, *The True Story of John Smyth, the Se-baptist, as Told by Himself and His Contemporaries* (Boston: Lee & Shepard, 1881), 75, nn. 55, 56. (A "se-baptist" is someone who has baptized him or herself.) John Norcott died on March 24, 1676, while serving as the pastor of the church in Gravel-lane, Wapping. William Brackney and Paul S. Fiddes, eds., *Pilgrim Pathways: Essays in Baptist History in Honour of B. R. White* (Macon, Ga.: Mercer University Press, 1999), 185.

[8] Known editions and reprintings after 1672 include 1675 (London), 1694 (London), 1700, 1709 (Dublin), 1721, 1722 (London), 1723 (Boston), 1740 (Dublin), 1747 (Boston), 1762, 1764 (Philadelphia), 1785 (Bennington, Vt.), 1799 (Mount Holly, N.J.), 1801 (Salem, Mass.), and 1878. Non-English translations include Welsh (1893) and Swedish (1908). The 1878 version was corrected and altered by Charles H. Spurgeon, the popular British Particular Baptist preacher. In the early twenty-first century, Norcott's treatise received a new publishing life with several reprintings, including one in 2011 by Ulan Press. This listing was compiled by the authors using http://www.worldcat .org and other printed sources, including Dexter, *The True Story of John Smyth*, 101; and Geoffrey F. Nuttall, "Another Baptist Ejection (1662): The Case of John Norcott," in *Pilgrim Pathways*, 185.

[9] John Eliot, *A Brief Answer to a Small Book Written by John Norcot Against Infant-Baptisme* (Boston: John Foster, 1679). In stark contrast to Norcott's book, Eliot's treatise does not appear to have been reprinted, nor were any subsequent editions issued. Regarding the spelling of Norcott, although Eliot renders it with one "t," Norcott's own 1675 edition has it with two, "Norcott," which is what we have chosen to use here. In his shorthand essay, Williams occasionally renders it "Norcut."

[10] Williams did not give a formal title to this new original essay that he wrote (in the margins of the book subtitled *An Essay Towards the Reconciling of Differences Among Christians*), although a title can be deduced from the first sentence of the shorthand essay: "A Brief Reply to a Small Book Written by John Eliot." For the purposes of this essay, we will refer to this new Williams shorthand essay as Roger Williams, "A Brief Reply to a Small Book Written by John Eliot," in *An Essay Towards the Reconciling of Differences Among*

Christians ([London], n.d.), 138–59. It is ironic, of course, that Williams' refutation of John Eliot on the contentious issue of infant baptism is contained within the margins of a book concerning the "Reconciling of Differences Among Christians."

[11] Williams' correspondence during this time illustrates his roles in and perspectives on King Philip's War. See Glenn W. LaFantasie, ed., *The Correspondence of Roger Williams* (Hanover, N.H.: University Press of New England, 1988), 2:690–730.

[12] King Philip's War has generated an extensive secondary literature, but one of the best books is Jill Lepore, *The Name of War: King Philip's War and the Origins of American Identity* (New York: Alfred A. Knopf, 1998).

[13] John Russell Bartlett, ed., *Records of the Colony and State of Rhode Island and Providence Plantations in New England*, 10 vols. (Providence: A Crawford Greene and Brothers, 1857), 2:531, 547; entries for August 14, August 29, August 30, 1676 (entry nos. 234–35, 242), and January 1677, *The Early Records of the Town of Providence*, Horatio Rogers and Edward Field, records commissioners (Providence: Snow & Farnham City Printers, 1899), 15:151–55.

[14] Although there was indeed a Widow Tweedy living in the Newport area at that time, the authors have been unable to establish any credible details concerning who Widow Tweedy was or how she came upon this book.

[15] The John Carter Brown Library (JCB) catalog lists the possible date of publication as 1646. The JCB copy of this book is the only known extant copy in the world.

[16] The book came with a short handwritten note, dated November 11, 1817, which reads, "The margin is filled with Short Hand Characters, Dates, Names of places &c. &c. by Roger Williams or it appears to be his hand Writing. . . . brot me from Widow Tweedy by Nicholas Brown Jr."

[17] Historians debate exactly when and where Coke took notice of Williams. Coke's daughter, Ann Sadleir, later recalled that Williams, "when he was a youth, would in a short hand take sermons and speeches in the Star Chamber, and presented them to my dear father." Henry Chupack, *Roger Williams* (New York: Twayne, 1969), 27. Other biographers doubt that Williams (coming from a middling background) would have had access to the Star Chamber prior to his patronage from Coke. Ernst, *Roger Williams*, 25. According to Cyclone Covey, "The likeliest reason Williams would 'present' his work to Coke is that Coke had hired him as a 'diarist' to take down a private record of the court proceedings." Covey, *The Gentle Radical: A Biography of Roger Williams* (New York: Macmillan, 1966), 4.

[18] The thirteen-year-old Roger Williams was already proficient in shorthand before Coke hired him as a personal scribe. Historians have speculated as to how he learned shorthand. Ola Winslow suggests that it might have been from John May, who wrote Williams' mother's will. Winslow, *Master Roger Williams: A Biography* (New York: Macmillan, 1957), 46. Cyclone Covey also guesses that it was a family friend: "John May, Roger's most probable teacher of shorthand." Covey, *The Gentle Radical*, 4. L. Raymond Camp believes that Williams learned it from John Willis' son, Robert Willis, "a popular a shorthand tutor" who lived in Cow Lane very near to the Williams family during Williams' boyhood. John Willis was the author of the 1602 shorthand textbook *The Art of Stenographie*, on which Williams' shorthand is based. Camp, *Roger Williams, God's Apostle of Advocacy: Biography and Rhetoric*, Studies in American Religion 36 (Lampeter, Wales: Edwin Mellen Press, 1989), vii, 20. In any event, Williams had learned shorthand, Dutch, and Latin in preparation for his entry into the family cloth trade business before his life was redirected by Sir Edward Coke.

[19] John Willis, *The Art of Stenographie* (London: For Cuthbert Burbie, 1602). Other scholars have come to the same conclusion. See, e.g., LaFantasie, *The Correspondence of Roger Williams*, 1:233, n. 14.

[20] Timothy Bright, *Characterie: An Arte of Short, Swifte, and Secrete Writing by Character* (London: I. Windet, 1588). John Willis' system was later improved and refined by Edmond Willis in *An Abreviation of Writing by Character* (London: G. Purslow, 1618).

[21] An overview of seventeenth-century shorthand can be found in Frances Henderson, " 'Swifte and Secrete Writing' in Seventeenth-Century England, and Samuel Shelton's Brachygraphy," *British Library Journal*, Article 5 (2008).

[22] And there are numerous discrepancies in relative character frequency between seventeenth- and twenty-first-century English.

[23] Peter Heylyn, *Cosmographie in Foure Bookes: Containing the Chorographie and Historie of the Whole World, and All the Principall Kingdomes, Provinces, Seas, and Isles Thereof* (London: Printed for Henry Seile, 1652). The authors are especially grateful to Tim Harris for the suggestion to look at Heylyn's *Cosmographie*. Peter Heylyn (1599–1662) was an Oxford-educated historian, theologian, and controversialist. A staunch supporter of Archbishop Laud and King Charles I, Heylyn was an acerbic critic of the Puritans.

[24] Thomas Bartholin, *Bartholinus Anatomy; Made from the Precepts of His Father, and from the Observations of All Modern Anatomists, Together with His Own* (London: Printed for John Streater, 1668). Special thanks to Harold Cook, who provided a short list of possible matches for the third section. *Bartholinus Anatomy* was then identified among these possibilities as the actual source text by closely examining the longhand flags in the third section. Thomas Bartholin (1616–1680), a Danish physician, mathematician, and theologian, is most famous for his discovery of the lymphatic system.

[25] Special thanks to the Rhode Island Historical Society for furnishing these shorthand samples. Additional verification was obtained by comparing the shorthand in question to the shorthand found in Williams' copy of the Eliot Bible at the Hay Library at Brown University. Other examples of Williams' shorthand can be found in LaFantasie, *The Correspondence of Roger Williams*, in images following vol. 2, p. 624.

[26] Williams, "A Brief Reply," 138. The ellipsis indicates a small portion of shorthand that has not been deciphered. The bracketed words are implied but missing from the shorthand. See the editorial note at the beginning of the Williams essay below for more information.

[27] Two sources served as limited source texts: first, the King James Bible (1611), from which Williams frequently quotes; second, Eliot's *A Brief Answer*, which Williams frequently either quotes from or paraphrases.

[28] Samuel Pepys, *The Diary of Samuel Pepys* (n.p.: BiblioLife, 2008).

[29] Williams, "A Brief Reply," 138.

[30] See, e.g., the shorthand transcriptions taken by Thomas Danforth of the 1668 Baptist Debate. Danforth clearly used shorthand for purposes of efficiency. William G. McLoughlin and Martha Whiting Davidson, "The Baptist Debate of April 14–15, 1668," *Proceedings of the Massachusetts Historical Society* 76 (1964): 91–133.

[31] "Roger Williams to the Town of Providence, 8 December 1680," in LaFantasie, *The Correspondence of Roger Williams*, 2:774. Additional examples can be found on 1:231, 1:233, n. 14, 2:525n, 2:773n, and 2:774n.

[32] "To Massachusetts Governor John Leverett, January 14, 1675/76," and "To Governor John Leverett or Governor Josiah Winslow, October 16, 1676," in LaFantasie, *The Correspondence of Roger Williams*, 2:714, 729. One can only wonder how many other books Williams made notes in that have been lost. Much of his correspondence has disappeared, and only a few of the books that he owned have managed to survive.

[33] This appears in *An Essay Towards the Reconciling of Differences Among Christians* on the page immediately preceding p. 1.

[34] As is common in many early modern shorthand systems, some symbols assume various meanings, depending on context and usage.

[35] The corresponding text in the original printed Heylyn book can be found in Peter Heylyn, *Cosmographie in Foure Bookes*, 2nd ed. (London: Printed for Henry Seile, 1657), 242. A perceptive reader will notice several minor discrepancies between the text of Heylyn's *Cosmographie* and Williams' shorthand transcription. Compare, e.g., Heylyn's "Pride from

the Goths" with Williams' "from the Goths pride." Such discrepancies are likely the result of hasty shorthand transcription.

[36] High-resolution images of the full text of the book into which Williams wrote his shorthand essay (*An Essay Towards the Reconciling of Differences Among Christians*) can be found at http://archive.org/details/essaytowardsreco00will.

[37] See, e.g., Perry Miller, *Roger Williams: His Contribution to the American Tradition* (New York: Atheneum, 1962); John M. Barry, *Roger Williams and the Creation of the American Soul: Church, State, and the Birth of Liberty* (New York: Viking, 2012); Samuel Hugh Brockunier, *The Irrepressible Democrat, Roger Williams* (New York: Ronald Press, 1940). The phrase "lively experiment" comes from the 1663 Rhode Island charter granted by Charles II, which can be found at http://livelyexperiment.org/read-the-charter/. The frequently used, but faux, old-fashioned spelling "livelie" seems to be a corruption of the original document, which simply has "lively." The growing scholarship on religious toleration and liberty in the early modern world places Williams in a much larger and multivocal movement that slowly forced pockets of religious toleration and liberty in the Atlantic world. See, e.g., Chris Beneke and Christopher S. Grenda, eds., *The First Prejudice: Religious Tolerance and Intolerance in Early America* (Philadelphia: University of Pennsylvania Press, 2010); Evan Haefeli, *New Netherland and the Dutch Origins of American Religious Liberty* (Philadelphia: University of Pennsylvania Press, 2012); Andrew R. Murphy, *Conscience and Community: Revisiting Toleration and Religious Dissent in Early Modern England and America* (University Park: Pennsylvania State University Press, 2003).

[38] With the exception of *Experiments in Spiritual Life and Health* (1652), all of Williams' published writings were related to transatlantic controversies, and all except *George Fox Digg'd out of his Burrowes* (1676) were published in England. His ca. 1680 rejoinder to Eliot marked his return to the transatlantic issues, but it is unlikely it was going to be published in New England. *Experiments in Spiritual Life and Health* had been written earlier in 1651 for the comfort of his wife during a spiritual crisis brought on by sickness, but was published while he was in England for the second time. Even *George Fox Digg'd out of his Burrowes*, which recounts his three-day debate with the Quakers in Rhode Island, was intended to be Williams' general response to the ideas of George Fox's *The Great Mystery of the Great Whore Unfolded; And Antichrists Kingdom Revealed Unto Destruction* (1659). See W. Clark Gilpin, *The Millenarian Piety of Roger Williams* (Chicago: University of Chicago Press, 1979), 166–67. Because Williams had attacked the Quakers, old enemies of Massachusetts Bay, his book was published in Boston, but it is improbable that he could have gotten anything else published there.

[39] Baptists have historically claimed Roger Williams as one of their own, from John Callender and Isaac Backus, to David Benedict, James Davis Knowles, Romeo Elton, Thomas Armitage, and William Cathcart, to recent times with Robert Torbet, Edwin Gaustad, H. Leon McBeth, William H. Brackney, Bill J. Leonard, and Everett Goodwin. See, e.g., John Callender, *An Historical Discourse on the Civil and Religious Affairs of the Colony of Rhode-Island,* ed. Romeo Elton (1739; Providence: Knowles, Vose, 1838); Isaac Backus, *A History of New England with Particular Reference to the Denomination of Christians Called Baptists*, 3 vols. (Boston, 1779–1796); David Benedict, *A General History of the Baptist Denomination in America and Other Parts of the World*, 2 vols. (Boston: Manning & Loring, 1813); James David Knowles, *Memoir of Roger Williams: The Founder of Rhode-Island* (Boston: Lincoln, Edmands, 1834); Romeo Elton, *Life of Roger Williams: The Earliest Legislator and True Champion for a Full and Absolute Liberty of Conscience* (New York: G. W. Putnam, 1852); William Cathcart, ed., *The Baptist Encyclopedia* (Philadelphia: Louis H. Everts, 1881); Thomas Armitage, *A History of the Baptists Traced by Their Vital Principles and Practices from the Time of Our Lord and Savior Jesus Christ to the Year 1886* (New York: Bryan, Taylor, 1887); Robert G. Torbet, *History of the Baptists*, 3rd ed. (Valley Forge, Pa.: Judson Press, 1963); H. Leon McBeth, *The Baptist*

Heritage: Four Centuries of Baptist Witness (Nashville: Broadman Press, 1987); William H. Brackney, *The Baptists* (Westport, Conn.: Praeger, 1994); Edwin Gaustad, *Liberty of Conscience: Roger Williams in America* (Valley Forge, Pa.: Judson Press, 1999); Everett Goodwin, *Down by the Riverside: A Brief History of Baptist Faith* (Valley Forge, Pa.: Judson Press, 2002); Bill J. Leonard, *Baptist Ways: A History* (Valley Forge, Pa.: Judson Press, 2003); Idem, *Baptists in America* (New York: Columbia University Press, 2005).

[40] There are those who argue that Williams was never a Baptist, let alone the founder of the first Baptist church in America. Many Landmark Baptists maintain that John Clarke founded the first Baptist church in America in Newport. The Newport church made no claim until 1847 that it was the first Baptist church in America. Their claim was based on their misunderstanding of the Portsmouth Compact of March 7, 1638, which established the Portsmouth settlement of the Antinomian exiles from Massachusetts. See John C. C. Clarke, "Dr. John Clarke, of Newport, R.I.," in *The First Baptist Church in America*, ed. Samuel Adlam and James Robinson Graves (Texarkana: Baptist Sunday School Committee, 1939). Louis F. Asher argues, "Whether or not an organized Baptist church existed at Providence before 1650 remains to be demonstrated by more than mere tradition." Asher, *John Clarke, 1609–1676* (Pittsburgh: Dorrance, 1997), 55. Asher further asserts, "In spite of an abundance of historical acumen alleging that Roger Williams was the first Baptist pastor in America, he was not a Baptist at all!" See Asher, "Was Roger Williams Really a Baptist?," reprinted at http://www.geocities.com/Athens/Delphi/8297/asherw.htm. Others argue that Williams really could not be considered a Baptist if he had not been immersed. See M. R. Ellis, "Was Roger Williams a Baptist?" *The Baptist* 9 (March 31, 1928): 408–10.

[41] At the time that Williams was a "Baptist," in 1638–1639, the label was not in use in New England; it was only developing in England in the 1640s. This is why we have chosen to describe Williams as "baptistic" in this essay. He accepted and continued to hold the most distinctive idea that characterized the Baptists of the seventeenth century—believer's baptism. According to H. Leon McBeth, the label "Baptists" was first applied to this movement by their opponents in the early 1640s. Baptists began to use this name themselves by the mid-1650s, but "not for a full century would *Baptist* be generally accepted." Those churches that eventually were called "Baptist" began as "brethren of the baptized way," "baptized Christians," "Baptized Church of Christ." However, their enemies called them "Anabaptists." See McBeth, *The Baptist Heritage*, 48–49.

[42] See LaFantasie, *The Correspondence of Roger Williams*, 1:170–200; *The Complete Writings of Roger Williams*, 7 vols., ed. John Russell Bartlett (New York: Russell & Russell, 1963), 7:117–37.

[43] This is the title of John Garrett's biography of Williams, *Roger Williams: Witness beyond Christendom, 1603–1683* (London: Collier-Macmillan, 1970), but Garrett regarded Williams as a "Seeker." See esp. chap. 7, pp. 145–75.

[44] *The Journal of John Winthrop, 1630–1645*, ed. James S. Dunn, James Savage, and Laetitia Yeandle (Cambridge, Mass.: Belknap Press of Harvard University Press, 1996), 286. Winthrop was referring to Catherine Scott, wife of Richard Scott and sister of Anne Hutchinson, as well as Ezekiel Holliman (Holyman). "Anabaptist" was the term that opponents used to slander the Baptists, trying to tie them to the wild excesses of the Anabaptists in Münster in Germany in 1534–1535. "Having no magistrates" meant that civil authorities had no role in church affairs, which meant separation of church and state.

[45] Raymond P. Stearns, *The Strenuous Puritan, Hugh Peter, 1599–1660* (Urbana: University of Illinois Press, 1954), 129.

[46] Stearns, *The Strenuous Puritan,* 130. Eight of those listed were founding members of the Providence church. Perhaps Peter's stay in New England softened his views and increased his tolerance, because when he returned to England in 1644 he called for "the toleration of all sects." This declaration so incensed the Presbyterian proponents of a national church

that Peter was singled out for special denunciation by the heresiologists, who called him a hypocrite, among other things, for his suppression of dissent in New England while calling for toleration in Old England. See Ann Hughes, *Gangraena and the Struggle for the English Revolution* (London: Oxford University Press, 2004), passim.

[47] Richard Scott, quoted in the introduction to *The Complete Writings of Roger Williams*, 5:li–liin. Scott penned this comment in a letter that became part of the Quaker response, entitled *A New-England Firebrand Quenched* (1678), to Williams' attack upon the Quakers in *George Fox Digg'd out of his Burrowes* (1676). Scott was said to have been the first Quaker convert in Providence, and he became an opponent of Williams after that conversion. In July 1639, Governor John Winthrop testified to the same development: "At Providence matters went after the old manner. Mr. Williams and many of his company, a few months since, were in all haste rebaptized, and denied communion with all others, and now he has come to question his rebaptism, not being able to derive the authority of it from the apostles." Winthrop, *Journal*, 300. All emphasis is original to the sources, unless otherwise noted.

[48] Williams replied to Governor Winthrop, who had asked him what he had gained from his stubborn Separatist position, "To his [Christ Jesus] all glorious Name I know I have gained the honour of one of his poore Witnesses, though in Sackcloth." "Williams to Governor John Winthrop, October 24, 1636," in LaFantasie, *The Correspondence of Roger Williams*, 1:66. The phrase "though in Sackcloth" is an allusion to God's witnesses in Revelation 11:3.

[49] Roger Williams never acknowledged the label of "Seeker," but it stuck to him and to the church he founded in Providence. The Puritan histories of New England described the Providence church as having "dissolved themselves and turned Seekers." William Hubbard, *A General History of New England from the Discovery to 1689* (1683; Cambridge: Massachusetts Historical Society, 1815), 208; Cotton Mather, *Magnalia Christi Americana or The Ecclesiastical History of New England* (London, 1702), 9. W. Clark Gilpin emphasizes Williams' characterization as a "Witness." See Gilpin, *The Millenarian Piety of Roger Williams*, 78–95.

[50] An example of this new, positive view of being a "Seeker" is when the Northern Baptists issued an undated booklet with a picture of Roger Williams on the cover over the title "Seeker." This was a reprint of the April 1954 issue of *Crusader*, the Northern Baptist denominational newspaper.

[51] J. M. McGregor, "Seekers and Ranters," in *Radical Religion in the English Revolution*, ed. J. M. McGregor and B. Reay (London: Oxford University Press, 1984), 122–24, argues that neither the Seekers nor the Ranters really existed. He bluntly states, "There was no sect of Seekers in revolutionary England." McGregor, "Seekers and Ranters," 129. Hughes explained that "heresiologists assumed that loosely connected ideas or even the teachings of one influential man had to be associated with a 'sect'—an organized group of people." Hughes, *Gangraena and the Struggle for the English Revolution*, 73.

[52] If the Seekers actually existed as an organized movement, they were held to believe in universal salvation, to deny the divinity of Jesus Christ, to say that there was no heaven or hell, to believe that God dwelled within each person, who could become sinless—all ideas which Williams utterly rejected. The one thing he shared with them was the view that a true visible church no longer existed and could be restored only by a new apostle commissioned by Christ. In all other respects he was, in theological doctrine, as Perry Miller wrote, a "conventional Calvinist." Perry Miller, "Roger Williams: An Essay in Interpretation," in *The Complete Writings of Roger Williams*, 7:21.

[53] The immersion of Williams was an article of Baptist orthodoxy until the late nineteenth century, when William H. Whitsitt, president of Southern Baptist Theological Seminary, wrote that Williams had not been dipped. Whitsitt penned a couple of anonymous articles that appeared in the summer of 1880 that questioned the immersion of Roger Williams, but he did not admit to them until 1896 when he published *A Question of Baptist*

History (Louisville, Ky.: Charles T. Dearing, 1896). He also wrote the entry on "Baptists" for the 1893 edition of *Johnson's Universal Cyclopedia*, where he said that English Baptists did not baptize by immersion until 1641 and that Roger Williams was not immersed. This provoked a great controversy, which helped his critics and opponents to oust him from the presidency of the seminary. He was already battling with the Landmark Baptists in the Southern Baptist Convention, and his assertion that the early English churches or American churches did not practice immersion before 1641 and 1644 was absolutely counter to one of the central dogmas of Landmarkism, which was that an unbroken line of immersing Baptists ran from the first church in Jerusalem to Baptists today. See Gregory A. Wills, *Southern Baptist Seminary, 1859–2009* (New York: Oxford University Press, 2009), 197–99. The most prominent counterattacker against Whitsitt was Henry Melville King, pastor of the First Baptist Church of Providence. King asserted that Whitsitt's conclusion was "unwarranted and unreasonable." King, *The Baptism of Roger Williams: A Review of Rev. Dr. W. H. Whitsitt's Inference* (Providence: Preston & Rounds, 1897), 3. Also see Wills, *Southern Baptist Seminary*, 199. King's book is still readily available in numerous reprint editions and online. Today, except for some Baptists still in thrall to Landmarkism, Baptist historians agree that Williams was not immersed.

[54] "Roger Williams to John Winthrop, Jr., November 10, 1649," in LaFantasie, *The Correspondence of Roger Williams*, 1:302.

[55] *Christenings Make Not Christians* was a short essay written in 1644, but not published until January 1645 in London. See Roger Williams, *Christenings Make Not Christians* (1645), in *The Complete Writings of Roger Williams*, vol. 7.

[56] Roger Williams, *Christenings Make Not Christians*, 7:36.

[57] Williams, *Christenings Make Not Christians*, 7:37.

[58] David W. Bebbington, *Baptists through the Centuries: A History of a Global People* (Waco, Tex.: Baylor University Press, 2010), 63; McGregor, "The Baptists," 41.

[59] Anabaptists in Switzerland, the Palatinate, and the Netherlands had already been forming congregations based on believer's baptism for almost a century. English Baptists and Anabaptists differed on many issues, but they did share a common belief in the need for a profession of faith and believer's baptism.

[60] William L. Lumpkin, *Baptist Confessions of Faith*, rev. ed. (Valley Forge, Pa.: Judson Press, 1969), 119, 120. On the other hand, John Spilsbury later argued that a church became a church by virtue of its covenant and confession of faith, not by baptism. A church thus formed elected its elders and teachers, who were empowered to administer baptism. Spilsbury, *A Treatise Concerning the Lawful Subject of Baptisme* (London, 1643). This was the first published piece on believer's baptism by a Calvinist Baptist. An issue for some early Baptists (including Roger Williams) was the authority to administer the ordinances of the church. Who had a valid warrant to administer baptism? Could an unbaptized person legitimately baptize someone else? Some felt that there must be a proper succession from the apostles. John Smyth completely rejected Apostolic Succession and baptized himself, as early Anabaptist leaders had a century prior in Switzerland. John Spilsbury denied that succession was necessary, and Williams was baptized by a member of his congregation, after which he baptized all the original members. However, within a few months Williams withdrew, having concluded that his rebaptism was invalid for lack of a proper succession from the apostles because the "Great Apostasy," which produced the Antichristian (Roman Catholic) church, had broken the chain of succession. For the same reasons, he regarded all visible church institutions and practices as invalid. Although Christianity remained, the visible church was dead. Most Baptists, however, simply started anew by accepting believer's baptism as being sufficient to form a church. See C. Douglas Weaver, *In Search of the New Testament Church: The Baptist Story* (Macon, Ga.: Mercer University Press, 2008), 19–20.

[61] Despite persecution and imprisonment, their numbers slowly increased, though they remained a small sect until the time of the English Civil War. Stephen Wright, *The Early English Baptists, 1603–1649* (Woodbridge, UK: Boydell Press, 2006), 58–61.

[62] See Charles Francis Adams, ed. and comp., *The Works of John Adams, Second President of the United States: With a Life of the Author, Notes and Illustrations*, 10 vols. (1850–1856; Freeport, N.Y.: Books for Libraries Press, 1969), 2:398. John Adams probably used the term in a more general sense of describing those who had been rebaptized, not linking them to the Münster radicals. On the other hand, he may have had the radical Anabaptists in mind, as he saw Baptist efforts to overthrow the Standing Order in Massachusetts as upsetting the social order. Christopher Hill observes, "The name [Anabaptist] came to be used in a general pejorative sense to describe those who were believed to oppose the existing social and political order." Hill, *The World Turned Upside Down: Radical Ideas during the English Revolution* (New York: Viking Press, 1972), 22.

[63] Wright, *The Early English Baptists*, 7. Bebbington generally agrees with this conclusion: *Baptists through the Centuries*, 25–41. Also see Barrington R. White, *The English Separatist Tradition: From the Marian Martyrs to the Pilgrim Fathers* (London: Oxford University Press, 1971); Idem, *The English Baptists in the Seventeenth Century* (London: Baptist Historical Society, 1983); William T. Whitley, *History of the British Baptists* (London: C. Griffin, 1923); Winthrop S. Hudson, "Baptists Are Not Anabaptists," *Chronicle* 16 (1953): 171–79; Michael R. Watts, *The Dissenters*, vol. 1, *From the Reformation to the French Revolution* (Oxford: Clarendon, 1978), 7–14; McGregor, "The Baptists: Fount of All Heresy," 26. For a representative view allowing for some influence of continental Anabaptists on English Baptists, see William Roscoe Estep, *The Anabaptist Story* (Grand Rapids: Eerdmans, 1975).

[64] Edward Barber, *A Small Treatise of Baptisme, or, Dipping: Wherein Is Cleerly Shewed that the Lord Christ Ordained Dipping for those only that professed Repentance and Faith* (London, 1641), preface, n.p.

[65] Lumpkin, *Baptist Confessions of Faith*, 153.

[66] Lumpkin, *Baptist Confessions of Faith*, 224.

[67] Henry Jacob (1563–1624) has been described as "a semi-separatist worshiping apart from the national church but refusing to repudiate it as false." He did not regard the Church of England as the Antichrist but instead worked to reform it. Jacob founded a church in 1616, the famous Jacob-Lathrop-Jessey church in Southwark, London, which, after debates and splits, gave rise to the Particular Baptists in the 1630s, during the pastorship of Henry Jessey. See Bebbington, *Baptists through the Centuries*, 46.

[68] Andrew Ritor, *A Treatis of the Vanity of Childish Baptism Wherein the deficiency of the Baptisme of the Church of England is considered in fine particulars thereof And wherein also is proved that Baptizing is Dipping, and Dipping Baptizing* (London, 1642), 12.

[69] Spilsbury, *A Treatise Concerning the Lawful Subject of Baptisme*, 31–35, 38.

[70] Samuel Fisher, *Baby-baptism mere babism, or an Answer to Nobody in Five Words, To Everybody Who Finds Himself Concerned in it* (London, 1653); Brackney, *The Baptists*, 57. About an equal number of books and tracts were published that defended infant baptism. Armitage, *A History of the Baptists*, 437. According to the OED, the word "babism" was first used in 1610 to denote "[c]hildish language or argument; a childish practice."

[71] While believer's baptism most distinguished the Baptists, whether one had to be rebaptized to become a member of a Baptist church was unsettled for some time. Some thought it absolutely necessary; others did not and were members of mixed communions. The early General Baptists in England thought rebaptism was required, but some of the early Particular Baptists did not. In Providence, Rhode Island, in 1638 Roger Williams began his church by baptism. On the other hand, there is no record of whether anyone, including John Clarke, was rebaptized to begin the Newport church in 1644. When John Myles gathered a church in Swansea in Plymouth Colony in 1663, it was a mixed communion of

pedeobaptists and antipedeobaptists. As the seventeenth century passed, Baptists in general hardened their stance to hold that believer's baptism was what the Scriptures required and that it must be done by immersion. After John Myles died in 1683, Samuel Luther became the pastor of the Swansea church and continued the mixed communion until 1705, when he decided that it was contrary to Scripture to allow pedeobaptists to join the church. The ensuing controversy led to a schism and the establishment of the Barrington Congregational Church. See William G. McLoughlin, "Barrington Congregationalists vs. Swansea Baptists, 1711," *Rhode Island History* 32 (1973): 19; William H. Brackney, "Historical Introduction to First Baptist, Swansea," in *Baptists in Early North America*, vol. 1, *First Baptist, Swansea*, ed. William H. Brackney and Charles Hartman (Macon, Ga.: Mercer University Press, 2013), xl–xlii, lix–lxi.

[72] Wright, *The Early English Baptists*, 56–57, quoting Helwys, who wrote, "if you had no other sin amongst you all, but this, you perish every man."

[73] McGregor, "The Baptists," 42.

[74] Stephen Brachlow, "Life Together in Exile: The Social Bond of Separated Ecclesiology," in *Pilgrim Pathways*, 119.

[75] Barber, *A Small Treatise of Baptisme*, 2–3.

[76] Ritor, *A Treatis of the Vanity of Childish Baptism*, 14–15. Others made the same point: Hanserd Knollys, *The Shining of a Flaming-fire in Zion, or, a clear Answer unto 13 Exceptions against the Grounds of New Baptism* (London: Jane Coe, 1645), 3; Thomas Nutt, *The Nutcracker Crackt by the Nutt and the Backers Cake Starke Dow: Being the Vindication of Honest Men, from the Scandalous Aspersions of Thomas Bakewell, the Baker* (London: 1645), n.p.

[77] *The London Confession* of 1644, Article 40, prescribed "dipping or plunging the body in water as the way and manner of dispensing this ordinance." Hanserd Knollys, William Kiffin, and Benjamin Coxe wrote *A Declaration Concerning a Public Dispute* (1647), which also laid out the Baptist position on baptism.

[78] Among the many attacks were P. B[arbor], *A Defence of the Lawfulness of Baptizing Infants* (1645); J. Stalham, *Vindiciae Redemptionis* (1647); T. Bakewell, *The Dippers Plunged* (1650); N. Stephens, *A Precept for the Baptizing of Infants* (1651); John Goodwin, *Catabaptism* (1655); R. Ballamie, *The Leper Clensed* (1657); A. Houghton, *An Antidote against Hen. Haggers poysonous pamphlet* (1658).

[79] Reay, "Radicalism and Religion," 13. George Thomason (ca. 1602–1666) collected more than twenty-two thousand books, broadsides, pamphlets, and tracts from 1640 to 1661, which today constitute the Thomason Collection of Civil War Tracts in the British Library. See also Joad Raymond, *Pamphlets and Pamphleteering in Early Modern Britain* (Cambridge: Cambridge University Press, 2003), chap. 6.

[80] Hill, *The World Turned Upside Down*, 16–31.

[81] Hughes, *Gangraena and the Struggle for the English Revolution*, 18.

[82] Central to Williams' argument was the assertion that government had no role to play in religious matters and that all consciences had to be free. Such ideas were regarded as rank heresy by the proponents of a national church and were denounced as such by the heresiologists.

[83] William Prynne, *Twelve Considerable Serious Questions touching on Church Government* (London: Michael Stark, Sr., September 16, 1644), 7. Prynne used Williams as a stick to attack the Independents, asking the question whether the national church proposed by the Independents would lead to the "detestable conclusion *That everyman, whither he be Jew, Turk, Pagan, Papist, Arminian, Anabaptist, etc. ought to be left to his own free liberty of conscience, without any coertion or restraint, to embrace & publickely to professe what Religion, Opinion, Church, Government he pleaseth, & conceiveth to be truest, though never so erroneous, false, seditious, detestable in it selfe?*" According to James Ernst, "More than one hundred pamphlets making similar sallies upon the doctrine of *The Bloudy Tenent* and Mr. Williams appeared before 1649." Ernst, *Roger Williams*, 248.

[84] The initial edition of *The Bloudy Tenent* spelled the word as "Tenet," but the second printing changed the spelling to "Tenent."

[85] Daniel Featley, D.D., *The Dippers Dipt, or, the Anabaptists Duck'd and Plung'e Over Head and Ears, at a Disputation at Southwark* (London, 1645), 6. Williams' mention of writing in milk referred not to himself but John Murton (1585–ca. 1626), who wrote a plea for religious freedom, *The Humble Supplication* (1620), with milk on paper smuggled to him in Newgate Prison, where he died in 1626.

[86] Hughes, *Gangraena and the Struggle for the English Revolution*, 42–54.

[87] Ephraim Pagitt, *Heresiography: Or a description of the Heretickes and Sectaries of these latter times* (London, 1645); Hughes, *Gangraena and the Struggle for the English Revolution*, 55.

[88] William Prynne, *A Fresh Discovery of Some Prodigious New Wandring Blasing-Stars & Firebrands, stiling themselves New Lights* (London, 1645); Robert Baillie, *A Dissuasive from the Errours of the Time* (London, 1645); Baillie, *Anabaptism: The True Fountaine of Independency, Brownism, Antimony, Familisme, and most of the other Errours which for the time doe trouble the Church of England* (London, 1647); Thomas Edwards, *Gangraena: or a Catalogue and Discovery of many of the Errors, Heresies, Blasphemies and pernicious Practices of the Sectaries of this time, three parts* (London, 1646).

[89] Hughes, *Gangraena and the Struggle for the English Revolution*, 2, 343.

[90] The Presbyterians sought to combat the "anabaptists and others of the brood of fractions and sectaries [that] swarmed in the parliamentary army." *Dictionary of National Biography*, ed. Leslie Stephen (New York: Macmillan, 1885), 3:433.

[91] By 1646 at least three dozen Baptist churches existed in London alone. Bebbington, *Baptists through the Centuries*, 43. One estimate of the number of Baptists in England by the time of the restoration of the monarchy in 1660 was about thirty thousand, with many more sympathizers. See Armitage, *A History of the Baptists*, 552.

[92] Curtis W. Freeman, "Visionary Women among Early Baptists," *Baptist Quarterly* 43, no. 5 (2010): 1–2. Arise Evans, a preaching "mechanic," declared, "I am as the Paul of this time; he was a mechanic, a tent-maker. Act. 18.3 I am a tailor." Quoted in Hill, *The World Turned Upside Down*, 75.

[93] Thomas Helwys, *A Short Declaration of the Mistery of Iniquity* (London, 1612). This was the first call for religious liberty written in English. For this Helwys was jailed and died in prison in 1616. By championing "freedom of conscience," English dissenters desired liberty regarding private belief and public worship.

[94] Featley, *The Dippers Dipt*, 4-6.

[95] Bebbington, *Baptists through the Centuries*, 48; Edwards, *Gangraena* (London, 1646).

[96] Thomas Edwards, *The Casting Down of the last and strongest hold of Satan or a Treatise against Toleration* (London, 1647).

[97] Quoted in Hughes, *Gangraena and the Struggle for the English Revolution*, 106.

[98] Quoted in Hughes, *Gangraena and the Struggle for the English Revolution*, 107.

[99] Robert Baillie, *Anabaptisme* (London: M. F. for Samuel Gallibrand, 1647). See McGregor, "The Baptists: Fount of All Heresy," 23–63. McGregor concludes that Baillie was basically correct, that Baptist ideas, preachers, and the like did stimulate the Levellers, Ranters, Quakers, Diggers, and others. McGregor, "The Baptists: Fount of All Heresy," 62–63.

[100] Quoted in Hughes, *Gangraena and the Struggle for the English Revolution*, 180. Also see references on pp. 112, 114, 120, 126, 180–81.

[101] Hughes, *Gangraena and the Struggle for the English Revolution*, 120.

[102] Edwards, *Gangraena*, pt. III, quoted in Hughes, *Gangraena and the Struggle for the English Revolution*, 91. As Christopher Hill has observed, "Nakedness is a relative concept: one critic of the Baptists expressed pious horror when, at a baptism, 'the nakedness of one of the women . . . was seen above her knees.' 'For this,' he added with relish, 'there were many witnesses.'" Hill, *The World Turned Upside Down*, 153.

[103] The immediate trigger for action was the uprising in January 1661 against the newly restored monarchy by some Fifth Monarchists led by Thomas Venner. Richard L. Greaves, *Deliver Us From Evil: The Radical Underground in Britain, 1660–1663* (New York: Oxford University Press, 1986), 49–53. See also Philip F. Gura, *A Glimpse of Sion's Glory: Puritan Radicalism in New England, 1620–1660* (Middletown, Conn.: Wesleyan University Press, 1984), 142–44; Bernard S. Capp, *The Fifth Monarchy Men: A Study in Seventeenth-Century English Millenarianism* (London: Faber & Faber, 1972). The Clarendon Code (named after Edward Hyde, the first Earl of Clarendon, who was Charles II's Lord Chancellor) was a post-Restoration (1660) series of acts that reestablished the Church of England. The Corporation Act (1661) excluded all nonconformists from public office. The Act of Uniformity (1662) required all clergy to use the *Book of Common Prayer*, resulting in the "ejection" of an estimated 1,700 pastors and 150 dons (university tutors) who refused to conform. The Conventicle Act (1664) penalized anyone who attended or preached to a dissenting meeting of worship. (Conventicles were small, private gatherings of dissenters, often led by laymen, a practice well developed by the Calvinists in France and Scotland in the sixteenth century and by Puritans in England in the seventeenth century to avoid detection by the authorities.) The Five-Mile Act (1665) forbade nonconforming ministers from coming within five miles of their former parishes and prohibited them from teaching school or taking in lodgers. Robert A. Beddard, "The Restoration Church," in *The Restored Monarchy, 1660–1688,* ed. J. R. Jones (Totowa, N.J.: Rowman & Littlefield, 1979), 155–75.

[104] Many pastors were "ejected" from their pulpits. John Bunyan (1628–1688), a dissenter but dubious Baptist, was jailed from 1660 to 1672. Hanserd Knollys (1599–1691) was jailed in 1661 and after his release fled to Wales, Germany, and Holland. In his absence his property was seized, and after his return to London he was arrested in 1670. Accounts of the persecution and punishment of Baptists appear in Joseph Ivimey, *A History of the English Baptists*, 4 vols. (London: Burdett & Morris, 1811), 1:335–60. See also Henry Jessey, *The Lord's Loud Call to England* (London: Chapman & Smith, 1660). In 1637 Jessey (1601–1663) became the pastor of the famous dissenting Independent church founded by Henry Jacob. He was baptized by Hanserd Knollys in 1645 and became the pastor of the Swan Alley Church, a Particular Baptist church. Cromwell appointed him to be the rector of St. George's church in London. After the restoration of the monarchy, he was one of those "ejected" from his church, was arrested, and died in prison.

[105] Nuttall, "Another Baptist Ejection (1662)," in *Pilgrim Pathways*, 185.

[106] In a humiliating reversal, Charles II was forced by Parliament to rescind his Declaration of Indulgence on May 7, 1673. Parliament then went further and passed the Test Act (1673), which required anyone holding public office to renounce Catholic dogma and to be an Anglican communicant, thereby disabling Charles' Catholic supporters. The suppression of Protestant dissenters resumed as well. Beddard, "The Restoration Church," in *The Restored Monarchy*, 169.

[107] The arguments of the Baptists going forward from the 1640s were fairly consistent and repetitious. Reading the tracts, one finds the same examples, the same points, and the same arguments used again and again. See, e.g., Edward Barber, *A Small Treatise of Baptisme, or, Dipping* (London, 1641); Spilsbury, *A Treatise Considering the Lawfull Subject of Baptisme;* Christopher Blackwood, *The Storming of Antichrist, in his two last and strongest Garrisons; Of Compulsion of Conscience and Infants Baptisme* (London, 1644); Christopher Blackwood, *Apostolic Baptisme: A Sober Rejoynder to a Book written by Mr. Thomas Blake* (London, 1645); Robert Garner, *A Treatis of Baptisme: Wherin is clearly proved the lawfulness and usefulness of Believers Baptisme* (London, 1645); Knollys, *The Shining of a Flaming-fire in Zion*; Henry Denne, *Antichrist Unmasked in two Treatises* (London, 1645); Thomas Nutt, *The Nut-cracker Crackt by the Nutt*; R.J., *Nineteen Arguments, Proving Circumcision No Seal of the Covenant of Grace* (London, 1646); Thomas Lambe, *Truth Prevailing against the fiercest Opposition* (London: G. Dawson, 1655).

[108] Gura, *A Glimpse of Sion's Glory*, argues that from the beginning the Puritan Establishment was vexed constantly and shaped by unorthodox, heretical individuals and movements, and was a nursery for radicals who often returned to England, such as Roger Williams, Hugh Peter, John Clarke, Samuel Gorton, William Aspinwall, and Thomas Venner. Also see Jonathan B. Field, *Errand into the Metropolis: New England Dissidents in Revolutionary London* (Hanover, N.H.: University Press of New England, 2009), which argues that dissidents coming and going to London shaped New England's religious and political landscape.

[109] For a fascinating study of Puritan and Quaker notions of their own persecution, see Adrian Chastain Weimer, *Martyrs' Mirror: Persecution and Holiness in Early New England* (New York: Oxford University Press, 2011).

[110] The Half-Way Covenant allowed baptized church members who had not yet made a public confession of their own faith to bring forward their children for baptism. The Puritan churches were confronted with a growing number of individuals who had never had a conversion experience to become a full church member, but who now had children and desired their own children to receive the nurture and spiritual benefits of the church, such as baptism.

[111] Gura, *A Glimpse of Sion's Glory*, 324–25.

[112] McLoughlin and Davidson, "The Baptist Debate," 96.

[113] Quoted from McLoughlin and Davidson, "The Baptist Debate," 98, n. 17.

[114] John Clarke, *Ill Newes from New-England, Or, a Narrative of New-Englands Persecution* (London: H. Hill, 1652); Obadiah Holmes, *Baptist Piety: The Last Will and Testament of Obadiah Holmes*, ed. Edwin Gaustad (Grand Rapids: Christian University Press, 1972).

[115] Brackney and Hartman, *Baptists in Early North America*, 1:xxx–xxxii; Nathan E. Wood, *The History of the First Baptist Church of Boston, 1665–1899* (Philadelphia: American Baptist Publication Society, 1899), 33; McBeth, *The Baptist Heritage*, 141–42. The Baptists in America were still a small sect at the beginning of the eighteenth century. New England had only about seventeen Baptist churches in 1700 (eleven of which were in the "hive of heretics," that is, Rhode Island), with only a few hundred members.

[116] McLoughlin and Davidson, "The Baptist Debate," 91–133.

[117] John Cotton (1585–1652), a graduate of Cambridge University, escaped arrest by Bishop Laud's agents and fled to Massachusetts in 1633, where he became the Teacher of the Boston church. He was involved in many theological controversies, including those with Roger Williams, Anne Hutchinson, and Samuel Gorton. His attack on the "Anabaptists" was *The Grounds and Ends of Baptisme of the Children of the Faithful* (London, 1647).

[118] Richard Mather (1596–1669) studied at Oxford, became a preacher, and was then suspended for nonconformity. In 1635, upon the advice of John Cotton and Thomas Hooker, he came to Massachusetts and was installed as the teacher at Dorchester. In approximately 1646, he attacked John Spilsbury's tract *A Treatise on the Lawful Subject of Baptism* with "Answer to Nine Reasons of John Spilsbury to Prove Infants Ought Not to Be Baptized." See Gura, *A Glimpse of Sion's Glory*, 113.

[119] Thomas Hooker (1586–1647), a graduate of Cambridge University, fled from the suppression of Bishop Laud to Holland and then to Massachusetts in 1633. He became the pastor of the church in Newtowne (now Cambridge), but left to found Hartford, Connecticut, in 1636. In 1644 he wrote a series of sermons to rebut John Spilsbury's tract *A Treatise on the Lawful Subject of Baptism*, but it was published posthumously in 1649 as *The Covenant of Grace Opened*.

[120] Thomas Shepard (1605–1649), a graduate of Cambridge University, sailed to Massachusetts in 1635 and became the pastor of the church in Cambridge, Massachusetts, succeeding Thomas Hooker. In the 1640s he wrote a tract called the *Church Membership of Children, And Their Right to Baptisme*, but it was not published until 1663 in London. In it he argued that the covenant included the church members and their children. Gura, *A Glimpse of Sion's Glory*, 114–15.

[121] George Phillips (1593–1644), a graduate of Cambridge University, sailed to America on the *Arbella* with John Winthrop in 1630. He became the first minister of the church in Watertown. After he discovered Thomas Lamb's *Confutation of Infant Baptism* (London, 1643), which attacked his defense of infant baptism, Phillips responded with *A Reply to a Confutation of some grounds for infants baptisme: as also, concerning the form of a church, put forth against mee by one Thomas Lamb* (London, 1645).

[122] Thomas Cobbett (1608–1685) was the pastor of the church in Lynn, Massachusetts, where John Clarke et al. were taken for forced worship upon their arrest in 1651. His rejoinder to John Spilsbury was entitled *A Just Vindication of the Covenant and Church-Estate of Children of Church-Members: As Also of their Right Unto Baptisme* (London, 1648).

[123] Gura, *A Glimpse of Sion's Glory*, 110–16; Weimer, *Martyrs' Mirror*, 93–96.

[124] Norcott, *Baptism Discovered Plainly*, 2–6. "Consider, there are multitudes of Examples of Believers Baptism . . . but there's not one Example of Infant-baptism." And "If it had been [God's] Will that Infants should have been baptized; surely he would have been so faithful as to have left us one word in his blessed Scriptures," 54. This was an argument made by all the Baptist writers.

[125] Eliot, *A Brief Answer*, 1.

[126] Eliot, *A Brief Answer*, 16.

[127] Williams, "A Brief Reply," 138.

[128] Williams, "A Brief Reply," 148–49.

[129] Eliot, *A Brief Answer*, 17; Williams, "A Brief Reply," 149.

[130] Norcott, *Baptism Discovered Plainly*, 45, 47, comparing believer's baptism with infant baptism, wrote, "But Infants know not any thing of their baptism. Infants remember not their baptism. . . . But Infants baptized are not converted, and may come into condemnation."

[131] About fourteen of the first seventeen pages were devoted to Eliot's covenant theory.

[132] Eliot, *A Brief Answer*, 7.

[133] Eliot, *A Brief Answer*, 11.

[134] Eliot, *A Brief Answer*, 3.

[135] Eliot, *A Brief Answer*, 5.

[136] Norcott, *Baptism Discovered Plainly*, 37-38. This particular point was based upon Romans 9:6b-8, which says that not all of the children of Abraham were counted as the children of promise. Those counted as children of the flesh were not regarded as the children of God.

[137] Williams, "A Brief Reply," 139-140, quoting Rom 8:14.

[138] Williams, "A Brief Reply," 146, quoting Rom 10:17.

[139] Norcott, *Baptism Discovered Plainly*, 11.

[140] Eliot, *A Brief Answer*, 17.

[141] Williams, "A Brief Reply," 150.

[142] 1 Cor 15:46: "Howbeit that was not first which is spiritual, but that which is natural, and afterward that which is spiritual."

[143] Williams, "A Brief Reply," 150, quoting John 3:6, 7. Williams here only quotes "Ye must be born again."

[144] Quoting Mark 16:15-16a; Norcott, *Baptism Discovered Plainly*, 10; Williams, "A Brief Reply," 148.

[145] Norcott, *Baptism Discovered Plainly*, 30.

[146] Norcott, *Baptism Discovered Plainly*, 31.

[147] Williams, "A Brief Reply," 155.

[148] Williams, "A Brief Reply," 141.

[149] Williams, "A Brief Reply," 150; or as Edward Barber had written in 1641 in the first published defense of dipping, "the Lord doth make his Covenant of the New Testament with those onely [sic] who know him by faith . . . at the hearing of faith." Barber, *A Small Treatise of Baptisme*, 7–8.

[150] Norcott, *Baptism Discovered Plainly*, 21.

[151] Eliot, *A Brief Answer*, 18.

[152] Eliot, *A Brief Answer*, 19.

[153] Eliot, *A Brief Answer*, 19.

[154] Barber and others used the same examples and arguments.

[155] Williams, "A Brief Reply," 152.

[156] Acts 8:38-39. For Williams' partial quotation of these verses, see Williams, "A Brief Reply," 152. See also Norcott, *Baptism Discovered Plainly*, 4-5, 12–13, 49–50.

[157] Eliot, *A Brief Answer*, 20.

[158] Eliot, *A Brief Answer*, 20.

[159] Eliot, *A Brief Answer*, 20–21.

[160] Williams, "A Brief Reply," 154.

[161] Eliot, *A Brief Answer*, 18, 19, 20.

[162] Eliot, *A Brief Answer*, 14, 23.

[163] For example, "but we are not therefore to be rebaptized: an error in the infant-subject, and in the manner of the action, as *you* suppose in our infant-baptism, is not essential, and therefore neither destroy baptism, nor require a rebaptizing, were the case as *you* say" [emphasis added]. Eliot, *A Brief Answer*, 25.

[164] Eliot, *A Brief Answer*, 9.

[165] Eliot, *A Brief Answer*, 8.

[166] Eliot, *A Brief Answer*, 23. He condescendingly and directly spoke to the Baptists as "your inconsiderable selves."

[167] Eliot, *A Brief Answer*, 8–10.

[168] Eliot, *A Brief Answer*, 14.

[169] Eliot, *A Brief Answer*, 9–10.

[170] Williams, "A Brief Reply," 145. These brief remarks directly defending Baptists are the only ones that can be deciphered presently in Williams' shorthand essay.

[171] Thomas Helwys, *A Short and Plain Proof, by the Word and Works of God, that God's Decree is not the Cause of any Man's Sin or Condemnation: and that all Men are Redeemed by Christ; and also that No Infants are Condemned* (1611). Also see Michel Walker, "The Relation of Infants to Church, Baptism and Gospel in Seventeenth Century Baptist Theology," *Baptist Quarterly* 2 (1966): 242–62.

[172] Spilsbury, *A Treatise Concerning the Lawful Subject of Baptisme*, 14. The "dark and mysterious subject" of what happened to infants was an issue that John Calvin himself confronted; he concluded that dying infants with believing parents were among the elect.

[173] Ivimey, *A History of the English Baptists,* 342. Keach (1640–1704) was a Particular Baptist preacher in London and one of the first proponents of congregational hymn singing (instead of psalms only) in Baptist churches. In 1664 Keach was fined, imprisoned, and forced to stand in the pillory. See Cathcart, *The Baptist Encyclopedia*, 637–38.

[174] Williams, "A Brief Reply," 141. Williams' responses were somewhat incomplete at times.

[175] Roger Williams had had plenty of trouble in governing Providence and Rhode Island over the years, and among his most vociferous and bitter opponents were such Baptists as William Harris, William Arnold, Robert Cole, William Carpenter, John Throckmorton, and Richard Scott. On the other hand, he had vigorously denounced the arrest and punishment in Massachusetts of John Clarke, Obadiah Holmes, and John Crandall in 1651; especially see his long letter excoriating Governor John Endicott, ca. August–September 1651, in LaFantasie, *The Correspondence of Roger Williams*, 1:337–46. When Williams debated the Quakers in 1672, his principal supporters were the Baptists, even to the point that Pardon Tillinghast, the pastor of the Providence church, stepped in to debate the last point on the fourth day when Williams stopped. Camp, *Roger Williams*, 197.

[176] Williams, "A Brief Reply," 138.

[177] The question of how to interpret *A Key* has caused considerable debate among historians. Earlier generations of historians said Williams "saw and carefully studied [the Indians] before they had become corrupted by the trade and the 'strong waters' of the English, or had added anything to their own native virtues or vices." Many recent historians have criticized this view, however, asserting that *A Key* merely served to further Williams' various agendas and reflected little of the actual life and culture of the Indians. See H. C. Dorr, *The Narragansetts*, Collections of the Rhode Island Historical Society 7 (Providence: Kellogg, 1885), 138 (quotation above); Miller, *Roger Williams*, 7:53; Jack L. Davis, "Roger Williams among the Narragansett Indians," *New England Quarterly* 43, no. 4 (1970): 594; Gilpin, *The Millenarian Piety of Roger Williams*, 123–25; Lepore, *The Name of War*, 30; Jennifer Reid, "Roger Williams' *Key*: Ethnography or Mythology?" *Rhode Island History* 56, no. 3 (1998): 77; J. Patrick Cesarini, "The Ambivalent Uses of Roger Williams's *A Key into the Language of America*," *Early American Literature* 38, no. 3 (2003): 469–94; Jessica R. Stern, "A Key into The Bloudy Tenent of Persecution: Roger Williams, the Pequot War, and the Origins of Toleration in America," *Early American Studies: An Interdisciplinary Journal* 9, no. 3 (2011): 576–616. For a positive recent assessment of *A Key*, see Ted Widmer, "A Nearer Neighbor to the Indians," in *A New Literary History of America*, ed. Greil Marcus and Werner Sollors (Cambridge, Mass.: Belknap Press of Harvard University Press, 2012).

[178] Patricia E. Rubertone, *Grave Undertakings: An Archaeology of Roger Williams and the Narragansett Indians* (Washington, D.C.: Smithsonian Institution Press, 2001); William S. Simmons, "Cultural Bias in the New England Puritans' Perception of Indians," *William and Mary Quarterly* 38, no. 1 (1981): 63; Cesarini, "The Ambivalent Uses"; Jonathan Beecher Field, *Errands into the Metropolis: New England Dissidents in Revolutionary London* (Dartmouth, N.H.: University Press of New England, 2009). See also John J. Teunissen and Evelyn J. Hinz, "Roger Williams, Thomas More, and the Narragansett Utopia," *Early American Literature* 11, no. 3 (1976): 281–95. On Williams' biblicism, see James P. Byrd Jr., *The Challenges of Roger Williams* (Macon, Ga.: Mercer University Press, 2002).

[179] Clark Gilpin has provided the most detailed analysis of Williams' views on Indian conversion, which Gilpin ties to Williams' eschatology, or his "millenarian piety." Gilpin argues that "immediately following his banishment from Massachusetts in 1636, Williams' knowledge of Indian speech and habit was directed toward much more pragmatic objectives than turning souls to God." Similarly, Gilpin interprets *Christenings Make Not Christians* in 1645 as Williams' statement that he had abandoned the missionary endeavor entirely. Gilpin, *The Millenarian Piety of Roger Williams*, 118, 126–28. See also LaFantasie, *The Correspondence of Roger Williams*; Richard W. Cogley, *John Eliot's Mission to the Indians before King Philip's War* (Cambridge, Mass.: Harvard University Press, 1999); Samuel Greene Arnold, *History of the State of Rhode Island and Providence Plantations* (New York: D. Appleton, 1859); Neal Salisbury, *Manitou and Providence: Indians, Europeans, and the Making of New England, 1500–1643* (New York: Oxford University Press, 1982), 194; Ernst, *Roger Williams*, 26–27; Arthur R. Railton, "Who Was Our First Missionary? Was It Roger Williams?" *Duke County Intelligencer* 36, no. 4 (1995): 182–90; Rubertone, *Grave Undertakings*.

[180] There are only seven extant letters and short pieces of writing from Roger Williams between January 1, 1679, and the end of Williams' life. Indeed, the very last piece of correspondence is from May 6, 1682. See LaFantasie, *The Correspondence of Roger Williams*, 2:768–80.

[181] On the New England Company, see William Kellaway, *The New England Company, 1649–1776: Missionary Society to the American Indians* ([London]: Longmans, 1961). Eliot was known in England and New England during his lifetime as the "Apostle to the Indians," an appellation he first received from Thomas Thorowgood in 1660. Eliot's biographers have invoked this title over the centuries, a trend some recent historians have continued. See

Michael Clark, *The Eliot Tracts: With Letters from John Eliot to Thomas Thorowgood and Richard Baxter* (Westport, Conn.: Praeger, 2003), 1; Martin Moore, *Memoirs of the Life and Character of Rev. John Eliot, Apostle of the N.A. Indians* (Boston: Flagg, 1822); Robert Boodey Caverly, *Life and Labors of John Eliot, the Apostle among the Indian Nations of New England: Together with an Account of the Eliots in England* (Lowell, Mass.: George M. Elliott, 1881); Cogley, *John Eliot's Mission.* Surprisingly, Cotton Mather's 1691 hagiographical account of Eliot does not use the term. Cotton Mather, *The Triumphs of the Reformed Religion, in America: The Life of the Renowned John Eliot* (Boston: Harris, Benjamin, 1691).

[182] Lawrence C. Wroth, *The Voyages of Giovanni Da Verrazzano, 1524–1528* (New Haven: Yale University Press, 1970), 134–38. See also Neal Salisbury, *Manitou and Providence: Indians, Europeans, and the Making of New England, 1500–1643* (New York: Oxford University Press, 1982), 52–54. Given the Narragansetts' hesitancies with Verrazzano's men, it is possible that they had contact with Europeans prior to 1524. Rubertone, *Grave Undertakings*, 72.

[183] Salisbury, *Manitou and Providence*, 26ff.

[184] "To an Assembly of Commissioners, November 17, 1677?" in LaFantasie, *The Correspondence of Roger Williams*, 2:750. On his early evangelistic ambitions, see also "To Governor John Winthrop, between July and December 1632," in LaFantasie, *The Correspondence of Roger Williams*, 1:8. Williams became well acquainted with several important Indian leaders, particularly Massasoit of the Wampanoags as well as Canonicus and his nephew Miantonomi of the Narragansetts. LaFantasie, *The Correspondence of Roger Williams*, 1:75, n. 4. Williams also began trading with the Indians while in Plymouth and set up a trading post in Narragansett country after his removal to Rhode Island. It remained a central part of his Indian interactions as well as provided financial security until he sold it in 1652 to pay for his trip to London. "To John Winthrop, Jr., 6 October 1651," in LaFantasie, *The Correspondence of Roger Williams*, 1:351.

[185] Gilpin, *The Millenarian Piety of Roger Williams*, 39–40; John Winthrop, *The Journal of John Winthrop, 1630–1649*, ed. Richard S. Dunn, James Savage, and Laetitia Yeandle, 3 vols. (Cambridge, Mass.: Harvard University Press, 1996), 1:113; *Winthrop Papers*, 6 vols. (Boston: Massachusetts Historical Society, 1929–1947), 3:147–48.

[186] The Massachusetts General Court repealed this banishment in the 1940s, more than three hundred years after the initial sentence. See Brockunier, *The Irrepressible Democrat*, 69.

[187] Miller, "Roger Williams," 7–8. See also John Winthrop, *The History of New England*, ed. James Savage (New York: Arno Press, 1972), 122–23, 170–71. Williams later stated that it was Winthrop who warned Williams that he was going to be physically removed to England, which is why he fled just days before Captain Underhill arrived at his Salem home. See Gaustad, *Liberty of Conscience*, 45. For more on Williams' relationship with Winthrop, see Francis Bremer, *John Winthrop: America's Forgotten Founding Father* (New York: Oxford University Press, 2003).

[188] "To Governor John Winthrop, between July and December 1632," in LaFantasie, *The Correspondence of Roger Williams*, 1:8.

[189] "To John Winthrop, 15 July 1637," in LaFantasie, *The Correspondence of Roger Williams*, 1:102.

[190] "To Governor John Winthrop, 28 February 1637/38," in LaFantasie, *The Correspondence of Roger Williams*, 1:146.

[191] Roger Williams, *A Key into the Language of America* (1643), in *The Complete Writings of Roger Williams*, vol. 1.

[192] On the abstention from their rituals, Williams states, "I confesse to have most of these their customes by their owne Relation, for after once being in their Houses and beholding what their Worship was, I durst never bee an eye witnesse, Spectatour, or looker on, least I should have been partaker of Sathans Inventions and Worships, contrary to *Ephes.* 5.14." Williams, *A Key into the Language of America*, 1:152.

[193] The core of the book is an extensive list of phrases; Williams additionally inserts various kinds of "observations" and summarizes the spiritual lessons of each section with a piquant, moralizing poem. Cesarini and others have noted that these poems especially tend to criticize English civility and spirituality, such as *"Boast not proud* Euglish, *of they birth & blood,* / *Thy brother* Indian *is by birth as Good.* / *Of one blood God made Him, and Thee & All,* / *As wise, as faire, as strong, as personall.* / *By nature wrath's his portiõ, thine no more* / *Till Grace his* soule *and* thine *in Christ restore* / *Make sure thy second birth, else thou shalt see,* / *Heaven ope to* Indians *wild, but shut to thee."* Williams, *A Key into the Language of America*, 1:81. See also Cesarini, "The Ambivalent Uses," 482–83.

[194] Williams, *A Key into the Language of America*, 1:26–27.

[195] Williams, *A Key into the Language of America*, 1:26. Williams states that "this was the summe of our last parting untill our great meeting," which is ambiguous but points in some fashion toward a future reunion. Williams, *A Key into the Language of America*, 1:27. Since the story was told in the context of the positive prospects of Indian conversion, however, it seems safe to assume Williams means he will see him in heaven, even though he wants to temper the optimism of *New England's First Fruits*, published in London in 1643. Kristina Bross reads even more certainty into Williams' rendering of Wequash's passing, asserting, "Wequash responds with a confession of sin and faith." Bross, *Dry Bones and Indian Sermons: Praying Indians in Colonial America* (Ithaca, N.Y.: Cornell University Press, 2004), 190.

[196] See especially Jonathan Beecher Field, "A Key for the Gate: Roger Williams, Parliament, and Providence," *New England Quarterly* 80, no. 3 (2007): 353–82; Cesarini, "The Ambivalent Uses."

[197] Field, "A Key for the Gate," 366.

[198] *New England's First Fruits*, 5–7. See Bross, *Dry Bones and Indian Sermons*, 190; Cesarini, "The Ambivalent Uses," 474–77; Karen Ordahl Kupperman, *Indians and English: Facing Off in Early America* (Ithaca, N.Y.: Cornell University Press, 2000), 204–5.

[199] In writing *A Key*, Williams was partly responding to critiques of nonevangelism coming from London, the printed versions of which appeared at least as early as 1641, when seventy-six British ministers criticized the colonies for conducting themselves, not "in pitty to mens soules, but in hope to possesse the land of those Infidels." Michael Clark, *The Eliot Tracts*, 1. Similarly, the resentful ex-Massachusetts resident Thomas Lechford published critiques of New Englanders in 1642, stating, "They have nothing to excuse themselves in this point of not laboring with the Indians to instruct them, but their want of a staple trade, and other businesses taking them up" (which Lechford said would only excuse them to a certain extent). Lechford, *Plain Dealing, or, Newes from New-England* (London: Printed by W. E. & I. G. for Nath. Butter, 1642), 21. And since *New England's First Fruits* was published in London just prior to Williams' *A Key*, Williams had extra motivation to show himself to be the most qualified linguist—and evangelist—in New England.

[200] Roger Williams, *Christenings Make Not Christians* (1645), in *The Complete Writings of Roger Williams*, vol. 7. There is good reason to think that Williams intentionally delayed the publication of *Christenings* until he had returned to New England because he anticipated an unfavorable reception of his pessimistic view of Indian conversion (especially on the heels of the rather optimistic *A Key*). Field, "A Key for the Gate," 374. *A Key* and *Christenings* were intimately connected and were apparently written around the same time; indeed, Williams had even promised his readers in *A Key* "a briefe Additionall discourse concerning this Great Point," namely, "what hopes of the *Indians* receiving the Knowledge of Christ!" Williams, *A Key into the Language of America*, 27.

[201] Williams, *Christenings Make Not Christians*, 7:36.

[202] Williams, *Christenings Make Not Christians*, 7:39–40.

[203] Williams, *Christenings Make Not Christians*, 7:40.

[204] Williams, *A Key into the Language of America*, 1:26–27.

[205] Williams, *A Key into the Language of America*, 1:155. By "theirs" Williams meant the Indians' estate.

[206] Williams, *A Key into the Language of America*, 1:155.

[207] Williams, *Christenings Make Not Christians*, 7:40. See also LaFantasie's essay on Williams and Indian Conversion in LaFantasie, *The Correspondence of Roger Williams*, 1:141–44. This lack of proper apostolic commission extended, in Williams' mind, to gathered churches and even forms of baptism for colonists.

[208] Williams, *Christenings Make Not Christians*, 7:40.

[209] Williams, *Christenings Make Not Christians*, 7:41.

[210] Williams, *Christenings Make Not Christians*, 7:38.

[211] Williams, *Christenings Make Not Christians*, 7:39.

[212] Williams, *Christenings Make Not Christians*, 7:38. See also Weimer, *Martyrs' Mirror*, chap. 2.

[213] "To the General Court of Massachusetts Bay, 5 October 1654," in LaFantasie, *The Correspondence of Roger Williams*, 2:409. See Richard Cogley's evaluation of both the frequency of such visits and the threats that were supposedly made: Cogley, *John Eliot's Mission*, 190–91.

[214] "To the General Court of Massachusetts Bay, 5 October 1654," in LaFantasie, *The Correspondence of Roger Williams*, 2:410.

[215] One rare example is in his public, printed disputes with George Fox, in which he mentions evangelistic methodology in passing: "When we deal with *Indians* about *Religion*, our work is to prove unto them by Reason, that the *Bible* is *Gods Word*, for by Nature they are much affected with a kind of Deity to be in Writing." Williams, *George Fox Digg'd out of his Burrowes*, in *The Complete Writings of Roger Williams*, 5:447.

[216] Eliot, *A Brief Answer*, 11.

[217] Eliot, *A Brief Answer*, 11.

[218] E. Brooks Holifield, *Theology in America: Christian Thought from the Age of the Puritans to the Civil War* (New Haven: Yale University Press, 2005), 53. More broadly, New England Congregationalist ministers were wrestling with the efficacy of the external covenant (including spiritual patrimony) as a means of grace. This is especially apparent in Increase Mather's 1678 sermon "Pray for the Rising Generation," where Mather asserts the importance of godly parents and especially godly mothers in salvation and yet in the end defers to the ultimate infusion of grace required by the Holy Spirit. See David D. Hall, ed., *Puritans in the New World: A Critical Anthology* (Princeton: Princeton University Press, 2004), 97–104; E. Brooks Holifield, *The Covenant Sealed: The Development of Puritan Sacramental Theology in Old and New England, 1570–1720* (New Haven: Yale University Press, 1974), chap. 6.

[219] Eliot, *A Brief Answer*, 11.

[220] For a larger discussion of Calvinist views on baptism in the seventeenth century, see Holifield, *Theology in America*, 53–55.

[221] Eliot, *A Brief Answer*, 11–12.

[222] Williams, "A Brief Reply," 146.

[223] Williams, "A Brief Reply," 146.

[224] Jorge Cañizares-Esguerra, *Puritan Conquistadors: Iberianizing the Atlantic, 1550–1700* (Stanford: Stanford University Press, 2006), 15–16; Nicholas Griffiths and Fernando Cervantes, *Spiritual Encounters: Interactions between Christianity and Native Religions in Colonial America* (Lincoln: University of Nebraska Press, 1999), 44–45.

[225] See, e.g., *David J. Silverman, Faith and Boundaries: Colonists, Christianity, and Community among the Wampanoag Indians of Martha's Vineyard, 1600–1871* (New York: Cambridge University Press, 2005); Cogley, *John Eliot's Mission*; James P. Ronda, "Generations of Faith: The Christian Indians of Martha's Vineyard," *William and Mary Quarterly* 38, no. 3 (1981):

369–94. See also the discussion of "sacred genealogy" in Edward E. Andrews, *Native Apostles: Black and Indian Missionaries in the British Atlantic World* (Cambridge, Mass.: Harvard University Press, 2013), 11–15.

[226] The primary purpose of Williams' essay was to critique the practice of infant baptism, most particularly in its reformed/Puritan manifestation. His extension of that critique to the missionary context is intertwined with his more basic disbelief in the appropriate apostolic commission for undertaking Indian evangelization.

[227] Cesarini, "The Ambivalent Uses," 470.

[228] Cesarini, "The Ambivalent Uses," 470–71.

[229] "To the General Court of Massachusetts Bay, 5 October 1654," in LaFantasie, *The Correspondence of Roger Williams*, 2:413. For a discussion of the role of domesticated animals in English notions of civility, see Virginia DeJohn Anderson, *Creatures of Empire: How Domestic Animals Transformed Early America* (New York: Oxford University Press, 2006).

[230] A detailed description of these developments can be found in Cogley, *John Eliot's Mission*. Regarding the number of Praying Towns (fourteen versus sixteen or even more), see Cogley, *John Eliot's Mission*, 158. For a full listing of the Indian language books and tracts, see "Books and Tracts in the Indian Language or Designed for the Use of Indians, Printed at Cambridge and Boston, 1653–1721," *Proceedings of the American Antiquarian Society* 61 (1873): 45–62. There was also a parallel evangelistic development on Cape Cod and Martha's Vineyard during this same time period, largely orchestrated by Thomas Mayhew Jr. and Sr. These efforts were similarly funded by the NEC and publicized in these same promotional pamphlets that were printed in London. See Silverman, *Faith and Boundaries*; James P. Ronda, "Generations of Faith: The Christian Indians of Martha's Vineyard," *William and Mary Quarterly* 38, no. 3 (1981): 369–94.

[231] "To the General Court of Massachusetts Bay, 5 October 1654," in LaFantasie, *The Correspondence of Roger Williams*, 2:410.

[232] *The Clear Sun-shine of the Gospel*, in Clark, *The Eliot Tracts*, 101. Clark's edition is the most recent and authoritative annotated edition of all of the Eliot Tracts. If *New England's First Fruits* is included in these promotional materials (as Clark suggests), readers in London started hearing such reports in 1643. But even if it was of a different tenor than these promotional tracts, Williams' *A Key* similarly fed the growing interest in Native conversion.

[233] These six are [Thomas Shepard?], *The Day-breaking, If Not the Sun-rising of the Gospell with the Indians in New-England* (London: Printed by Rich. Cotes, 1647); Thomas Shepard, *The Clear Sun-shine of the Gospel Breaking Forth upon the Indians in New-England* (London: R. Cotes, 1648); Edward Winslow, *The Glorious Progress of the Gospel Amongst the Indians in New England* (London: Printed for Hannah Allen, 1649); Henry Whitfield, *The Light Appearing More and More Towards the Perfect Day* (London: Printed by T. R. & E. M., 1651); Henry Whitfield, *Strength Out of Weaknesse; or A Glorious Manifestation of the Further Progresse of the Gospel Among the Indians in New-England* (London: Printed by M. Simmons, 1652); John Eliot and Thomas Mayhew, *Tears of Repentance: Or, A Further Narrative of the Progress of the Gospel Amongst the Indians in New-England* (London: Printed by P. Cole in Leaden-hall, 1653). An additional four were published between 1655 and 1670. See Clark, *The Eliot Tracts*.

[234] "To the General Court of Massachusetts Bay, 5 October 1654," in LaFantasie, *The Correspondence of Roger Williams*, 2:410.

[235] Regarding warfare and evangelization, Williams stated, "I beseech You consider how the name of the most holy and jealous God may be preserved betweene the clashings of these Two: Viz: The Glor [Glorious] Conversion of the Indians in N Engl. and the Unnecessary Warrs and cruel Destructions of the Indians in New Engl." "To the General Court of Massachusetts Bay, 5 October 1654," in LaFantasie, *The Correspondence of Roger Williams*, 2:410.

[236] In 1649 Parliament created the Society for the Propagation of the Gospel in New England with the explicit purpose of raising funds for Indian evangelization in New England,

from which Eliot and other missionaries received money in the seventeenth century. This society was rechartered in 1662 as the Company for the Propagation of the Gospel in New England and Parts Adjacent, which scholars usually refer to as the NEC. Kellaway, *The New England Company*; Linford D. Fisher, *The Indian Great Awakening: Religion and the Shaping of Indian Cultures in Early America* (New York: Oxford University Press, 2012), 230, n. 57.

[237] There are only a few sparse references in the records to any kind of direct interchange between Eliot and Williams. There are at least several instances of Williams receiving letters from Eliot. See Williams, *The Complete Writings of Roger Williams*, 6:172; LaFantasie, *The Correspondence of Roger Williams*, 1:281. In the early 1650s, Williams sent a book to Eliot on the Seekers (a Protestant sect in England whose members considered all churches to be corrupt) titled *A Sober Word to a Serious People*, anonymously written (but identified as by John Jackson) and published in London, 1651. Eliot, after receiving the book from Williams, sent it along to John Cotton for his input. In it, Jackson (a "Seeker" sympathizer) suggested that the present-day ministry had been corrupted (something Williams agreed with); it is tempting to interpret this as Williams suggesting to Eliot that he had no proper authority to evangelize Native Americans. See John Cotton, *The Correspondence of John Cotton* (Chapel Hill: University of North Carolina Press, 2001), 63, 446; McGregor, "Seekers and Ranters," 123. Late in his life, in 1682, Williams said he wrote to Eliot and several other individuals in Massachusetts for assistance in printing and distributing the summary of a collection of sermons he had preached among English colonists in Rhode Island. "To Governor Simon Bradstreet, 6 May 1682," in LaFantasie, *The Correspondence of Roger Williams*, 2:777. Nonetheless, direct and active correspondence over the years appears to have been minimal. Williams and Eliot both—but independently—were involved in the attempts to remove the autonomous Native man Pumham from land on Warwick Neck that was previously sold to the English. Williams eventually negotiated Pumham's removal after he was paid off by the English to move. See Robert Carr to Lord Arlington, April 9, 1666, Colonial Office (CO) 1/20, no. 43, Calendar of State Papers Online, National Archives of the United Kingdom (NA); Roger Williams to Robert Carr, March 1, 1666, CO 1/20, no. 43.1, Calendar of State Papers Online (NA). For further analysis of the Pumham affair, see Teresa M. Bejan, "Mere Civility: Toleration and its Limits in Early Modern England and America" (Ph.D. diss., Yale University, 2013), 125–27. For additional discussion of the relationship between Eliot and Williams, see Teresa M. Bejan, " 'The Bond of Civility': Roger Williams on Toleration and Its Limits," *History of European Ideas* 37, no. 4 (2011): 409–20.

[238] "To John Winthrop, Jr., ca. 13 April 1649," and "To Governor Simon Bradstreet, 6 May 1682," in LaFantasie, *The Correspondence of Roger Williams*, 1:281, 2:777.

[239] Cogley, *John Eliot's Mission*, 47, 277, n. 42. Eliot was surely part of the proceedings against Roger Williams in 1635, for, shortly after Williams fled, Eliot defended the colony's banishment in writing. See "A Reply to Mr. Williams His Examination," in *The Complete Writings of Roger Williams*, 2:43. See also Cogley, *John Eliot's Mission*, 47. Even if Williams might have felt ambivalent about Hutchinson's views, he seems to have disagreed with the Massachusetts Bay's handling of her case. At the very least, he aided her (temporary) settlement in Rhode Island. And in 1638 (after Hutchinson's banishment in 1637), Williams wrote to John Winthrop, "The Lord mercifully redeeme them, and all of us from all our delusions." "To Governor John Winthrop, 16 April 1638," in LaFantasie, *The Correspondence of Roger Williams*, 2:777. See also Lafantasie's discussion of Williams' relationship with Hutchinson in LaFantasie, *The Correspondence of Roger Williams,* 2:151–52, n. 8.

[240] Shepard, *The Clear Sun-shine of the Gospel*, 31. See also Clark, *The Eliot Tracts*, 134.

[241] John Cotton, *The Way of Congregational Churches Cleared* (London: Printed by Matthew Simmons, 1648), Part 1, 79.

[242] Cotton, *The Way of Congregational Churches Cleared*, Part 1, 77.

²⁴³ John Cotton, *A Letter of Mr. John Cottons, Teacher of the Church in Boston in New-England, to Mr. Williams* (London: Printed for Benjamin Allen, 1643); Roger Williams, *The Bloudy Tenent, of Persecution, for Cause of Conscience, in a Conference Betweene Truth and Peace* (London, 1644); John Cotton, *The Bloudy Tenent Washed and Made White in the Bloud of the Lambe* (London: Matthew Symmons, 1647); Roger Williams, *The Bloody Tenent yet More Bloody* (London: G. Calvert, 1652).

²⁴⁴ Roger Williams, *The Bloody Tenent yet More Bloody*, in *The Complete Writings of Roger Williams*, 4:371–72.

²⁴⁵ Williams, *The Bloody Tenent yet More Bloody*, 4:373. For a brief discussion of this critique of Eliot, see Clark, *The Eliot Tracts*, 34n2.

²⁴⁶ Williams, *The Bloody Tenent yet More Bloody*, 4:374.

²⁴⁷ John Eliot, *Mamusse Wunneetupanatamwe Up-Biblum God Naneeswe Nukkone Testament Kah Wonk Wusku Testament* (Cambridge, Mass.: Printeuoop nashpe Samuel Green kah Marmaduke Johnson, 1663).

²⁴⁸ Williams' copy of *Mamusse Wunneetupanatamwe Up-Biblum God* is at the John Hay Library, Brown University. The shorthand notations are mostly in the blank spaces at the front and back of the Bible, although there are at least two pages near the middle where the margins contain Williams' shorthand. Some of the shorthand consists of Williams' notes on John Foxe's *The Book of Martyrs* (first published in London in 1563 as *Actes and Monuments of these Latter and Perillous Days, Touching Matters of the Church*). Other sections of the shorthand in the Indian Bible include a listing of Indian-language phrases, much like *A Key*, as well as a few other mostly indecipherable lists.

²⁴⁹ Williams, "A Brief Reply," 138. Although, to be fair, Williams also refers to Eliot as "Brother Eliot." "A Brief Reply," 142.

²⁵⁰ Williams, "A Brief Reply," 146.

²⁵¹ Williams, "A Brief Reply," 146.

²⁵² Williams, *Christenings Make Not Christians*, 7:36.

²⁵³ Williams, "A Brief Reply," 146.

²⁵⁴ John Easton, "A Relation of the Indian War," in *A Narrative of the Causes Which Led to Philip's Indian War, of 1675 and 1676*, ed. Franklin B. Hough (Albany: J. Munsell, 1858), 10.

²⁵⁵ For a sympathetic contemporary account of the activity of New England's Christian Indians (that was not published until much later), see Daniel Gookin, "An Historical Account of the Doings and Sufferings of the Christian Indians in New England," in *Archaeologia Americana: Transactions and Collections of the American Antiquarian Society* (Cambridge, Mass.: Folsom, Wells, & Thurston, 1836).

²⁵⁶ Lepore, *The Name of War*, 138–40.

²⁵⁷ Mary White Rowlandson, *The Soveraignty & Goodness of God, Together, with the Faithfulness of His Promises Displayed; Being a Narrative of the Captivity and Restauration of Mrs. Mary Rowlandson*, 2nd ed. (Cambridge: Samuel Green, 1682).

²⁵⁸ Mary White Rowlandson and Neal Salisbury, *The Soveraignty and Goodness of God: Together with the Faithfulness of His Promises Displayed: Being a Narrative of the Captivity and Restoration of Mrs. Mary Rowlandson and Related Documents*, Bedford Series in History and Culture (Boston: Bedford Books, 1997), 98. See also Bross, *Dry Bones and Indian Sermons*, 183.

²⁵⁹ David J. Silverman, *Red Brethren: The Brothertown and Stockbridge Indians and the Problem of Race in Early America* (Ithaca: Cornell University Press, 2010), 27–28. Part of this was that the experience of the war irreparably damaged the reputation of the Praying Indians that John Eliot had worked so hard to cultivate, as Jill Lepore has noted. Lepore, *The Name of War*, 139–40.

²⁶⁰ The war did not bring an end to Eliot's and the NEC's evangelistic attempts, however. A second edition of *Mamusse Wunneetupanatamwe Up-Biblum God* was issued in 1685, in part to replace volumes that had been damaged or destroyed during the war, and missionary and

publishing activity continued well into the eighteenth century. See Fisher, *The Indian Great Awakening*, 28–29; chap. 2.

[261] "To the General Court of Massachusetts Bay, 7 May 1668," in LaFantasie, *The Correspondence of Roger Williams*, 2:577. Williams seems to be using "barbarous" in the most straightforward sense possible, namely, pertaining to a peoples' cultures and customs; in this context, according to the OED, it would mean "[u]ncultured, uncivilized, unpolished; rude, rough, wild, savage. (Said of men, their manners, customs, products.) The usual opposite of *civilized*."

[262] "Roger Williams to John Winthrop, Jr., 18 December 1675," in LaFantasie, *The Correspondence of Roger Williams*, 2:708.

[263] Glenn W. LaFantasie, introduction to *The Correspondence of Roger Williams*, 1:xliii. See also Ernst, *Roger Williams*, 497; W. R. Staples, "Annals of the Town of Providence," in *Collections of the Rhode Island Historical Society* vol. 5 (Providence: The Rhode Island Historical Society, 1843), 170. Regarding Williams' militia service during the war, see John Russell Bartlett, ed., *Records of the Colony and State of Rhode Island and Providence Plantations in New England*, 10 vols. (Providence: A Crawford Greene and Brothers, 1857), 2:531, 547; entries for August 14, August 29, and August 30, 1676, and January 1677, *The Early Records of the Town of Providence*, Horatio Rogers and Edward Field, records commissioners (Providence: Snow & Farnham City Printers, 1899), 15:151–55. Historians have noted that Roger Williams and the Rhode Island residents were less harsh in their treatment of the Indians than the Massachusetts Bay Puritans, since they did not ship their Indians off to the Caribbean as "real" slaves, but instead set time limits for their enslavement on their own lands. John Sainsbury, "Indian Labor in Early Rhode Island," *New England Quarterly* 48 (1995): 260–63. But there seems to be some evidence that some Indians *were* shipped out from Rhode Island as slaves, even in a boat owned by Providence Williams, Roger Williams' own son. See Staples, "Annals of the Town of Providence," 172. Jessica Stern has suggested that the Pequot War caused Williams to lean more definitively toward nonviolent approaches to matters of religion in society (and, by extension, a more generous view of Natives). See Stern, "A Key into The Bloudy Tenent of Persecution," 578. In fact, the opposite trend seems to be observable over the course of his lifetime. Williams started his time in New England relatively sympathetic to Native religion and culture but drifted over time to a more typical English view of Native lifeways by King Philip's War. He justified violence and enslavement against the Pequots in the 1630s and did so once again in the 1670s against the Narragansetts and other Natives.

[264] Daniel Gookin, Eliot's collaborator and contemporary, gives two reasons for this intransigence: "The reasons whereof, I conjecture, are principally these two. First, the averseness of their sachems. Secondly, the bad example of the English in those parts, where civil government and religion among the English runs very low." Richard Cogley suggests that Eliot and his Native associates "may have been the only ones who attempted to evangelize Rhode Island's two major Indian groups, the Narragansetts and the Eastern Niantic, in the period before King Philip's War." Daniel Gookin, *Historical Collections of the Indians in New England* (Boston: Joseph Belknap, 1792), 70; Cogley, *John Eliot's Mission*, 187. On the 1698 NEC survey, see Fisher, *The Indian Great Awakening*, 33.

[265] LaFantasie, *The Correspondence of Roger Williams*, 1:144 and n. 7. For a full account of Native involvement in the First Great Awakening, see Fisher, *The Indian Great Awakening*. For the primary source account of the revival, see Joseph Park, "An Account of the late Propagation of Religion at Westerly and Charlestown in Rhode-Island Colony, in a Letter from the Rev. Mr. Parks Pastor of a Church newly gathered there," August 27, 1743, no. 26, and September 3, 1743, no. 27; *The Christian History: Containing Accounts of the Revival and Propagation of Religion in Great Britain & America* 26:208, 27:1. See also William S. Simmons, "Red Yankees: Narragansett Conversion in the Great Awakening," *American Ethnologist* 10,

no. 2 (1983): 253–71; Cheryl L. Simmons and William S. Simmons, *Old Light on Separate Ways: The Narragansett Diary of Joseph Fish, 1765–1776* (Hanover, N.H.: University Press of New England, 1982).

[266] Fisher, *The Indian Great Awakening*, 113–17.

II

ROGER WILLIAMS

"A Brief Reply to a Small Book Written by John Eliot" (ca. 1680)

EDITORIAL NOTE

The text of Williams' essay poses a variety of interpretive challenges. Williams' shorthand system is personalized and idiosyncratic. For many English words, there is no standard shorthand correlate, and Williams appears to have improvised new symbols and constructions while drafting the essay. Moreover, as with any shorthand system, the writing is highly abbreviated. Most words have been condensed to two or three shorthand characters, and many articles, prepositions, and "to be" verbs have been omitted. Finally, the quality of the handwriting is consistently poor. For these reasons, a complete verbatim translation is difficult, if not impossible.

We have indicated with italics the portions of the original manuscript for which we have not been able to produce an exact word-for-word translation. In these instances, the italicized text represents an approximate translation, based on contextual clues and what shorthand we can decipher. Bracketed text is not derived from the original shorthand, but has been inserted to clarify the meaning of the translated text. Punctuation is rarely included in the original shorthand text, probably because most punctuation marks are instead employed as arbitrary symbols for common words, letters, and suffixes. Therefore, punctuation has been added to the translated document. For the sake of readability, we have elected not to bracket inserted punctuation. Ellipses have been inserted to indicate undeciphered text, and each ellipsis has been footnoted to indicate approximately how much text is undeciphered. Williams' system, like most shorthand systems, is strictly case-indifferent; it cannot distinguish between uppercase and lowercase letters. We have done our best to capitalize the translated text in a historically plausible manner, using Eliot's book and Williams' published essays as guides.

[138]¹

[Preface]

[Here is a] brief reply to a small book written *by* John Eliot² called, "an Answer to John Norcut³ *Against* Infant Baptism," a plea to the parents of the children of Christ. [Argued] from "Acts" . . .⁴ and other *Scriptures*, [written] with love and salutations. . . .⁵ [I will] plant here a seed to [take] root . . .⁶ *Written as an Answer to John Eliot, in his Answer to John Norcott. John Eliot felt* Norcott's Book to move him to write these few lines. But the words of the Great King⁷ enjoin [us] to *protect* the Gospel, whose written word *refutes* John Eliot . . .⁸ and whose Word must prevail over the Book of John Eliot. [I hope a] beam of light will appear to you by my labor. . . .⁹ I [shall] not weary the reader with a large and onerous discourse. I shall not [let it be so that] principles themselves prevail over *the written Word of God.*

[Body]

John Eliot feareth the author¹⁰ to be a Godly though erring brother who, acting the cause of a roaring Lyon, craftily seeks to devour the poor Lambs of Christ.¹¹

Answer: Eliot's voice sounds *like* the voice of a grievous Wolf, *who will enter among us and* devour the Lambs of the flock . . .¹² Acts 20.29. Christ

---

¹ These bracketed numbers indicate the printed page numbers in *An Essay Towards the Reconciling of Differences Among Christians*, the subtitle of the book in which the shorthand text was found, located in the John Carter Brown Library in Providence, Rhode Island. Williams' shorthand essay fills the margins of pp. 138–59.

² John Eliot, *A Brief Answer to a Small Book Written by John Norcot Against Infant-Baptisme* (Boston: John Foster, 1679). The word "Eliot" is written out in standard longhand English. "Eliot" and "Norcut" are the only two longhand words included in this section of short-hand marginalia.

³ The word "Norcut" is written out in standard longhand English. "Norcut" is a mis-spelling of "Norcott," the author of the book to which Eliot was responding: John Nor-cott, *Baptism Discovered Plainly and Faithfully, According to the Word of God* (London, 1672). Everywhere else, Williams writes Norcott's name in shorthand. To avoid confusion, when translating his name from shorthand, we have always used the standard spelling (Norcott).

⁴ Three to five words undeciphered.

⁵ Two to three words undeciphered.

⁶ One to two words undeciphered.

⁷ I.e., God.

⁸ Four to five words undeciphered.

⁹ Six to eight words undeciphered.

¹⁰ I.e., John Norcott.

¹¹ Here Williams paraphrases an accusation made by Eliot on p. 1 of *A Brief Answer*. Eliot's "roaring Lyon" is a biblical allusion. See 1 Peter 5:8: "Be sober, be vigilant; because your adversary the devil, as a roaring lion, walketh about, seeking whom he may devour."

¹² Nine to eleven words undeciphered.

sayeth, in Matthew 18.6, "It were better [for him] that a millstone [were] hanged about his neck, and that he were drowned in the depth of the sea than to offend one of these children who believes in me."[13] . . .[14] For ours is surely a reasonable God, brethren. . . .[15]

The next *thing* Eliot sayeth is that the words of Norcott's discourse hang upon the [belief] that there is no place for the baptism of infants in the Scriptures.

[139]

His words are: "The baptism of Believers and their infants is one of the first Gospel Apostolical Institutions commanded in the Gospel politie."[16] *"Therefore, let all the house of Israel know assuredly that God hath made him both Lord, and Christ, this Jesus, I say, whom ye have crucified. Now when they heard it, they were pricked in their heart, and said unto Peter and the other apostles, 'Men and brethren, what shall we do?' Then Peter said unto them, 'Amend your lives, and be baptized every one of you in the Name of Jesus Christ for the remission of sins: and ye shall receive the gift of the Holy Ghost. For the promise is made unto you, and to your children, and to all that are far off, even as many as the Lord our God shall call.' "*[17]

Answer: This was not the first *such Command appearing in the Gospel.* The first was the teacher John the Baptist to those that came to *be* baptized: "Bring forth therefore *fruit worthy of life*. And think not to say with your selves, We have Abraham to our father" Matthew 3.[18] [This Scripture is] contrary to the *argument* of John Eliot's book. . . .[19]

---

[13] Matthew 18:6 reads, "But whoso shall offend one of these little ones which believe in me, it were better for him that a millstone were hanged about his neck, and that he were drowned in the depth of the sea." Williams' quotations from the Bible are not always accurate. Occasionally he alters the wording, and much less frequently miscites the verse. This suggests that Williams was quoting Scripture from memory. The scriptural quotations by John Norcott, John Eliot, and Williams are generally consistent with the 1611 King James Version (KJV) of the Bible. Therefore, we have used the KJV to translate scriptural quotations included in the shorthand when a verbatim translation is impossible. Although the Puritan-Separatist-Baptists favored the Geneva Bible, it was no longer in print by the 1670s–1680s. The last known edition of the Geneva Bible was printed in Amsterdam in 1644, and it had not been printed in England since being banned in 1616. Alister McGrath, *In the Beginning: The Story of the King James Bible and How It Changed a Nation, a Language, and a Culture* (New York: Anchor Books, 2001), 280–84.

[14] Two to three words undeciphered.

[15] One short paragraph undeciphered.

[16] Eliot, *A Brief Answer*, 1.

[17] The shorthand here is difficult to decipher, but our best guess is that Williams is quoting Acts 2:36-37, as Eliot cites precisely these verses.

[18] Matthew 3:8-9.

[19] One short paragraph undeciphered. Williams is arguing against Eliot's belief in the benefits of spiritual patrimony

[It is] written that God made a promise and a covenant with Abraham and his seed. . . .[20] Acts 2: "[un]to you, and to your children,"[21] is [what] the verse sayeth. . . .[22]

[Answer]: The men of the Spirit are the true children of the Promise; for the teaching of the Spirit is first for the removal of thy *desires*,[23] both negative and affirmative. Romans 9.9 sayeth, "Neither because they are the seed of Abraham are they all children. But, in Isaac shall thy seed be called. That is, they which are the children of the flesh, these are not the children of God. But the children of the promise are counted for the seed."[24] . . .[25]

[140]

Romans 8.[14]: "For as many as are led by the spirit of God, they are the sons of God." . . .[26] Galatians 3.16: "Now to Abraham and his seed were the promises made." . . .[27] Romans 4[28] *"For the promise that he should be the heir of the world was not given to Abraham, or to his seed, through the Law, but through the* righteousness of faith." . . .[29] "If ye were Abraham's children, ye would do the works of Abraham" John 8.39. . . .[30] "born, not of blood, nor of the will of the flesh, nor of the will of man, but of God" John 1.13. . . .[31] [I] Peter 2.9: "But ye are a chosen generation, a royal priesthood, a holy nation, a peculiar people that ye show forth the praises of him who hath called you out of darkness into his marvelous light." . . .[32]

[141]

Here sayeth John Eliot there is a clear practice and example of the baptism of believers and their children.[33] . . .[34]

---

[20] Eight to ten words undeciphered.

[21] Acts 2:39.

[22] One paragraph undeciphered.

[23] This word, no doubt crucial to the meaning of the passage, is unclear. The shorthand consists of only a "d" and an "s."

[24] The citation Williams provides is incorrect. The verse quoted is Romans 9:7-8.

[25] One short paragraph undeciphered.

[26] Five to six words undeciphered.

[27] One short paragraph undeciphered.

[28] The verse number is illegible. Given the context of the passage and the few words we can make out, our best guess is Romans 4:13.

[29] Seven to eight words undeciphered.

[30] One paragraph undeciphered.

[31] One short paragraph undeciphered.

[32] One short paragraph undeciphered.

[33] Eliot, *A Brief Answer*, 2, where Eliot writes, "*Act* 2.41 *then they that gladly received his Word were baptized,* viz, they and their Children were baptized. For I ask, did they receive the whole Word of Apostolical Institution? or only a part of the Word? sure you will say, they received the whole Word of Institution, therefore these Believers and their Children at first or at last were baptized."

[34] One paragraph undeciphered.

Answer: . . .[35] Eliot adds to the word more than is written and contrary to the Holy *Scripture. For Peter says only those that gladly received his
words* were baptized. . . .[36]

Next Eliot sayeth that baptism is the Seal of the Covenant and the
Children of Believers are of the Covenant, therefore the Seal belongs to
them.[37]

Answer: The great Seal of the new Covenant is the blood of Jesus
Christ. Jeremiah 9.11,[38] Hebrews 10.29,[39] Matthew 26.28,[40] Luke 22.20.[41]
. . .[42] There is a new Covenant; baptism was a seal of the old Covenant
. . .[43] and the children of the new Covenant, it is written, are only born of
the Spirit. . . .[44] John 8.36[45] . . .[46] Galatians 4.20[47] . . .[48]

Further, Eliot sayeth the Church, with the Testimony of the Father,
Son, and Holy Ghost, *may* receive infants to their communion.[49]

Answer: Thus is Paul[50] [admitted unto communion by sufficient tes-
timony] but we are [admitted unto communion with Christ] by acts of
faith. . . .[51] Neither do we exclude the infants from the kingdom of God
(*as is* supposed) . . .[52] they[53] belong to the Lord. . . .[54]

---

[35] Four to five words undeciphered.

[36] One short paragraph undeciphered.

[37] Eliot, *A Brief Answer*, 3.

[38] "And I will make Jerusalem heaps, and a den of dragons; and I will make the cities of
Judah desolate, without an inhabitant" (Jer 9:11).

[39] "Of how much sorer punishment, suppose ye, shall he be thought worthy, who hath
trodden under foot the Son of God, and hath counteth the blood of the covenant, where-
with he was sanctified, an unholy thing, and hath done despite unto the Spirit of grace?"
(Heb 10:29).

[40] "For this is my blood of the new testament, which is shed for many for the remission
of sins" (Matt 26:28).

[41] "Likewise also the cup after supper, saying, this cup is the new testament in my blood,
which is shed for you" (Luke 22:20).

[42] One short paragraph undeciphered.

[43] Four to five words undeciphered.

[44] Four to five words undeciphered.

[45] "If the Son therefore shall make you free, ye shall be free indeed" (John 8:36).

[46] Seven words undeciphered.

[47] "My little children, of whom I travail in birth again until Christ be formed in you,
I desire to be present with you now, and to change my voice; for I stand in doubt of you"
(Gal 4:19-20).

[48] Seven to eight words undeciphered.

[49] Eliot, *A Brief Answer*, 4.

[50] Williams is referring to the testimony of Barnabas in Acts 9:26-28.

[51] One paragraph undeciphered.

[52] One short paragraph undeciphered.

[53] I.e., the infants.

[54] One short paragraph undeciphered.

[142]

And Eliot sayeth, from Romans 11, "if the first fruit be holy, the lump is also holy; and if the root be holy, so are the branches."[55]

Answer: . . .[56] I Corinthians 15[57] . . .[58] The lump and branches are holy. . . .[59]

Eliot *so truly* believes the words that he here has written, *but not the* words of Adam, Abraham, Isaac, Elijah, David, Aaron, and more. . . .[60] Eliot sayeth from John 21[61] [that] Christ has appointed [as part of our] ministry to feed the *little* Lambs, which Eliot sayeth are the infants. They are to be fed by baptism.[62]

Answer: The lambs of Christ *are* to be fed by our ministry. . . .[63] [I] Peter 1.24.[64] . . .[65] So Paul sayeth, "My little children, of whom I travail [in birth again] until Christ be formed in you."[66] . . .[67] The spiritual life and *feeling* of the new born baby in Christ is the milk of the Word.[68] . . .[69]

Brother Eliot sayeth [that] God from the first creation *hath* comprehended Parents and children together in his Covenant. Children were comprehended in the Covenant of works: so they were in the covenant of Grace.[70]

[143]

Answer: Eliot [sayeth] the Lord *did not* exclude the infants from the grace of Christ. The word is *from* Romans 5.18, 19.[71] But why is this a matter of

---

[55] Romans 11:16; Eliot, *A Brief Answer*, 4.

[56] Eight words undeciphered.

[57] Although the verse is not specified, given the context of the passage and the overall thrust of Williams' argument, 1 Corinthians 15:44-50 seems like a plausible guess. In these verses, Paul contrasts the natural and spiritual bodies and declares that the natural body came first. Verse 47: "The first man [Adam] is of the earth, earthy; the second man is the Lord from heaven." Verse 50: "Now this I say, brethren that flesh and blood cannot inherit the kingdom of God; neither doth corruption inherit incorruption."

[58] Five to seven words undeciphered.

[59] Four to five words undeciphered.

[60] Eleven to twelve words undeciphered.

[61] The verse to which Williams refers is John 21:15: "So when they had dined, Jesus saith to Simon Peter, Simon, son of Jonas, lovest thou me more than these? He saith unto him, Yea, Lord; thou knowest that I love thee. He saith unto him, Feed my lambs."

[62] Eliot, *A Brief Answer*, 6.

[63] One short paragraph undeciphered.

[64] "For all flesh is as grass, and all the glory of man as the flower of grass. The grass withereth, and the flower thereof falleth away" (1 Pet 1:24).

[65] One short paragraph undeciphered.

[66] Galatians 4:19.

[67] One short paragraph undeciphered.

[68] Allusion to 1 Peter 2:2: "As newborn babes, desire the sincere milk of the word, that ye may grow thereby."

[69] One short paragraph undeciphered.

[70] Eliot, *A Brief Answer*, 7.

[71] "Therefore as by the offence of one judgment came upon all men to condemnation;

believer's children being the right *ones for* baptism? If there be a thing that argues for the baptism of infants it [is that] all Adam's seed was comprehended with him in the Covenant of works. And by this *reason* you *conclude* [that] baptism is only for children which you call believer's children. But Indians and unbelievers of all *kinds* must then *also be* comprehended in the Covenant of Grace with Adam. . . .[72]

We do not *intend to* exclude neither the seed nor their children from the generous grace of God. [It] must be their *actions* that exclude them. . . .[73] I Corinthians 7.14: "The unbelieving husband is sanctified by the believing wife and the unbelieving wife is sanctified by the believing husband. Else were [your] children unclean *but now they are holy.*" . . .[74]

[144]

. . .[75] The next is a grave charge against the people whom Eliot calls Anabaptists[76] of uncharitableness and censoriousness.[77] . . .[78]

Answer: . . .[79] Faith *in the* wisdom of the *Scripture* is not uncharitableness or censoriousness . . .[80] John 3.4[81] . . .[82] This is not uncharitableness but the will of God. . . .[83]

Brother Eliot sayeth they[84] are without natural affection to their children in the highest degree for they exclude them from sharing with them in Christ.[85]

Answer: We do *consider it* a gross *sin* to be without natural affection [for one's children] but this charge is without a true grounding. . . .[86]

---

even so by the righteousness of one the free gift came upon all men unto justification of life. For as by one man's disobedience many were made sinners, so by the obedience of one shall many be made righteous" (Rom 5:18-19).

[72] One paragraph undeciphered.

[73] One short paragraph undeciphered.

[74] One paragraph undeciphered.

[75] One short paragraph undeciphered.

[76] "Anabaptist" was a term used by opponents of the Baptists, linking them to the infamous radicalism of some of the sixteenth-century Anabaptist movements, a rhetorical move clearly intended to discredit the Baptists. See the discussion of Anabaptists in part I (pp. 21–22).

[77] Eliot, *A Brief Answer*, 8–9.

[78] Seven to nine words undeciphered.

[79] One short paragraph undeciphered.

[80] Five to six words undeciphered.

[81] "Nicodemus saith unto him, How can a man be born when he is old? Can he enter the second time into his mother's womb, and be born? Jesus answered, Verily, verily I say unto thee, Except a man be born of water and of the Spirit, he cannot enter into the kingdom of God. That which is born of the flesh, is flesh; and that that is born of the Spirit is spirit" (John 3:4-6).

[82] One short paragraph undeciphered.

[83] One paragraph undeciphered.

[84] I.e., the Anabaptists.

[85] Eliot, *A Brief Answer*, 10.

[86] One paragraph undeciphered.

[145][87]

[146]

. . .[88] The next *thing* that Eliot writes of is three to four pages[89] [about] parental Covenant or a spiritual Patrimony,[90] which, sayeth Eliot, the Anabaptists deny. [On] Page 12 Eliot sayeth *that* spiritual Patrimony is a great and sanctified means of conversion, though not the only means thereof; the Indians are converted without it. But, sayeth Eliot, in our churches all of the converts are converted by the improvement of their Patrimony or Covenant only, and this appears, sayeth Eliot, by their confessions when they come into full communion with the church.[91]

Answer: As for the conversion of the Indians by the Gospel (for those are [the] words written)[92] it would be [a] cause of great joy if they were feeling true.[93] But if the shepherd of their chiefs[94] [uses] treachery and seduction, [it] is much a sore to the wisdom of the gospel of Christ. As the first treatise[95] doth declare, there is first *grounding*[96] to prepare one's soul before conversion. Eliot speaks out against the Indians.[97] They might

---

[87] Nothing on this page has been deciphered (the equivalent of several full paragraphs).

[88] One short paragraph undeciphered.

[89] Eliot, *A Brief Answer*, 10–14.

[90] Eliot, *A Brief Answer*, 11, defines spiritual patrimony as "our Estate in Religion which our Parents conveigh unto us," a benefit that remained with baptized children throughout their lifetime, comforting them in difficult times and aiding them to make their own profession of faith.

[91] For many Congregational churches in seventeenth-century New England, full membership (and therefore access to Communion, or the Lord's Supper) was reserved for individuals who could narrate their own conversion either to a minister or to the congregation. The "Halfway Covenant" of 1662 created an alternate possibility for parents who had been baptized as children in their local Congregational church but had not yet made the confession of faith to become full members to still bring their own children forward for baptism (full membership would previously have been required to have one's children baptized). See Robert G. Pope, *The Half-Way Covenant: Church Membership in Puritan New England* (Princeton: Princeton University Press, 1969); David D. Hall, ed., *Puritans in the New World: A Critical Anthology* (Princeton: Princeton University Press, 2004), chap. 11.

[92] Phrase means: "for those are the words Eliot has written."

[93] I.e., "if their feelings were genuine"; indicates sincerity.

[94] The shorthand is a bit unclear here, but the most straightforward rendering is "shepherd of their chiefs," meaning John Eliot.

[95] Here Williams is likely referring to Norcott's 1672 treatise *Baptism Discovered Plainly and Faithfully, According to the Word of God*, to which Eliot's essay was a response.

[96] This likely means "scriptural authority" or "grounding in the Scripture."

[97] This phrase is not entirely clear. One possible interpretation: Eliot does not have the interest of the Indians in mind (there are parallel phrases elsewhere in the essay in which Williams accuses Eliot of speaking out against the word of God). This phrase could also imply betrayal, i.e., "Eliot betrays the word of God / betrays the Indians." There is, however, an alternate reading of the shorthand, namely: "For Eliot speaks out against this. Indians,

speak [or] do *something*[98] as they are taught[99] and *this* conversion [of the] Indians appears as the French and Spanish [conversions].[100] But if their leaders be prepared in error, how can their duties be considered true or according to the Gospel?

As for those whom Eliot calls true converts, [we must] wonder of the wisdom of their conversion.[101] *In contrast to the Indians whom Eliot says are converted by the gospel, Christians are converted* [102] only by the improvement of spiritual Patrimony and by the Covenant of the Spirit. Surely we be *cautious* of such conversions[103] to Christ. The Apostle Paul [in] Romans 10.17 speaks clearly against this: "faith cometh by hearing and hearing by the word of God" to join the gospel out of *feeling*[104] not by patrimony. . . .[105]

[147]

"Therefore it is of faith, that it might be by grace; to the end the promise might be sure to all the seed; not to that only which is of the law, but to that also which is of the faith of Abraham, who is the father of us all."[106] Romans 4.16. . . .[107] 2 Corinthians 11.13–18[108] . . .[109]

---

then, might speak. . . ." One possible interpretation is that Williams sees the Indians and the Baptists (as articulated by Norcott) to be in the same position of preparation apart from patrimony. By speaking out against Norcott, Williams argues, Eliot is inadvertently also speaking out against the Indians, since they, too, come to Christ apart from spiritual patrimony.

[98] Literally "some."

[99] Gloss: "They simply say and do what they have been taught" (i.e., the Indians are simply performing for the missionaries).

[100] This is a pointed critique of Eliot's program of Indian evangelization.

[101] Here Williams broadens his argument to include non-Natives, once again picking up the theme of the inefficacy of spiritual patrimony.

[102] Only a few isolated phrases here are decipherable, including "to the Indians" and "by the Gospel."

[103] Williams here is talking about the "conversions" of Christians (or people already in the church) through spiritual patrimony.

[104] The shorthand here is ambiguous, but the citation of Romans 10:17 is clearly intended to refute Eliot's claims about the role of spiritual patrimony in conversion.

[105] One paragraph undeciphered.

[106] The shorthand here is difficult to decipher, but the citation of Romans 4:16 indicates that Williams is quoting Scripture.

[107] One short paragraph undeciphered.

[108] "For such are false apostles, deceitful workers, transforming themselves into the apostles of Christ. And no marvel; for Satan himself is transformed into an angel of light. Therefore it is no great thing if his ministers also be transformed as the ministers of righteousness; whose end shall be according to their works. I say again, Let no man think me a fool; if otherwise, yet as a fool receive me, that I may boast myself a little. That which I speak, I speak *it* not after the Lord, but as it were foolishly, in this confidence of boasting. Seeing that many glory after the flesh, I will glory also" (2 Cor 11:13–18).

[109] One short paragraph undeciphered.

Philippians 3.4[110] . . .[111] Galatians 2.20,[112] Hebrews 10.38.[113]

Compare these testaments with John Eliot's words of Patrimony and Covenant and then appreciate *that his* advice [is] against the example of the Gospel of Christ. Acts 13.32,[114]

Luke 1.69, 70, 71[115] . . .[116]

[148]

. . .[117] Acts 13.26, 46,[118] Acts 5.2[119] . . .[120]

Furthermore, sayeth Eliot, this opinion is pernicious and destructive to the Churches of Christ, [it] killeth them in their bud, [it] robbeth them of their Lambs, and will make the Churches poor and thin.[121]

Answer: . . .[122] First, the children are not of *the* flesh . . .[123] but they are born of God the children of the new Covenant. . . .[124]

Eliot sayeth [on] page 12 that converts [are] converted by the improvement of their patrimony and *so* the conversions have no grounding in Christ. . . .[125]

---

[110] "Though I might also have confidence in the flesh. If any other man thinketh that he hath whereof he might trust in the flesh, I more" (Phil 3:4).

[111] One short paragraph undeciphered.

[112] "I am crucified with Christ: nevertheless I live; yet not I, but Christ liveth in me: and the life which I now live in the flesh I live by the faith of the Son of God, who loved me, and gave himself for me" (Gal 2:20).

[113] "Now the just shall live by faith: but if *any* man draw back, my soul shall have no pleasure in him" (Heb 10:38).

[114] "And we declare unto you glad tidings, how that the promise which was made unto the fathers, God hath fulfilled the same unto us their children, in that he hath raised up Jesus again; as it is also written in the second psalm, Thou art my Son, this day have I begotten thee" (Acts 13:32-33).

[115] "And hath raised up an horn of salvation for us in the house of his servant David; As he spake by the mouth of his holy prophets, which have been since the world began: That we should be saved from our enemies, and from the hand of all that hate us" (Luke 1:69-71).

[116] Nine to eleven words undeciphered.

[117] One short paragraph undeciphered.

[118] "Men and brethren, children of the stock of Abraham, and whosoever among you feareth God, to you is the word of this salvation sent" (Acts 13:26). "Then Paul and Barnabas waxed bold, and said, It was necessary that the word of God should first have been spoken to you: but seeing ye put it from you, and judge yourselves unworthy of everlasting life, lo, we turn to the Gentiles" (Acts 13:46).

[119] "And kept back part of the price, his wife also being privy to it, and brought a certain part, and laid it down at the apostles' feet" (Acts 5:2).

[120] One paragraph undeciphered.

[121] Eliot, *A Brief Answer*, 14.

[122] Eleven to twelve words undeciphered.

[123] Five to six words undeciphered.

[124] One short paragraph undeciphered.

[125] One short paragraph undeciphered.

The next thing Eliot sayeth was, "I shall [now] take brief consideration of the Book,[126] and I will give one direction to such as read it, which being observed will quite enervate the whole Book, *viz.* when the Book mentioneth baptism of believers, do you add in your mind 'and their Seed.' "[127]

Answer: When the book[128] mentioneth this [the baptism of believers], it is from the *Word of God.*[129] Matthew 28,[130] Mark 16: "He that believeth and is baptized shall be saved."[131] Acts 8.18: "The Corinthians, hearing [it], believed and were baptized."[132]

To add in the mind "and their Seed, the infants" [whenever Baptism of Believers is mentioned] is not to add only to Norcott's

[149]

book, but to add to the book of Holy Scripture[133] . . .[134] contrary to the plain word of God, Deuteronomy 4.2: "Ye shall not add [un]to the word that I command you, neither shall you diminish [ought] from it." . . .[135]

The children of the flesh, these are not the children of God, but the children of the promise are counted for the Seed. When you read [on] page 17[136] that believers' infants had the privilege to be born Disciples, add in your mind: "that which is born of the flesh is flesh and that which is born of the Spirit is spirit."[137] . . .[138]

On the first chapter of his[139] book, Eliot sayeth that had baptism been instituted when Jesus was an Infant, he would have submitted to it.[140]

Answer: Had it been instituted for infants, as circumcision was, [there is] no doubt that he would [have submitted to baptism]. . . .[141] But that it

---

[126] I.e., Norcott's book.

[127] Eliot, *A Brief Answer*, 16.

[128] I.e., Norcott's book.

[129] The verses cited subsequently are precisely those cited by Norcott on p. 10 of *Baptism Discovered Plainly.*

[130] Verse not specified. The most relevant verses from Matthew are the following: "And when they saw him, they worshipped him: but some doubted. And Jesus came and spake unto them, saying, All power is given unto me in heaven and in earth. Go ye therefore, and teach all nations, baptizing them in the name of the Father, and of the Son, and the Holy Ghost" (Matt 28:17-19).

[131] Mark 16:16.

[132] Here Williams has transposed chapter and verse. The correct citation is Acts 18:8.

[133] Adding to the Bible was a serious accusation for early modern Bible-believing Protestants.

[134] Fourteen to fifteen words undeciphered.

[135] One paragraph undeciphered.

[136] Eliot, *A Brief Answer*, 17.

[137] John 3:6.

[138] One paragraph undeciphered.

[139] I.e., Eliot's book.

[140] Eliot, *A Brief Answer*, 17.

[141] Eight to nine words undeciphered.

was no so instituted. . .[142] *when* he was of age, it shows that it was the Lord's desire that *the privilege* shall belong only to . . .[143] believers. . . .[144]

Matthew 28: "First teach them and then baptize them,"[145] Acts 8: "If thou believest with all thine heart, thou mayest."[146] . . .[147]

[150]

. . .[148] Eliot sayeth that Infants are taught and made Disciples, in that their parents are so.[149]

Answer: . . .[150] For the *command* of Christ is first for teaching and then for baptizing. . .[151]

In the third chapter, [Norcott] *takes an* example [from] John 4.1, 2: "Jesus made [Disciples] and baptized." They [the Disciples] were made, not born so. John Eliot answers that it was so with the first believers, but their Infants had the privilege of being born Disciples. This was, sayeth Eliot, at the beginning of the public ministry of Christ. The order of the Gospel Churches was not yet instituted and fixed.[152]

[Answer:] . . .[153] But we read not anywhere of *Infants* that were born Disciples. John 3: "Ye must be born again."[154] For if children are born Disciples, as Eliot sayeth, then there is no difference between being born of the flesh and being born of the Spirit, contrary to the word of Paul in I Corinthians 15.46 : "Howbeit that was not first which is spiritual, but that which is natural, and afterward that which is spiritual." . . .[155]

[151]

. . .[156] The example of the Jaylor affordeth no weight to the *practice* of infant baptism, but much to the contrary. . .[157] 2.[158] [It is] said plainly that

---

[142] One short paragraph undeciphered.

[143] One to two words undeciphered.

[144] Eight to nine words undeciphered.

[145] Matthew 28:19.

[146] I.e., "thou mayest be baptized" (Acts 8:37).

[147] One short paragraph undeciphered.

[148] One short paragraph undeciphered.

[149] Eliot, *A Brief Answer*, 17.

[150] One short paragraph undeciphered.

[151] One short paragraph undeciphered.

[152] Eliot, *A Brief Answer*, 17.

[153] One short paragraph undeciphered.

[154] John 3:7.

[155] One paragraph undeciphered.

[156] One paragraph undeciphered.

[157] One short paragraph undeciphered.

[158] The numerals in this paragraph correspond to numbered items in a list, the first point of which remains undeciphered.

the Apostles[159] spake the word of the Lord to him and to all those that were in his household. They are the *persons* to whom it was spoken. 3. He[160] rejoiced, believing in God with all his household, plainly declaring that those that were baptized were no infants but believers.

[As for] Lydia, Acts 16.14[161] is the verse that sayeth who was baptized: "and her household," who *we* must declare to be Believers and not Infants. . . .[162] It is written, in Acts 40:[163] "They entered into the house of Lydia, and when they had seen the brethren, they comforted them and departed." For it is written plainly that her household were brethren that were comforted. . . .[164]

The fourth chapter *concerns* dipping.[165] Eliot sayeth first [that] the Holy Scriptures have left it indifferent; baptism *either way may be lawful*.[166] . . .[167]

Answer: . . .[168] Sayeth Paul [in] I Corinthians 11.[1], "Be ye followers of me, even as I am of Christ."

[152]

. . .[169] For the word of God *Almighty* was dipping, for when Jesus was baptized "he went straightway out of the water," Matthew 3.16. "And Philip and the Eunuch then went both down into the water," Acts 8.38. Acts [8].39: "and when they were come out of the water." . . .[170] I Timothy 6.3 speaks of such teachers that do not consenteth to the wholesome words of our Lord Jesus and the doctrine that is according to godliness. . . .[171]

[153]

. . .[172] Eliot *concludes* his answer to the fourth chapter of Norcott's book with the *claim* . . .[173] first, that the great administration of baptism Acts 2 was performed in the Temple where was no River.[174]

---

[159] I.e., Paul and Silas. See Acts 16:32.

[160] I.e., the jailer.

[161] This citation is incorrect. The baptism of Lydia and her household is declared in Acts 16:15, not Acts 16:14.

[162] Six to eight words undeciphered.

[163] Acts 16:40.

[164] One short paragraph undeciphered.

[165] I.e., baptism by full immersion into water.

[166] Eliot was probably referring to dipping and sprinkling. But pouring and washing were two more modes of baptism in the seventeenth century. By the 1640s the Baptists had universally adopted dipping, to the exclusion of the three other modes.

[167] One short paragraph undeciphered.

[168] One short paragraph undeciphered.

[169] One paragraph undeciphered.

[170] One paragraph undeciphered.

[171] One paragraph undeciphered.

[172] One paragraph undeciphered.

[173] One short clause undeciphered.

[174] Eliot, *A Brief Answer*, 20.

Answer: . . .[175] It doth not appear clear that the *Pentecost* was in the Temple, when Peter spake to them.[176] The text sayeth, "they were all with one accord in one place."[177] . . .[178] Luke *makes* no mention of their being in the Temple till the great addition of the three thousand.[179] And all *throughout* Luke does not mention the place where they were baptized. Yet it is not to be doubted that they followed their Lord's example who . . .[180] came straightaway out of the water. Matthew 3.16. . . .[181]

Second, Eliot sayeth: of the Jaylor, there was no going to a River for dipping.

Answer: . . .[182] *The Scripture* sayeth no such thing to negate or affirm.[183]

Third, Eliot sayeth Paul was baptized in the room where he lay sick. Acts 9.[18].

[154]

Answer: . . .[184] contrary to the plain word of Christ. . . .[185] It is plain there was more to this *story*.[186] For *Paul is commanded to* arise and be baptized. But there was no *mention* of rising according to Eliot's *account*.[187]

Fourth, Cornelius and his family were (sayeth Eliot) baptized in the place where the Word was preached to them. Nothing *intimated* of the assemblies removing to a River.[188]

[Answer:] . . .[189] There is nothing but the bare *speculation*[190] against the written Word of the Lord, as has been said. For if there be nothing [said] of going to a riverside and nothing is said they were baptized in the house, it must be *inferred* [that] there is better grounding to affirm they went to

---

[175] One short paragraph undeciphered.

[176] That is, the people who were converted and baptized.

[177] Acts 2:46.

[178] One short paragraph undeciphered.

[179] The first mention of a "temple" appears in Acts 2:46. At this point, all three thousand converts have already been baptized.

[180] One clause undeciphered.

[181] One paragraph undeciphered.

[182] One short paragraph undeciphered.

[183] I.e., the scriptural passage does not specify the details of the jailer's baptism.

[184] Fifteen to sixteen words undeciphered.

[185] Fifteen to seventeen words undeciphered.

[186] Williams is accusing Eliot of omitting important details in the story of Paul's baptism as described in Acts 9:18.

[187] Eliot, *A Brief Answer*, 21: "*Paul* was baptized in the room where he lay sick."

[188] Eliot, *A Brief Answer*, 21.

[189] Eleven to twelve words undeciphered.

[190] Between "bare" and "against" is a two-to-three-word phrase, which, judging by context, has the same general meaning as "speculation."

some water . . .[191] then to affirm they were baptized in the house of which [there is] no example nor *consideration* in the Scripture. . . .[192]

Fifth, Eliot sayeth baptism is to be administered in the public assembly as a part of God's worship.[193] . . .[194]

Answer: . . .[195] For we do not read that Christ nor Paul nor the Eunuch *best* of all were baptized in the Assembly. . . .[196]

Eliot passes by chapters 5, 6, and 7 of the book[197] without any answer.

Chapter 8 [gives] answers to 22 objections. Eliot leaves out 19 and takes notice only of 3. *Eliot dismisses the* first objections as hardly worth writing *about*.[198]

The first he answers to is the objection about circumcision. . . .[199] First I shall take notice of the *argument* . . .[200] that baptism comes in the room[201] of circumcision.[202] Romans 4 plainly said of Abraham: "He received Circumcision, a Seal of the of the Righteousness of Faith, which he had yet being uncircumcised, that he might be the father of all those that believe."[203]

Answer: . . .[204] here is not an *example* of Baptism coming in the room of Circumcision. . . .[205]

[155]

. . .[206] Verse 9: "*Cometh this blessedness then upon the circumcision only, or upon the uncircumcision also? For we say the faith was imputed to Abraham for righteousness.*"[207] Verse 11 cited to prove baptism is to come in the room of Circumcision. He [Abraham] sayeth that he might be the father of all that believe.

Verse 12: He [Abraham] is the father of those of Circumcision. . . .[208] See also Romans 9.7: "Neither because they are of the seed of Abraham

---

[191] One clause undeciphered.
[192] One paragraph undeciphered.
[193] Eliot, *A Brief Answer*, 21.
[194] Six words undeciphered.
[195] Eleven to thirteen words undeciphered.
[196] One short paragraph undeciphered.
[197] I.e., Norcott's book.
[198] Eliot, *A Brief Answer*, 21.
[199] One short paragraph undeciphered.
[200] Three words undeciphered.
[201] Meaning "place."
[202] Eliot, *A Brief Answer*, 21–22.
[203] Romans 4:11.
[204] Eight to nine words undeciphered.
[205] One short paragraph undeciphered.
[206] One short paragraph undeciphered.
[207] Romans 4:9.
[208] One paragraph undeciphered.

are they children but, in Isaac shall thy seed be called." That is, sayeth he,[209] Verse 8, "They which are the children of the flesh, these are not the children of God, but the children of the promise, they are counted for the seed."[210] . . .[211]

Neither will the *epistles* define Baptism [as] coming in the room of Circumcision. . . .[212] For though Circumcision was a Seal of Abraham's faith, yet it cannot become a Seal of the Righteousness of the male's faith, who is to be *cast* out of the family. . . .[213] The covenant of Circumcision *shuts out* their female children: Circumcision was only for the males.[214] . . .[215]

[156]

. . .[216] Furthermore Eliot sayeth, "Why they deny baptism to come in the room of circumcision I know not, unless it be for fear of an argument that it affordeth for infant baptism which they know not how to evade."[217]

Answer: I know not the argument it affordeth at all. . . .[218] For Abraham's children are . . .[219] of the faith of Abraham and we deny not Baptism to come in the room of Circumcision [but] it is those who worship God in the spirit and rejoice in Christ Jesus who are the true Circumcision. Philippians 3.3. So sayeth Paul, Romans 2.[29], that Circumcision is that of the heart, in the spirit not in the letter, whose praise is not of men but of God.

As to the *objection to* Infant Baptism that there [is] need [for] new rebaptisms, Eliot sayeth that the parent giveth consent to the baptismal covenant and acteth faith in behalf of the child and the child is trained up and taught to do it himself and this is accepted of God.[220]

Answer: . . .[221] Nor do I believe that I exclude Infants from the ministry of God. Romans 15.18.[222]

Eliot furthermore sayeth that in Acts 19 that they were not rebaptized but instructed by the Apostle that they were rightly baptized.[223]

---

[209] I.e., Paul.

[210] Romans 9:8.

[211] One short paragraph undeciphered.

[212] One short paragraph undeciphered.

[213] One short paragraph undeciphered.

[214] Norcott makes a similar argument on p. 31 of *Baptism Discovered Plainly*.

[215] One short paragraph undeciphered.

[216] One short paragraph undeciphered.

[217] Eliot, *A Brief Answer*, 22.

[218] Twelve to thirteen words undeciphered.

[219] Three to four words undeciphered.

[220] Eliot, *A Brief Answer*, 23.

[221] One short paragraph undeciphered.

[222] "For I will not dare to speak of any of those things which Christ hath not wrought by me, to make the Gentiles obedient, by word and deed" (Rom 15:18).

[223] Eliot, *A Brief Answer*, 23.

Answer: . . .[224] [It is] plainly declared that when they heard that [they] should believe on Jesus they were baptized in the name of the Lord Jesus . . .[225] they were believers yet rebaptized according to the Church's *customs* . . .[226] to nullify that which [has] been called baptism that *was* neither the right ministry nor the right *spirit* nor performed in the right manner.[227]

[157]

But Eliot sayeth of the Baptists . . .[228] that they are inconsiderable.[229]

Answer: *The word* was to Christ's flock. Luke 12.42: "Fear not, little flock, it is your father's pleasure to give you the kingdom."[230] . . .[231]

As for the rest of chapters 9 and 10, he[232] slights them. It is, [as] I said, *an* insult [to] Norcott's book. . . .[233]

The 11th chapter, Eliot sayeth, [is] a chapter of *considerations*,[234] being 29 as *in* chapter 10.[235] But no *one* can know by his answers what they be. Eliot sayeth he shall answer them[236] with his considerations,[237] which considerations of John Eliot are not considerations but nothing but *whims*. . . .[238]

The 12th consideration Eliot sayeth: "If the salvation of my soul lay upon it, I dare affirm with holy boldness that believers and their Infants were baptized in the Primitive Church."

Answer: . . .[239]

[158]

. . .[240] But Eliot adds in the 18th consideration . . .[241] that the infants in Lydia's house be not named yet the whole household is mentioned and who shall teach the Holy Ghost to speak.[242]

---

[224] Eleven to twelve words undeciphered.

[225] One short paragraph missing.

[226] Six to eight words undeciphered.

[227] Williams is referring to the account in Acts 19:1-5 of the rebaptism of the disciples of John.

[228] Eleven to twelve words undeciphered.

[229] Eliot, *A Brief Answer*, 23. That is, Eliot suggests that Baptists are not very numerous.

[230] The citation Williams provides is incorrect. The verse quoted is Luke 12:32.

[231] One long paragraph undeciphered.

[232] I.e., Eliot.

[233] Five words undeciphered.

[234] In chapter 11, Norcott lists out twenty-nine "Considerations by way of Conclusion." Norcott, *Baptism Discovered Plainly*, 51–59.

[235] Although chapter 10 of Norcott's book indeed contains twenty-nine Scripture verses, chapter 11 contains thirty, not twenty-nine, considerations.

[236] I.e., Norcott's twenty-nine considerations.

[237] Eliot, *A Brief Answer*, 24.

[238] One short paragraph undeciphered.

[239] One short paragraph undeciphered.

[240] One short paragraph undeciphered.

[241] Four words undeciphered.

[242] Eliot, *A Brief Answer*, 26.

Answer: That which the Holy Ghost hath spoken and taught Lydia and her household is true. . . .[243] Yet the household doth not *necessarily* include an infant nor can any such [thing] be inferred. . . .[244]

All of Eliot's argument (that can be understood) is that the only households being mentioned [are those with] Infants. Now consider: . . .[245] that where household appears [it] means friends. [It] be the same argument when [Paul] sayeth (Romans 16), "salute them of Aristobulus' household and the household of Narcissus,"[246] and adds to Timothy, "Salute the household of Sosipater."[247] And to the Philippians, "All the saints salute you, chiefly they of Caesar's household."[248] And to the Colossians, "Salute the brethren of Laodicea and Nymphas and the church that is in his house."[249] . . .[250]

[159]

. . .[251] For there is but one Fold and one Shepherd.[252] . . .[253] higher duty [to] defy the old way . . .[254] and ye shall find rest [un]to your souls.[255]

EDITORIAL NOTE

Williams' essay ends here. The marginalia, which fills only a small section of page 159, is capped off with a short horizontal line.

---

[243] One short paragraph undeciphered.

[244] One short paragraph undeciphered.

[245] One clause undeciphered.

[246] Romans 16:10-11.

[247] Romans 16:21.

[248] Philippians 4:22.

[249] Colossians 4:15.

[250] One paragraph undeciphered.

[251] One paragraph undeciphered.

[252] Allusion to John 10:16: "And other sheep I have, which are not of this fold: them also I must bring, and they shall hear my voice; and there shall be one fold, and one shepherd."

[253] Five to six words undeciphered.

[254] Seven to nine words undeciphered.

[255] Matthew 11:29.

An Essay Towards the Reconciling
of Differences Among Christians
[138–159]

FIGURES 19–40 (following)

Pages from Williams, "A Brief Reply to a Small Book Written by John Eliot," written in the margins of An Essay Towards the Reconciling of Differences Among Christians. *Courtesy of the John Carter Brown Library at Brown University.*

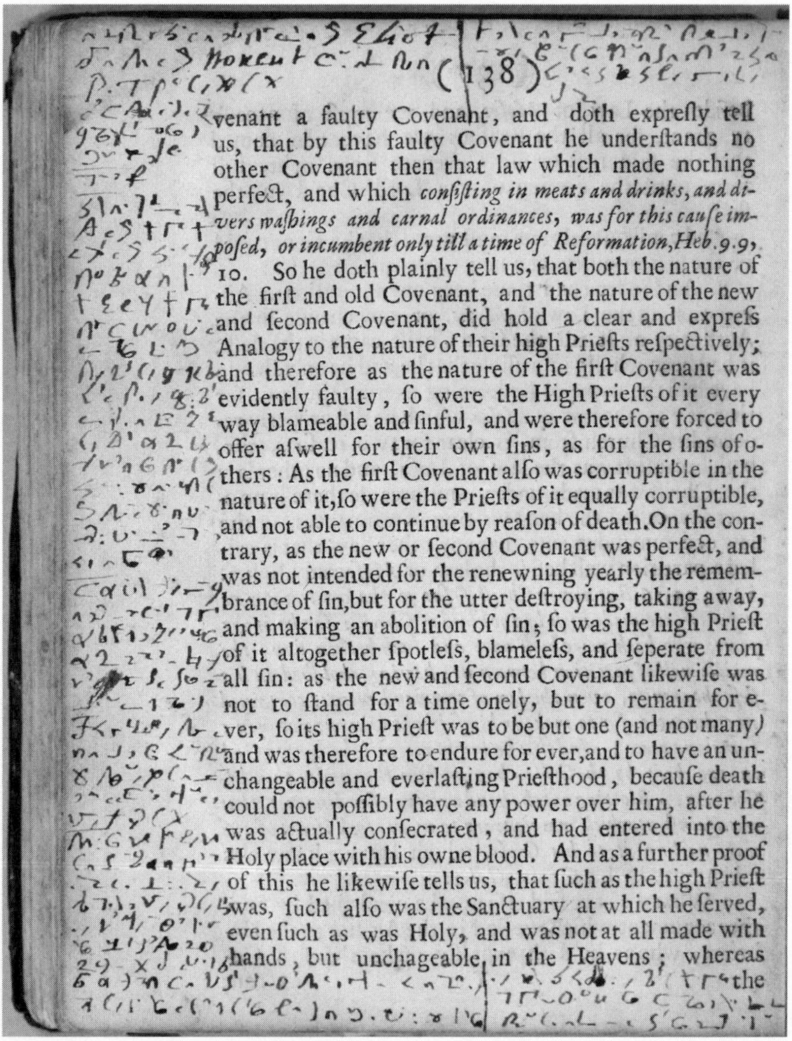

(138)

...venant a faulty Covenant, and doth exprefly tell us, that by this faulty Covenant he underſtands no other Covenant then that law which made nothing perfect, and which *confiſting in meats and drinks, and divers waſhings and carnal ordinances, was for this cauſe impoſed, or incumbent only till a time of Reformation, Heb. 9. 9, 10.* So he doth plainly tell us, that both the nature of the firſt and old Covenant, and the nature of the new and ſecond Covenant, did hold a clear and exprefs Analogy to the nature of their high Prieſts reſpectively; and therefore as the nature of the firſt Covenant was evidently faulty, ſo were the High Prieſts of it every way blameable and ſinful, and were therefore forced to offer aſwell for their own ſins, as for the ſins of others: As the firſt Covenant alſo was corruptible in the nature of it, ſo were the Prieſts of it equally corruptible, and not able to continue by reaſon of death. On the contrary, as the new or ſecond Covenant was perfect, and was not intended for the renewning yearly the remembrance of ſin, but for the utter deſtroying, taking away, and making an abolition of ſin; ſo was the high Prieſt of it altogether ſpotleſs, blameleſs, and ſeperate from all ſin: as the new and ſecond Covenant likewiſe was not to ſtand for a time onely, but to remain for ever, ſo its high Prieſt was to be but one (and not many) and was therefore to endure for ever, and to have an unchangeable and everlaſting Prieſthood, becauſe death could not poſſibly have any power over him, after he was actually conſecrated, and had entered into the Holy place with his owne blood. And as a further proof of this he likewiſe tells us, that ſuch as the high Prieſt was, ſuch alſo was the Sanctuary at which he ſerved, even ſuch as was Holy, and was not at all made with hands, but unchageable in the Heavens; whereas the

FIGURE 19

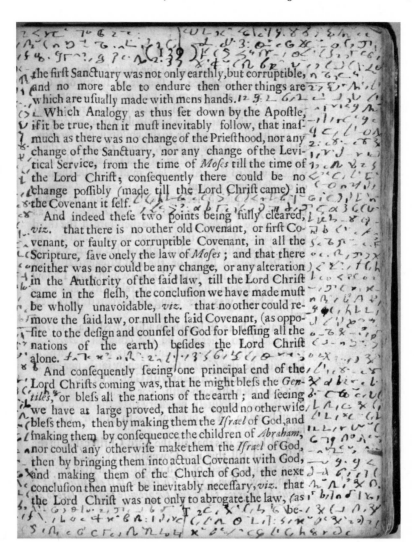

the firſt Sanctuary was not only earthly, but corruptible,
and no more able to endure then other things are
which are uſually made with mens hands. Which Analogy as thus ſet down by the Apoſtle, if it be true, then it muſt inevitably follow, that inaſmuch as there was no change of the Prieſthood, nor any change of the Sanctuary, nor any change of the Levitical Service, from the time of *Moſes* till the time of the Lord Chriſt; conſequently there could be no change poſſibly (made till the Lord Chriſt came) in the Covenant it ſelf.

And indeed theſe two points being fully cleared, *viz.* that there is no other old Covenant, or firſt Covenant, or faulty or corruptible Covenant, in all the Scripture, ſave onely the law of *Moſes*; and that there neither was nor could be any change, or any alteration in the Authority of the ſaid law, till the Lord Chriſt came in the fleſh, the concluſion we have made muſt be wholly unavoidable, *viz.* that no other could remove the ſaid law, or null the ſaid Covenant, (as oppoſite to the deſign and counſel of God for bleſſing all the nations of the earth) beſides the Lord Chriſt alone.

And conſequently ſeeing one principal end of the Lord Chriſts coming was, that he might bleſs the *Gentiles*, or bleſs all the nations of the earth; and ſeeing we have at large proved, that he could no otherwiſe bleſs them, then by making them the *Iſrael* of God, and making them by conſequence the children of *Abraham*, nor could any otherwiſe make them the *Iſrael* of God, then by bringing them into actual Covenant with God, and making them of the Church of God, the next concluſion then muſt be inevitably neceſſary, *viz.* that the Lord Chriſt was not only to abrogate the law, (as

FIGURE 20

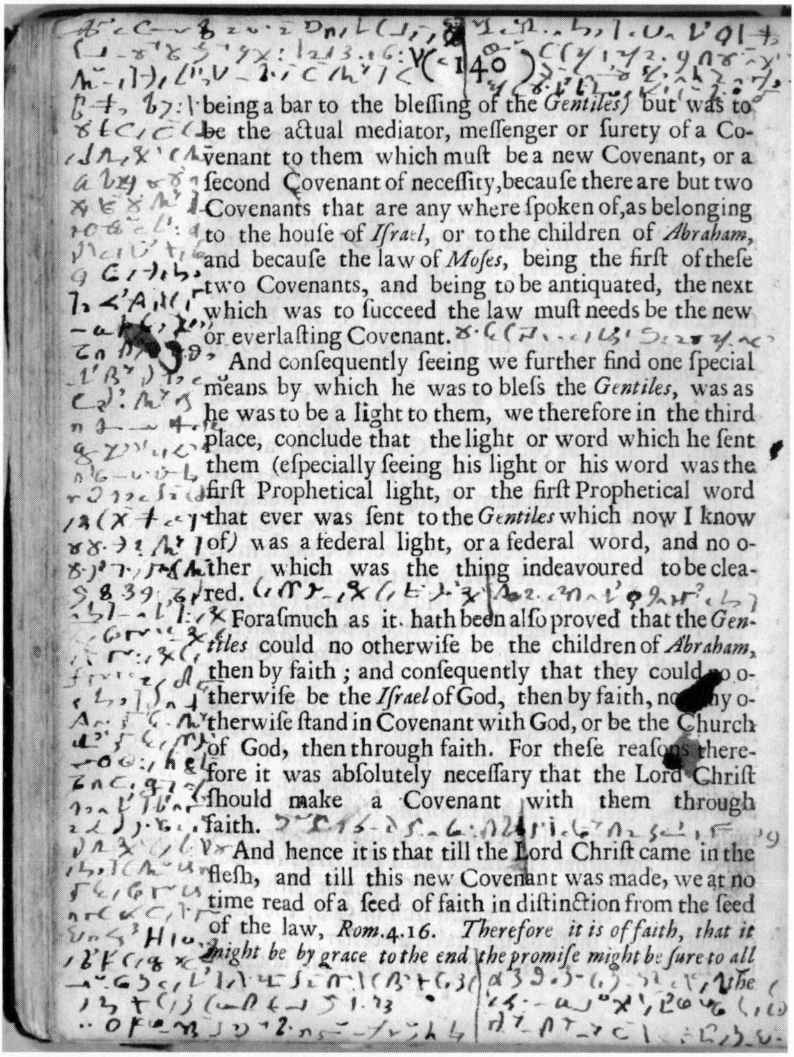

being a bar to the blessing of the *Gentiles;* but was to be the actual mediator, messenger or surety of a Covenant to them which must be a new Covenant, or a second Covenant of necessity, because there are but two Covenants that are any where spoken of, as belonging to the house of *Israel,* or to the children of *Abraham,* and because the law of *Moses,* being the first of these two Covenants, and being to be antiquated, the next which was to succeed the law must needs be the new or everlasting Covenant.

And consequently seeing we further find one special means by which he was to bless the *Gentiles,* was as he was to be a light to them, we therefore in the third place, conclude that the light or word which he sent them (especially seeing his light or his word was the first Prophetical light, or the first Prophetical word that ever was sent to the *Gentiles* which now I know of) was a federal light, or a federal word, and no other which was the thing indeavoured to be cleared.

Forasmuch as it hath been also proved that the *Gentiles* could no otherwise be the children of *Abraham,* then by faith; and consequently that they could no otherwise be the *Israel* of God, then by faith, no any otherwise stand in Covenant with God, or be the Church of God, then through faith. For these reasons therefore it was absolutely necessary that the Lord Christ should make a Covenant with them through faith. And hence it is that till the Lord Christ came in the flesh, and till this new Covenant was made, we at no time read of a seed of faith in distinction from the seed of the law, *Rom.* 4.16. *Therefore it is of faith, that it might be by grace to the end the promise might be sure to all*

FIGURE 21

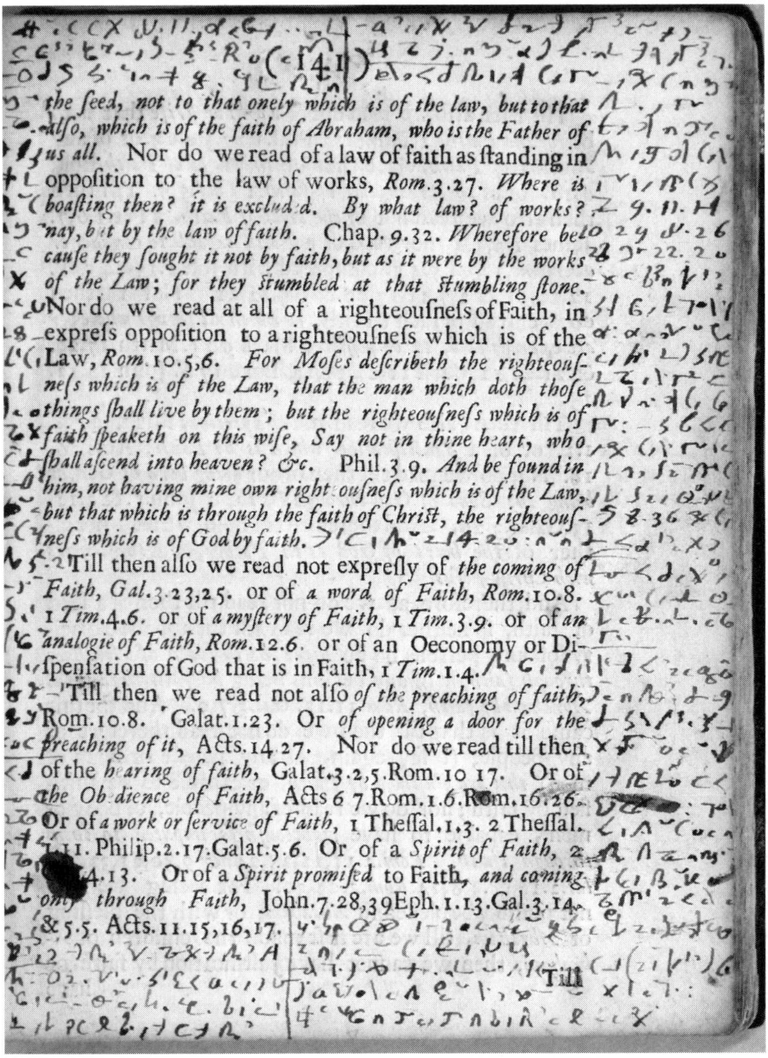

the feed, not to that onely which is of the law, but to that
also, which is of the faith of Abraham, who is the Father of
us all. Nor do we read of a law of faith as standing in
opposition to the law of works, Rom. 3.27. Where is
boasting then? it is excluded. By what law? of works?
nay, but by the law of faith. Chap. 9.32. Wherefore because they sought it not by faith, but as it were by the works
of the Law; for they stumbled at that stumbling stone.
Nor do we read at all of a righteousness of Faith, in
express opposition to a righteousness which is of the
Law, Rom. 10.5,6. For Moses describeth the righteouf-
ness which is of the Law, that the man which doth those
things shall live by them; but the righteousness which is of
faith speaketh on this wise, Say not in thine heart, who
shall ascend into heaven? &c. Phil. 3.9. And be found in
him, not having mine own righteousness which is of the Law,
but that which is through the faith of Christ, the righteouf-
ness which is of God by faith. Till then also we read not expresly of the coming of
Faith, Gal. 3.23,25. or of a word of Faith, Rom. 10.8.
1 Tim. 4.6. or of a mystery of Faith, 1 Tim. 3.9. or of an
analogie of Faith, Rom. 12.6. or of an Oeconomy or Di-
spensation of God that is in Faith, 1 Tim. 1.4.
Till then we read not also of the preaching of faith,
Rom. 10.8. Galat. 1.23. Or of opening a door for the
preaching of it, Acts. 14.27. Nor do we read till then
of the hearing of faith, Galat. 3.2,5. Rom. 10 17. Or of
the Obedience of Faith, Acts 6 7. Rom. 1.6. Rom. 16.26.
Or of a work or service of Faith, 1 Theffal. 1.3. 2 Theffal.
1.11. Philip. 2.17. Galat. 5.6. Or of a Spirit of Faith, 2
4.13. Or of a Spirit promised to Faith, and coming
only through Faith, John. 7.28,39 Eph. 1.13. Gal. 3.14.
&5.5. Acts. 11.15,16,17.

FIGURE 22

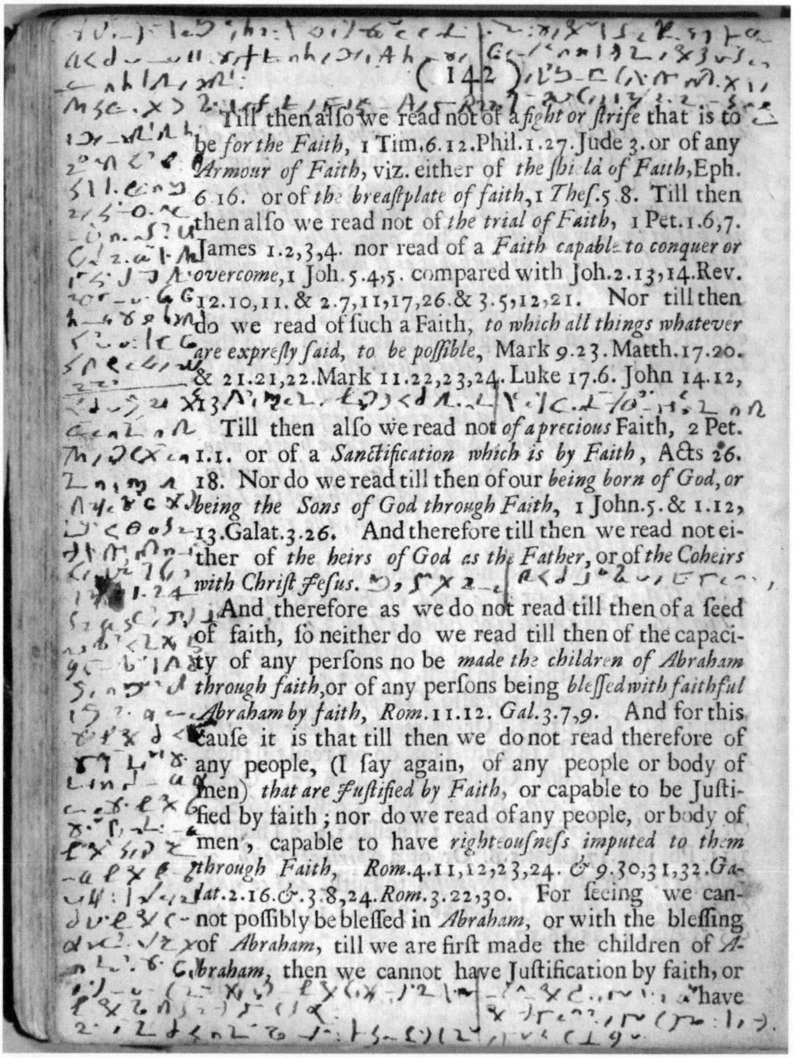

(142)

Till then also we read not of a *fight or strife* that is to
be *for the Faith*, 1 Tim.6.12.Phil.1.27.Jude 3. or of any
Armour of Faith, viz. either of *the shi la of Faith*,Eph.
6.16. or of *the breastplate of faith*,1 Thes.5.8. Till then
then also we read not of *the trial of Faith*, 1 Pet.1.6,7.
James 1.2,3,4. nor read of a *Faith capable to conquer or
overcome*,1 Joh.5.4,5. compared with Joh.2.13,14.Rev.
12.10,11. & 2.7,11,17,26.& 3.5,12,21. Nor till then
do we read of such a Faith, *to which all things whatever
are expresly said, to be possible*, Mark 9.23.Matth.17.20.
& 21.21,22.Mark 11.22,23,24.Luke 17.6. John 14.12,

Till then also we read not *of a precious* Faith, 2 Pet.
1.1. or of a *Sanctification which is by Faith*, Acts 26.
18. Nor do we read till then of our *being born of God, or
being the Sons of God through Faith*, 1 John.5.& 1.12,
13.Galat.3.26. And therefore till then we read not either of *the heirs of God as the Father*, or of *the Coheirs
with Christ Jesus.*

And therefore as we do not read till then of a seed
of faith, so neither do we read till then of the capacity of any persons no be *made the children of Abraham
through faith*,or of any persons being *blessed with faithful
Abraham by faith*, Rom.11.12. Gal.3.7,9. And for this
cause it is that till then we do not read therefore of
any people, (I say again, of any people or body of
men) *that are Justified by Faith*, or capable to be Justified by faith ; nor do we read of any people, or body of
men`, capable to have *righteousness imputed to them
through Faith*, Rom.4.11,12,23,24. & 9.30,31,32.Ga-
lat.2.16.& 3.8,24.Rom.3.22,30. For seeing we cannot possibly be blessed in *Abraham*, or with the blessing
of *Abraham*, till we are first made the children of A-
braham, then we cannot have Justification by faith, or
have

FIGURE 23

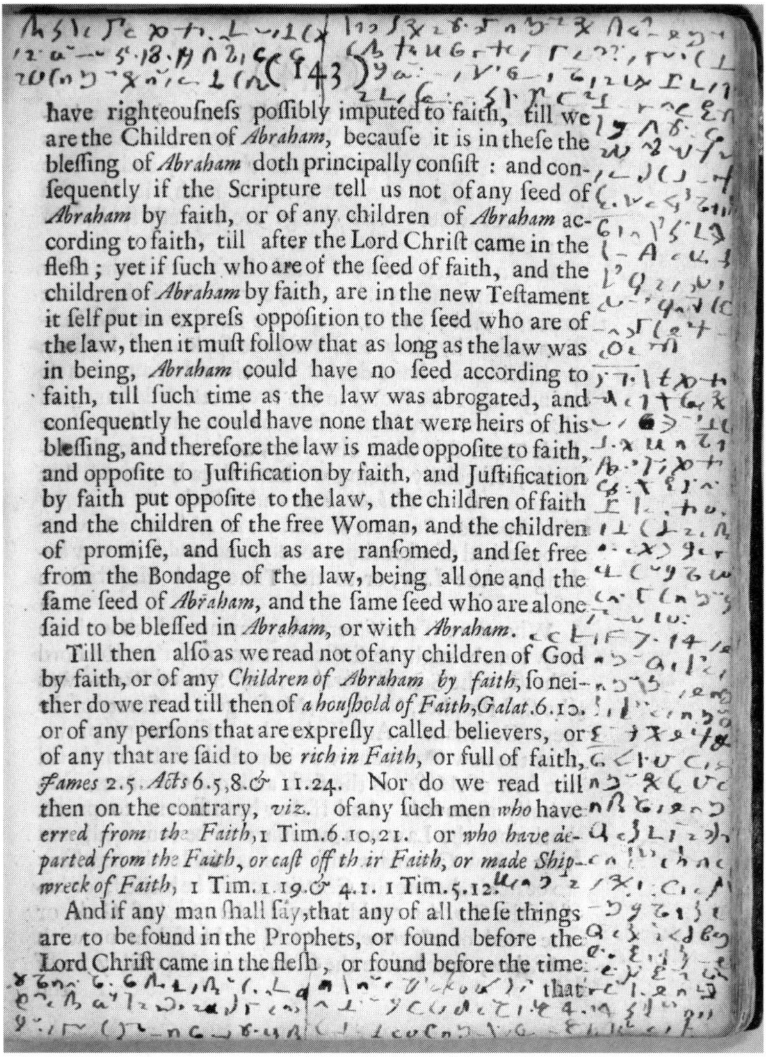

(143)

have righteouſneſs poſſibly imputed to faith, till we are the Children of *Abraham*, becauſe it is in theſe the bleſſing of *Abraham* doth principally conſiſt: and conſequently if the Scripture tell us not of any ſeed of *Abraham* by faith, or of any children of *Abraham* according to faith, till after the Lord Chriſt came in the fleſh; yet if ſuch who are of the ſeed of faith, and the children of *Abraham* by faith, are in the new Teſtament it ſelf put in expreſs oppoſition to the ſeed who are of the law, then it muſt follow that as long as the law was in being, *Abraham* could have no ſeed according to faith, till ſuch time as the law was abrogated, and conſequently he could have none that were heirs of his bleſſing, and therefore the law is made oppoſite to faith, and oppoſite to Juſtification by faith, and Juſtification by faith put oppoſite to the law, the children of faith and the children of the free Woman, and the children of promiſe, and ſuch as are ranſomed, and ſet free from the Bondage of the law, being all one and the ſame ſeed of *Abraham*, and the ſame ſeed who are alone ſaid to be bleſſed in *Abraham*, or with *Abraham*.

Till then alſo as we read not of any children of God by faith, or of any *Children of Abraham by faith*, ſo neither do we read till then of *a houſhold of Faith*, *Galat*. 6. 10. or of any perſons that are expreſly called believers, or of any that are ſaid to be *rich in Faith*, or full of faith, *James* 2. 5. *Acts* 6. 5, 8. & 11. 24. Nor do we read till then on the contrary, *viz*. of any ſuch men *who* have *erred from the Faith*, 1 Tim. 6. 10, 21. or *who have departed from the Faith, or caſt off their Faith, or made Shipwreck of Faith*, 1 Tim. 1. 19. & 4. 1. 1 Tim. 5. 12.

And if any man ſhall ſay, that any of all theſe things are to be found in the Prophets, or found before the Lord Chriſt came in the fleſh, or found before the time that

FIGURE 24

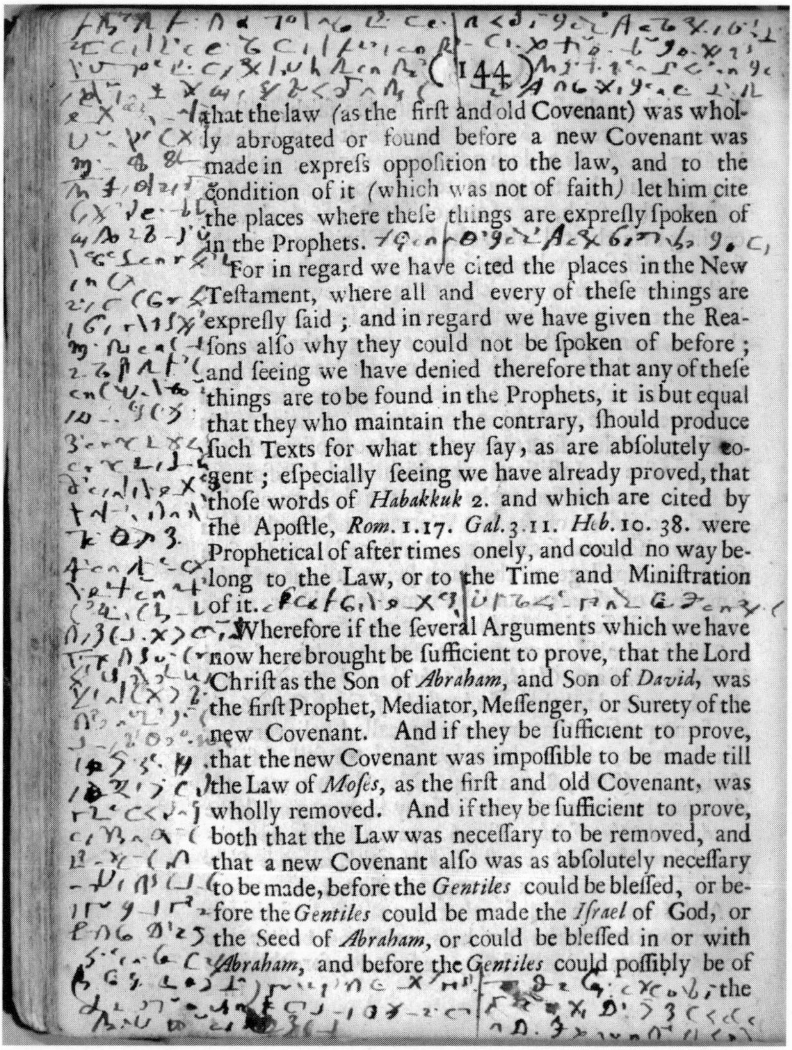

(144)

that the law (as the firſt and old Covenant) was wholly abrogated or found before a new Covenant was
made in expreſs oppoſition to the law, and to the
condition of it (which was not of faith) let him cite
the places where theſe things are expreſly ſpoken of
in the Prophets. For in regard we have cited the places in the New
Teſtament, where all and every of theſe things are
expreſly ſaid ; and in regard we have given the Rea-
ſons alſo why they could not be ſpoken of before ;
and ſeeing we have denied therefore that any of theſe
things are to be found in the Prophets, it is but equal
that they who maintain the contrary, ſhould produce
ſuch Texts for what they ſay, as are abſolutely co-
gent ; eſpecially ſeeing we have already proved, that
thoſe words of *Habakkuk* 2. and which are cited by
the Apoſtle, *Rom.* 1.17. *Gal.* 3.11. *Heb.* 10. 38. were
Prophetical of after times onely, and could no way belong to the Law, or to the Time and Miniſtration
of it. Wherefore if the ſeveral Arguments which we have
now here brought be ſufficient to prove, that the Lord
Chriſt as the Son of *Abraham*, and Son of *David*, was
the firſt Prophet, Mediator, Meſſenger, or Surety of the
new Covenant. And if they be ſufficient to prove,
that the new Covenant was impoſſible to be made till
the Law of *Moſes*, as the firſt and old Covenant, was
wholly removed. And if they be ſufficient to prove,
both that the Law was neceſſary to be removed, and
that a new Covenant alſo was as abſolutely neceſſary
to be made, before the *Gentiles* could be bleſſed, or before the *Gentiles* could be made the *Iſrael* of God, or
the Seed of *Abraham*, or could be bleſſed in or with
Abraham, and before the *Gentiles* could poſſibly be of
the

FIGURE 25

the Church of God, or could be the rightful Inheritance of the Lord Chrift. And if they be likewife fufficient to prove, that the Condition of the new Covenant, I mean, that to which all its Promifes were made, could not be the fame with the Condition, on which all the Promifes were made under the Law of *Mofes*; but was exprefly to be oppofite to it, and was to have all its Promifes made unto faith, and was confequently to have no other People than what were to be ἐν πίςεως, of faith.

I fay, if the Arguments we have here brought are fufficient fully to prove thefe things, then in as much as it muft be wholly abfurd, and wholly unfcriptural, to fay, there was no faith at all before the Lord Chrift came in the flefh, (in regard the Scripture doth abundantly teftifie the contrary) we muft confequently of neceffity diftinguifh between faith and faith ; I mean, between the faith which was in *Abraham*, and bleffed *Abraham*, and did refpect the time after *Abraham*, which *Abraham* was capable to be the father of, and through which he was to have a Seed according to promife, (even as God had from the beginning appointed him to be the father of many Nations:) And the faith, which being long before *Abraham* was, he could therefore in no fenfe poffibly be faid to be the father truly of; between that faith which is purely Federal, and which is a Myftery ; and which hath promifes not onely fpecial, but explicitly made to it, and which hath a Seal annexed to the faid promifes; and that faith, which though it be capable to pleafe God, yet hath neither any promifes exprefly annexed to it, nor any feal given it.

Which diftinction is the more abfolutely neceffary alfo, becaufe without this the Scripture can no way be

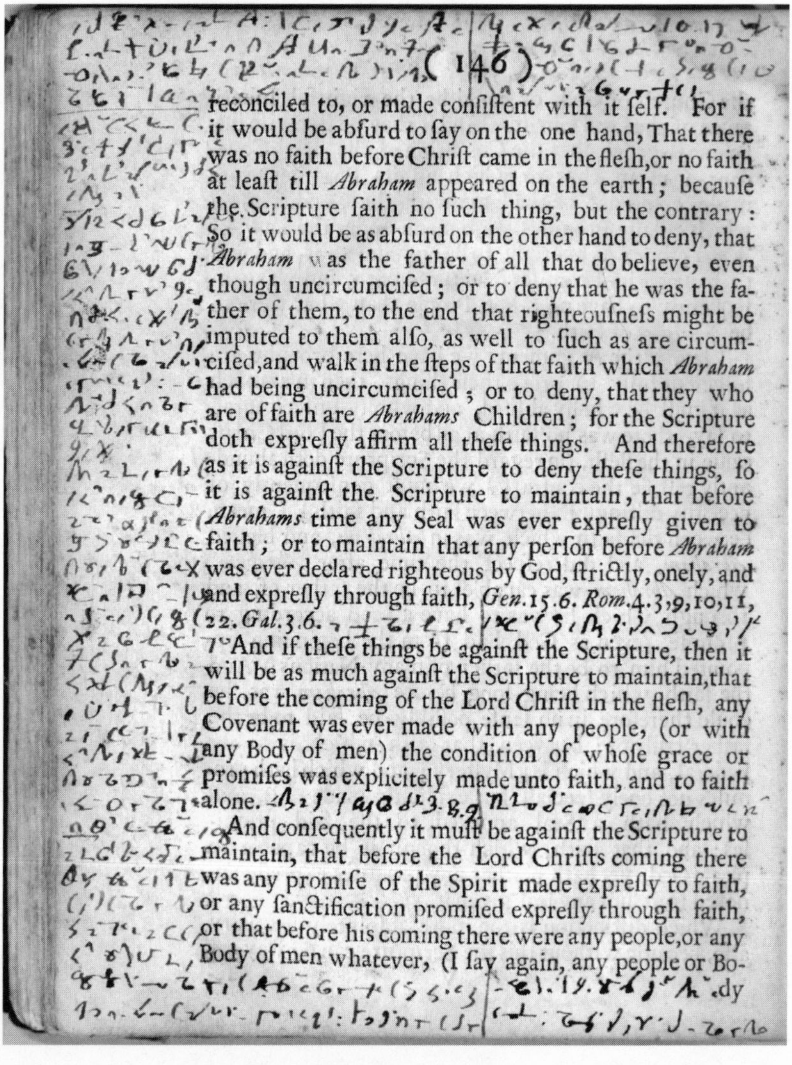

(146)

reconciled to, or made confiftent with it felf. For if it would be abfurd to fay on the one hand, That there was no faith before Chrift came in the flefh, or no faith at leaft till *Abraham* appeared on the earth; becaufe the Scripture faith no fuch thing, but the contrary : So it would be as abfurd on the other hand to deny, that *Abraham* was the father of all that do believe, even though uncircumcifed; or to deny that he was the father of them, to the end that righteoufnefs might be imputed to them alfo, as well to fuch as are circum-cifed, and walk in the fteps of that faith which *Abraham* had being uncircumcifed ; or to deny, that they who are of faith are *Abrahams* Children; for the Scripture doth exprefly affirm all thefe things. And therefore (as it is againft the Scripture to deny thefe things, fo it is againft the Scripture to maintain, that before *Abrahams* time any Seal was ever exprefly given to faith; or to maintain that any perfon before *Abraham* was ever declared righteous by God, ftrictly, onely, and exprefly through faith, *Gen.* 15.6. *Rom.* 4.3,9,10,11, 22. *Gal.* 3.6.

7. And if thefe things be againft the Scripture, then it will be as much againft the Scripture to maintain, that before the coming of the Lord Chrift in the flefh, any Covenant was ever made with any people, (or with any Body of men) the condition of whofe grace or promifes was explicitely made unto faith, and to faith alone. And confequently it muft be againft the Scripture to maintain, that before the Lord Chrifts coming there was any promife of the Spirit made exprefly to faith, or any fanctification promifed exprefly through faith, or that before his coming there were any people, or any Body of men whatever, (I fay again, any people or Bo-

FIGURE 27

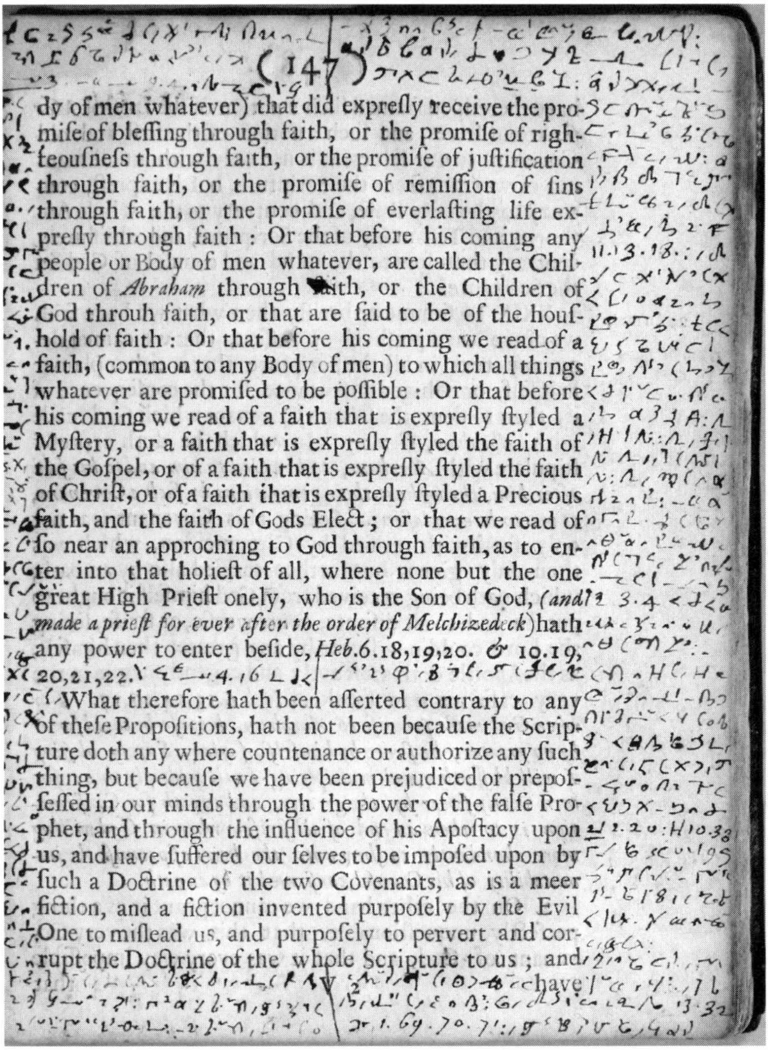

(147)

dy of men whatever) that did expresly receive the promise of blessing through faith, or the promise of righteousness through faith, or the promise of justification
through faith, or the promise of remission of sins
through faith, or the promise of everlasting life expresly through faith : Or that before his coming any
people or Body of men whatever, are called the Children of *Abraham* through faith, or the Children of
God throuh faith, or that are said to be of the houf-
hold of faith : Or that before his coming we read of a
faith, (common to any Body of men) to which all things
whatever are promised to be possible : Or that before
his coming we read of a faith that is expresly styled a
Mystery, or a faith that is expresly styled the faith of
the Gospel, or of a faith that is expresly styled the faith
of Christ, or of a faith that is expresly styled a Precious
faith, and the faith of Gods Elect; or that we read of
so near an approching to God through faith, as to enter into that holiest of all, where none but the one
great High Priest onely, who is the Son of God, *(and*
made a priest for ever after the order of Melchizedeck)hath
any power to enter beside, *Heb.*6.18,19,20. *&* 10.19,
20,21,22. ✓ What therefore hath been asserted contrary to any
of these Propositions, hath not been because the Scripture doth any where countenance or authorize any such
thing, but because we have been prejudiced or prepos-
sessed in our minds through the power of the false Prophet, and through the influence of his Apostacy upon
us, and have suffered our selves to be imposed upon by
such a Doctrine of the two Covenants, as is a meer
fiction, and a fiction invented purposely by the Evil
One to mislead us, and purposely to pervert and corrupt the Doctrine of the whole Scripture to us ; and

FIGURE 28

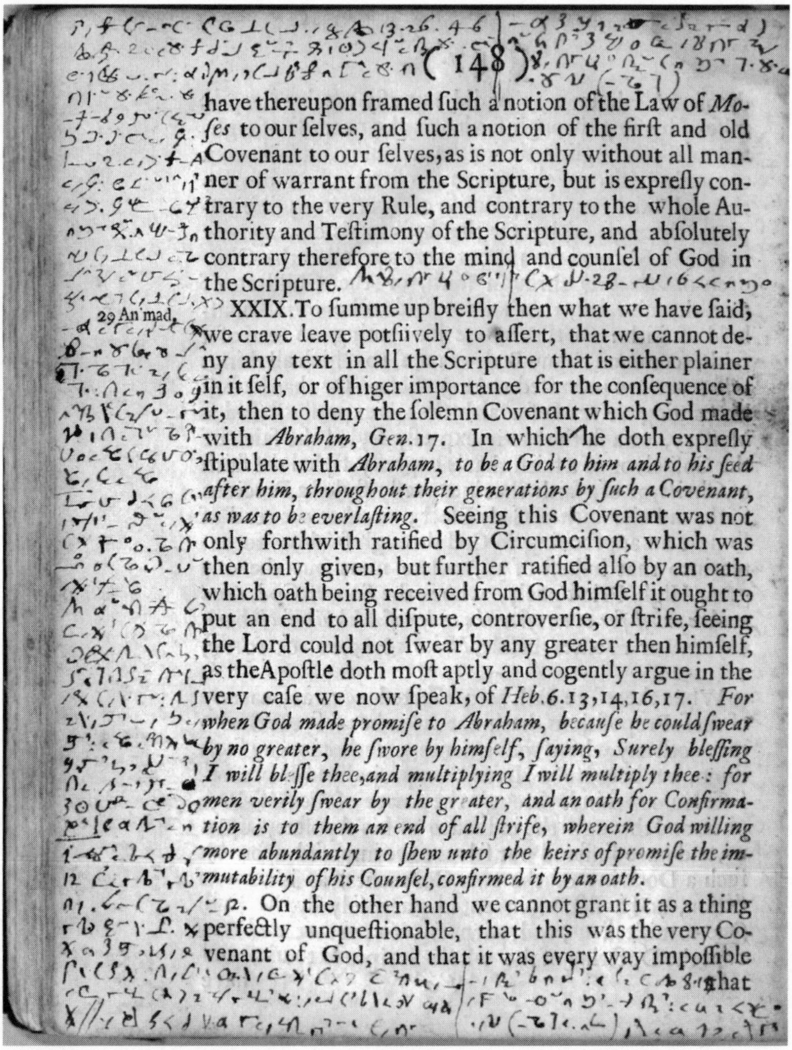

(148)

have thereupon framed such a notion of the Law of *Mo-ses* to our selves, and such a notion of the first and old Covenant to our selves, as is not only without all manner of warrant from the Scripture, but is expresly contrary to the very Rule, and contrary to the whole Authority and Testimony of the Scripture, and absolutely contrary therefore to the mind and counsel of God in the Scripture.

29 An'mad. XXIX. To summe up briefly then what we have said, we crave leave potsively to assert, that we cannot deny any text in all the Scripture that is either plainer in it self, or of higer importance for the consequence of it, then to deny the solemn Covenant which God made with *Abraham, Gen.* 17. In which he doth expresly stipulate with *Abraham, to be a God to him and to his seed after him, throughout their generations by such a Covenant, as was to be everlasting.* Seeing this Covenant was not only forthwith ratified by Circumcision, which was then only given, but further ratified also by an oath, which oath being received from God himself it ought to put an end to all dispute, controversie, or strife, seeing the Lord could not swear by any greater then himself, as the Apostle doth most aptly and cogently argue in the very case we now speak, of *Heb.* 6.13,14,16,17. *For when God made promise to Abraham, because he could swear by no greater, he swore by himself, saying, Surely blessing I will blesse thee, and multiplying I will multiply thee: for men verily swear by the greater, and an oath for Confirmation is to them an end of all strife, wherein God willing more abundantly to shew unto the heirs of promise the immutability of his Counsel, confirmed it by an oath.* On the other hand we cannot grant it as a thing perfectly unquestionable, that this was the very Covenant of God, and that it was every way impossible that

FIGURE 29

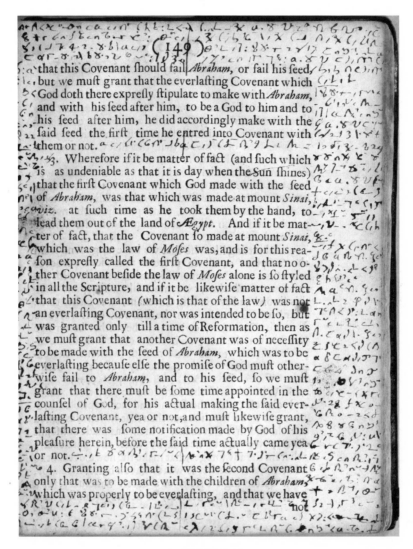

that this Covenant fhould fail *Abraham*, or fail his feed, but we muft grant that the everlafting Covenant which God doth there exprefly ftipulate to make with *Abraham*, and with his feed after him, to be a God to him and to his feed after him, he did accordingly make with the faid feed the firft time he entred into Covenant with them or not. §. 43. Wherefore if it be matter of fact (and fuch which is as undeniable as that it is day when the Sun fhines) that the firft Covenant which God made with the feed of *Abraham*, was that which was made at mount *Sinai*, *viz.* at fuch time as he took them by the hand, to lead them out of the land of *Ægypt*. And if it be matter of fact, that the Covenant fo made at mount *Sinai*, which was the law of *Mofes* was, and is for this reafon exprefly called the firft Covenant, and that no other Covenant befide the law of *Mofes* alone is fo ftyled in all the Scripture, and if it be likewife matter of fact that this Covenant (which is that of the law) was not an everlafting Covenant, nor was intended to be fo, but was granted only till a time of Reformation, then as we muft grant that another Covenant was of neceffity to be made with the feed of *Abraham*, which was to be everlafting becaufe elfe the promife of God muft otherwife fail to *Abraham*, and to his feed, fo we muft grant that there muft be fome time appointed in the counfel of God, for his actual making the faid everlafting Covenant, yea or not, and muft likewife grant, that there was fome notification made by God of his pleafure herein, before the faid time actually came yea or not. §. 4. Granting alfo that it was the fecond Covenant only that was to be made with the children of *Abraham*, which was properly to be everlafting, and that we have not

FIGURE 30

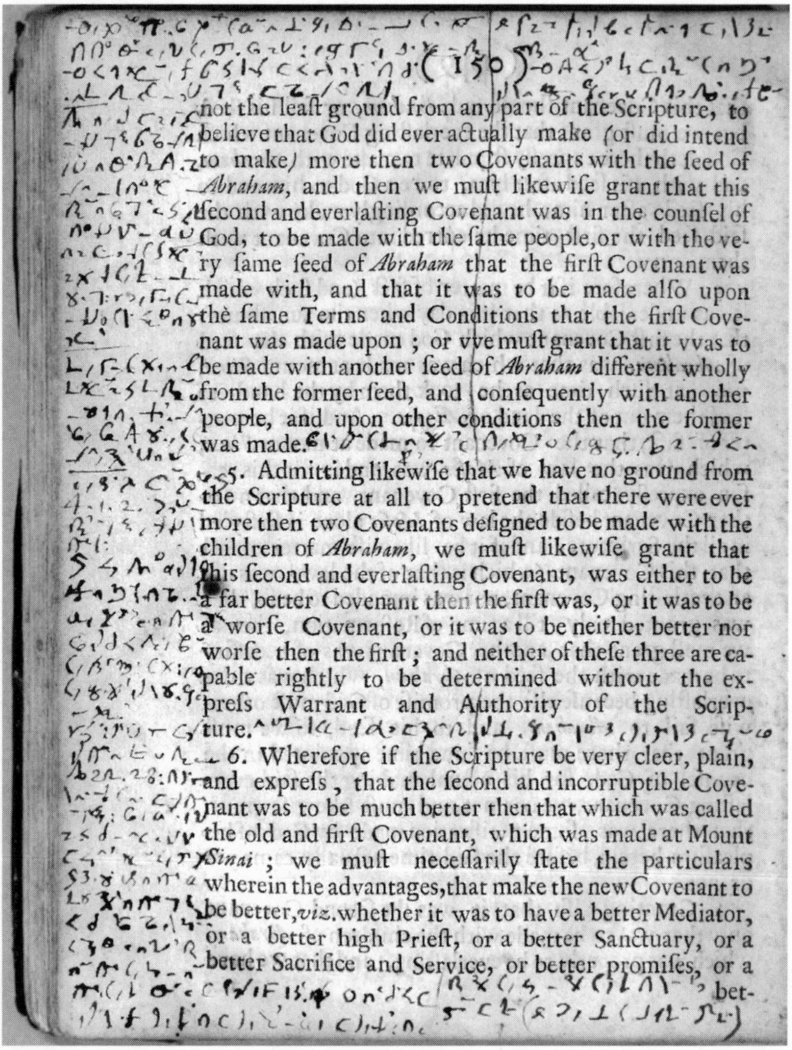

(150)

... not the least ground from any part of the Scripture, to believe that God did ever actually make (or did intend to make) more then two Covenants with the seed of *Abraham*, and then we must likewise grant that this second and everlasting Covenant was in the counsel of God, to be made with the same people, or with the very same seed of *Abraham* that the first Covenant was made with, and that it was to be made also upon the same Terms and Conditions that the first Covenant was made upon ; or vve must grant that it vvas to be made with another seed of *Abraham* different wholly from the former seed, and consequently with another people, and upon other conditions then the former was made.

5. Admitting likewise that we have no ground from the Scripture at all to pretend that there were ever more then two Covenants designed to be made with the children of *Abraham*, we must likewise grant that this second and everlasting Covenant, was either to be a far better Covenant then the first was, or it was to be a worse Covenant, or it was to be neither better nor worse then the first ; and neither of these three are capable rightly to be determined without the express Warrant and Authority of the Scripture.

6. Wherefore if the Scripture be very cleer, plain, and express, that the second and incorruptible Covenant was to be much better then that which was called the old and first Covenant, which was made at Mount *Sinai* ; we must necessarily state the particulars wherein the advantages, that make the new Covenant to be better, *viz.* whether it was to have a better Mediator, or a better high Priest, or a better Sanctuary, or a better Sacrifice and Service, or better promises, or a bet-

FIGURE 31

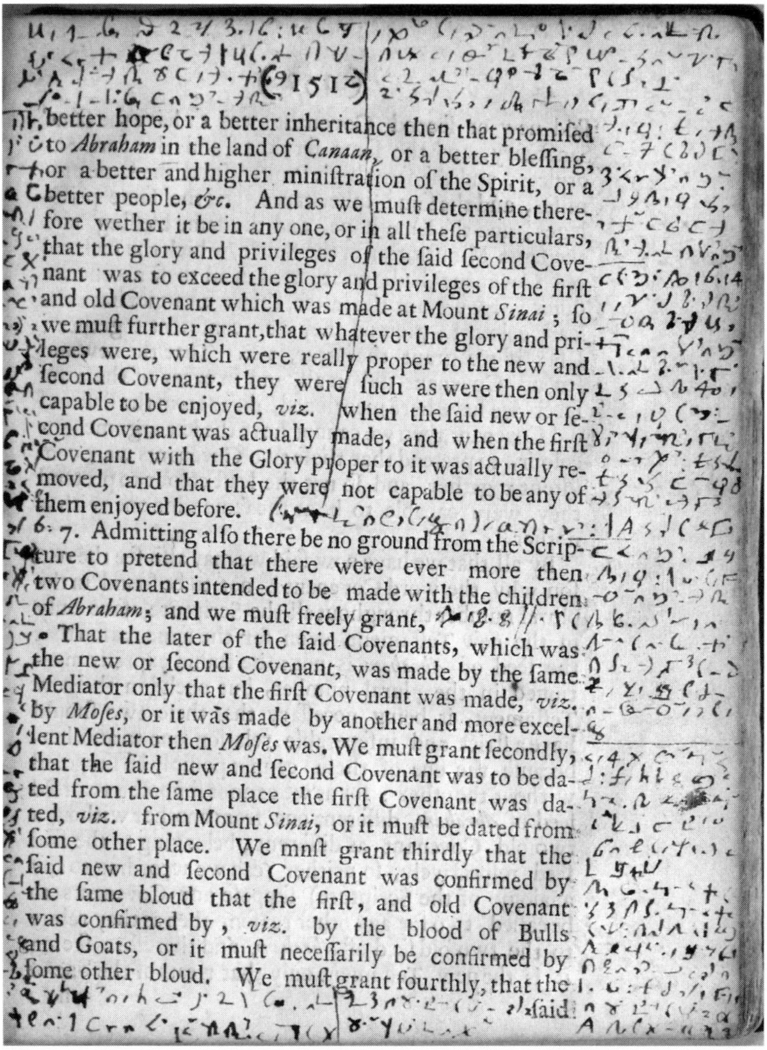

better hope, or a better inheritance then that promised to *Abraham* in the land of *Canaan*, or a better bleſſing, or a better and higher miniſtration of the Spirit, or a better people, &c. And as we muſt determine therefore wether it be in any one, or in all theſe particulars, that the glory and privileges of the ſaid ſecond Covenant was to exceed the glory and privileges of the firſt and old Covenant which was made at Mount *Sinai* ; ſo we muſt further grant, that whatever the glory and priʋleges were, which were really proper to the new and ſecond Covenant, they were ſuch as were then only capable to be enjoyed, *viz.* when the ſaid new or ſecond Covenant was actually made, and when the firſt Covenant with the Glory proper to it was actually removed, and that they were not capable to be any of them enjoyed before.

6. 7. Admitting alſo there be no ground from the Scripture to pretend that there were ever more then two Covenants intended to be made with the children of *Abraham*; and we muſt freely grant, That the later of the ſaid Covenants, which was the new or ſecond Covenant, was made by the ſame Mediator only that the firſt Covenant was made, *viz.* by *Moſes*, or it was made by another and more excel\lent Mediator then *Moſes* was. We muſt grant ſecondly, that the ſaid new and ſecond Covenant was to be dated from the ſame place the firſt Covenant was dated, *viz.* from Mount *Sinai*; or it muſt be dated from ſome other place. We mnſt grant thirdly that the ſaid new and ſecond Covenant was confirmed by the ſame bloud that the firſt, and old Covenant was confirmed by, *viz.* by the blood of Bulls and Goats, or it muſt neceſſarily be confirmed by ſome other bloud. We muſt grant fourthly, that the ſaid

FIGURE 32

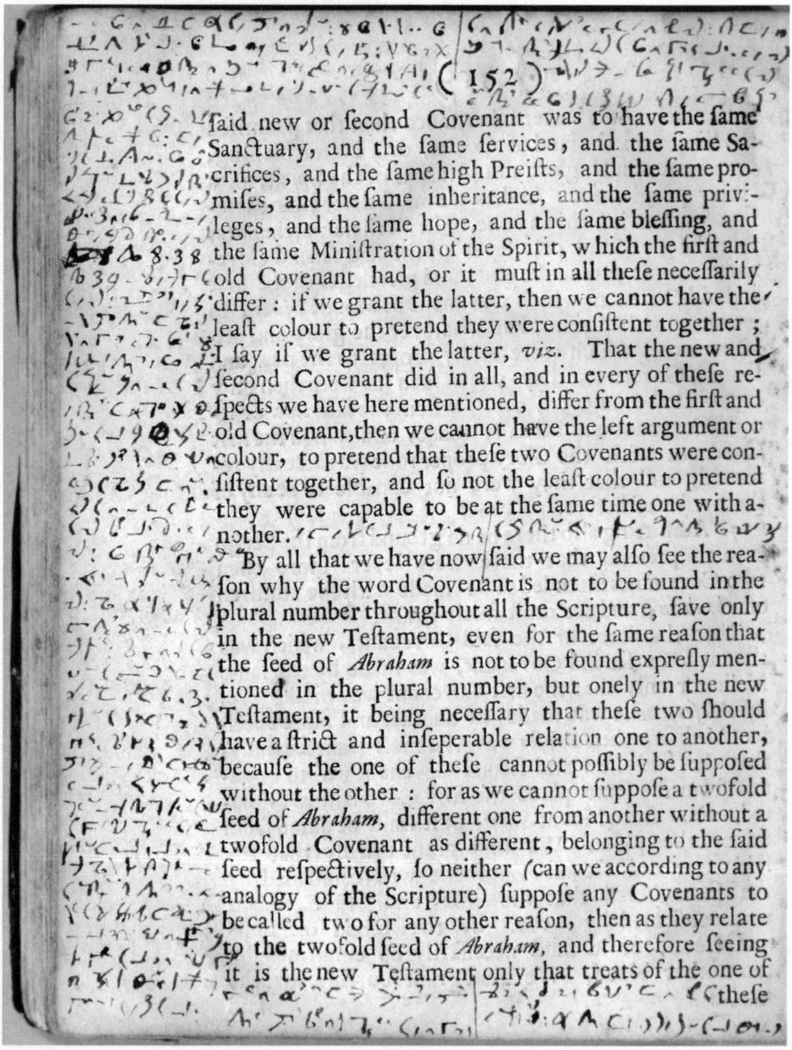

(152)

said new or second Covenant was to have the same
Sanctuary, and the same services, and the same Sacrifices, and the same high Preists, and the same promises, and the same inheritance, and the same privileges, and the same hope, and the same blessing, and
the same Ministration of the Spirit, which the first and
old Covenant had, or it must in all these necessarily
differ: if we grant the latter, then we cannot have the
least colour to pretend they were consistent together;
I say if we grant the latter, viz. That the new and
second Covenant did in all, and in every of these respects we have here mentioned, differ from the first and
old Covenant, then we cannot have the left argument or
colour, to pretend that these two Covenants were consistent together, and so not the least colour to pretend
they were capable to be at the same time one with a-
nother.

By all that we have now said we may also see the reason why the word Covenant is not to be found in the
plural number throughout all the Scripture, save only
in the new Testament, even for the same reason that
the feed of *Abraham* is not to be found expresly mentioned in the plural number, but onely in the new
Testament, it being necessary that these two should
have a strict and inseperable relation one to another,
because the one of these cannot possibly be supposed
without the other: for as we cannot suppose a twofold
seed of *Abraham*, different one from another without a
twofold Covenant as different, belonging to the said
seed respectively, so neither (can we according to any
analogy of the Scripture) suppose any Covenants to
be called two for any other reason, then as they relate
to the twofold seed of *Abraham*, and therefore seeing
it is the new Testament only that treats of the one of
these

FIGURE 33

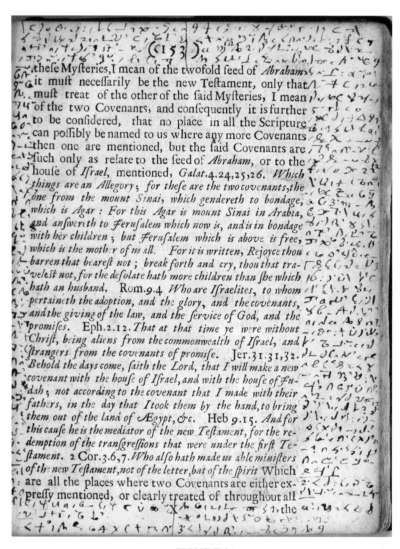

FIGURE 34

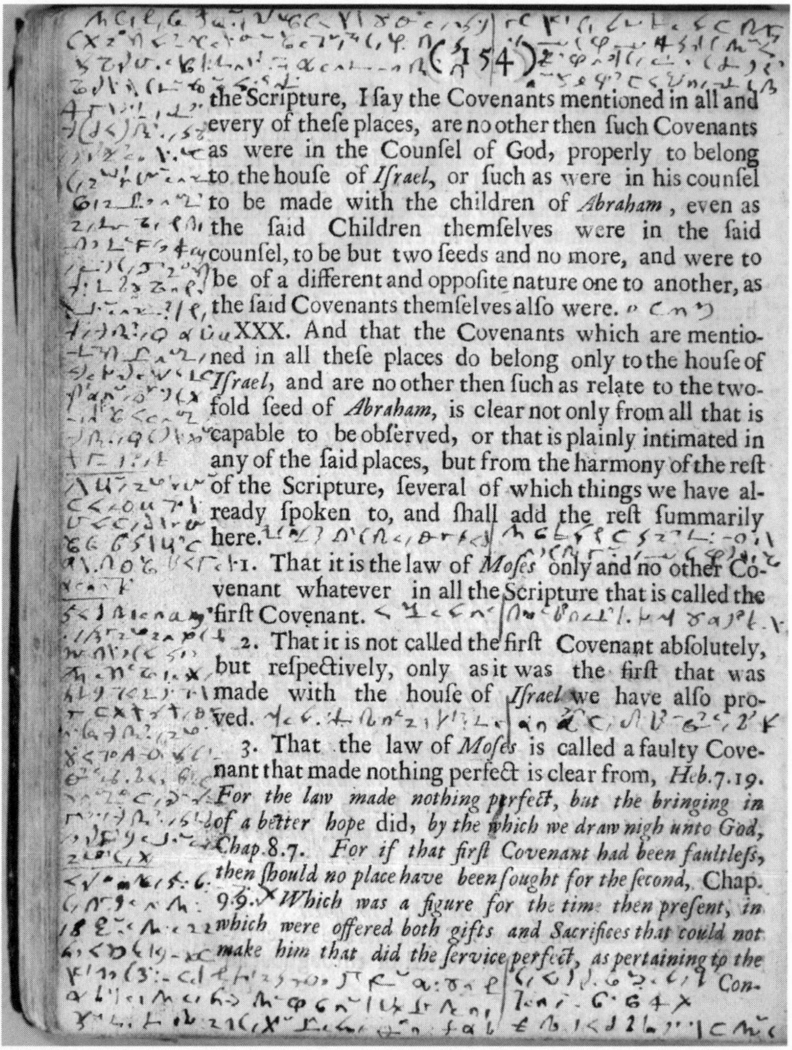

(454)

the Scripture, I say the Covenants mentioned in all and every of these places, are no other then such Covenants as were in the Counsel of God, properly to belong to the house of *Israel*, or such as were in his counsel to be made with the children of *Abraham*, even as the said Children themselves were in the said counsel, to be but two seeds and no more, and were to be of a different and opposite nature one to another, as the said Covenants themselves also were.

XXX. And that the Covenants which are mentio-ned in all these places do belong only to the house of *Israel*, and are no other then such as relate to the two-fold seed of *Abraham*, is clear not only from all that is capable to be observed, or that is plainly intimated in any of the said places, but from the harmony of the rest of the Scripture, several of which things we have already spoken to, and shall add the rest summarily here.

1. That it is the law of *Moses* only and no other Co-venant whatever in all the Scripture that is called the first Covenant.

2. That it is not called the first Covenant absolutely, but respectively, only as it was the first that was made with the house of *Israel* we have also pro-ved.

3. That the law of *Moses* is called a faulty Cove-nant that made nothing perfect is clear from, *Heb.*7.19. *For the law made nothing perfect, but the bringing in of a better hope did, by the which we draw nigh unto God,* *Chap.*8.7. *For if that first Covenant had been faultless, then should no place have been sought for the second,* Chap. 9.9. *Which was a figure for the time then present, in which were offered both gifts and Sacrifices that could not make him that did the service perfect, as pertaining to the* Con-

FIGURE 35

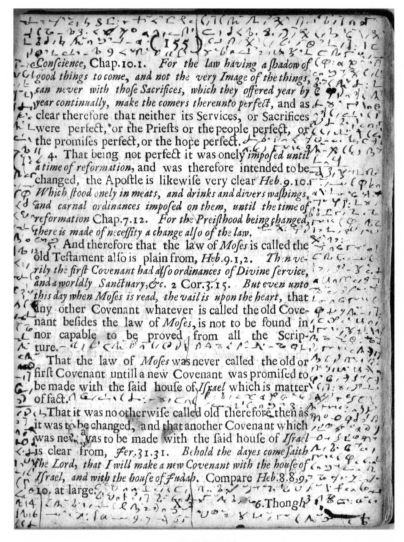

Confcience, Chap. 10. 1. *For the law having a fhadow of good things to come, and not the very Image of the things, can never with thofe Sacrifices, which they offered year by year continually, make the comers thereunto perfect,* and as clear therefore that neither its Services, or Sacrifices were perfect, or the Priefts or the people perfect, or the promifes perfect, or the hope perfect.

4. That being not perfect it was onely *impofed until a time of reformation,* and was therefore intended to be changed, the Apoftle is likewife very clear *Heb. 9. 10.* *Which ftood onely in meats, and drinks and divers wafhings, and carnal ordinances impofed on them, until the time of reformation* Chap. 7. 12. *For the Preifthood being changed, there is made of neceffity a change alfo of the law.*

5. And therefore that the law of *Mofes* is called the old Teftament alfo is plain from, *Heb. 9. 1, 2. Then verily the firft Covenant had alfo ordinances of Divine fervice, and a worldly Sanctuary,&c.* 2 *Cor. 3. 15. But even unto this day when Mofes is read, the vail is upon the heart, that* any other Covenant whatever is called the old Covenant befides the law of *Mofes,* is not to be found in nor capable to be proved from all the Scripture.

That the law of *Mofes* was never called the old or firft Covenant untill a new Covenant was promifed to be made with the faid houfe of *Ifrael* which is matter of fact.

That it was no otherwife called old therefore then as it was to be changed, and that another Covenant which was never was to be made with the faid houfe of *Ifrael* is clear from, *Jer. 31. 31. Behold the dayes come faith the Lord, that I will make a new Covenant with the houfe of Ifrael, and with the houfe of Judah.* Compare *Heb. 8. 8, 9, 10.* at large

6. Though

FIGURE 36

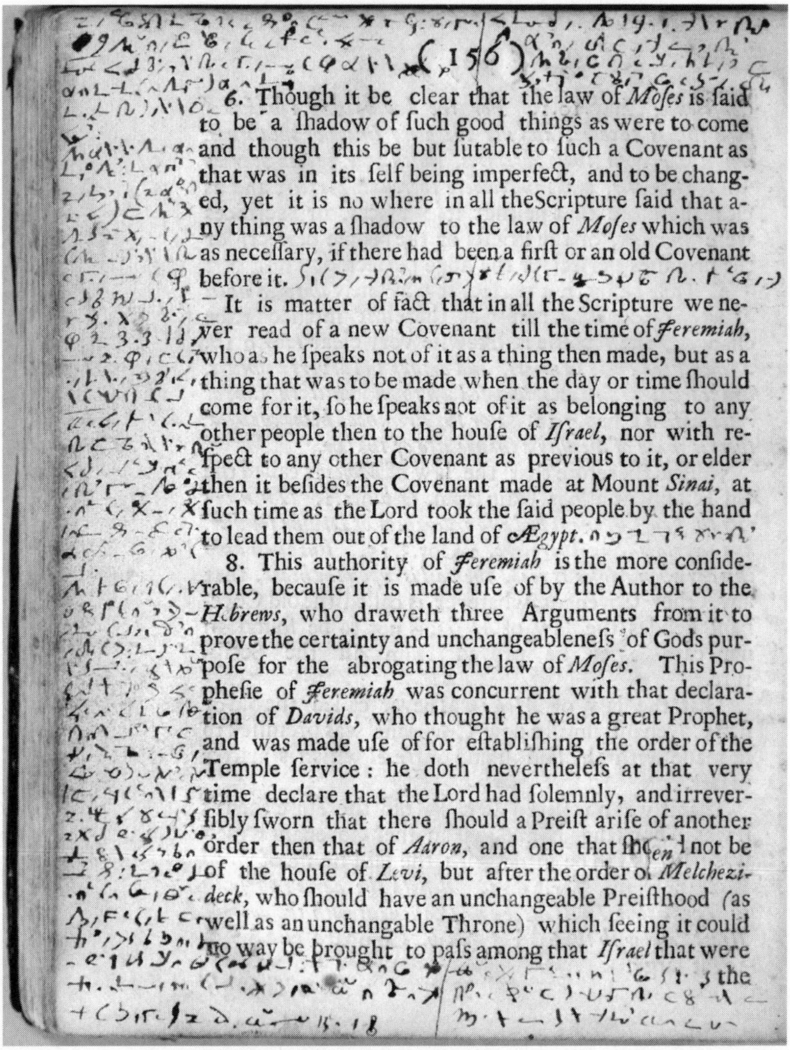

6. Though it be clear that the law of *Moses* is said to be a shadow of such good things as were to come and though this be but sutable to such a Covenant as that was in its self being imperfect, and to be changed, yet it is no where in all the Scripture said that any thing was a shadow to the law of *Moses* which was as necessary, if there had been a first or an old Covenant before it.

It is matter of fact that in all the Scripture we never read of a new Covenant till the time of *Jeremiah*, who as he speaks not of it as a thing then made, but as a thing that was to be made when the day or time should come for it, so he speaks not of it as belonging to any other people then to the house of *Israel*, nor with respect to any other Covenant as previous to it, or elder then it besides the Covenant made at Mount *Sinai*, at such time as the Lord took the said people by the hand to lead them out of the land of *Ægypt*.

8. This authority of *Jeremiah* is the more considerable, because it is made use of by the Author to the *Hebrews*, who draweth three Arguments from it to prove the certainty and unchangeableness of Gods purpose for the abrogating the law of *Moses*. This Prophesie of *Jeremiah* was concurrent with that declaration of *Davids*, who thought he was a great Prophet, and was made use of for establishing the order of the Temple service: he doth nevertheless at that very time declare that the Lord had solemnly, and irreversibly sworn that there should a Preist arise of another order then that of *Aaron*, and one that should not be of the house of *Levi*, but after the order of *Melchezideck*, who should have an unchangeable Preisthood (as well as an unchangable Throne) which seeing it could no way be brought to pass among that *Israel* that were

FIGURE 37

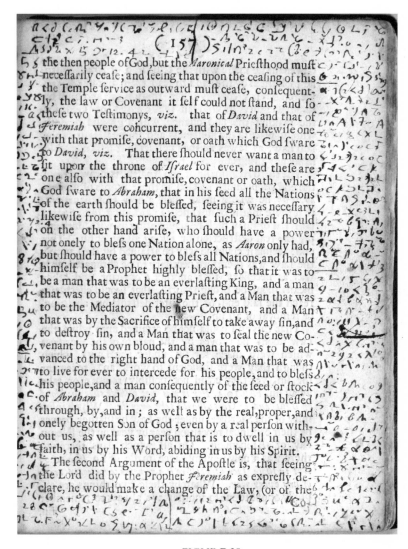

(157)

... the then people of God, but the *Aaronical* Priesthood muſt neceſſarily ceaſe; and ſeeing that upon the ceaſing of this the Temple ſervice as outward muſt ceaſe, conſequently, the law or Covenant it ſelf could not ſtand, and ſo theſe two Teſtimonys, *viz.* that of *David* and that of *Jeremiah* were concurrent, and they are likewiſe one with that promiſe, covenant, or oath which God ſware to *David*, *viz.* That there ſhould never want a man to ſit upon the throne of *Iſrael* for ever, and theſe are one alſo with that promiſe, covenant or oath, which God ſware to *Abraham*, that in his ſeed all the Nations of the earth ſhould be bleſſed, ſeeing it was neceſſary likewiſe from this promiſe, that ſuch a Prieſt ſhould on the other hand ariſe, who ſhould have a power not onely to bleſs one Nation alone, as *Aaron* only had, but ſhould have a power to bleſs all Nations, and ſhould himſelf be a Prophet highly bleſſed, ſo that it was to be a man that was to be an everlaſting King, and a man that was to be an everlaſting Prieſt, and a Man that was to be the Mediator of the new Covenant, and a Man that was by the Sacrifice of himſelf to take away ſin, and to deſtroy ſin, and a Man that was to ſeal the new Covenant by his own blood, and a man that was to be advanced to the right hand of God, and a Man that was to live for ever to intercede for his people, and to bleſs his people, and a man conſequently of the ſeed or ſtock of *Abraham* and *David*, that we were to be bleſſed through, by, and in ; as well as by the real, proper, and onely begotten Son of God ; even by a real perſon without us, as well as a perſon that is to dwell in us by faith, in us by his Word, abiding in us by his Spirit.

The ſecond Argument of the Apoſtle is, that ſeeing the Lord did by the Prophet *Jeremiah* as expreſly declare, he would make a change of the Law, (or of the

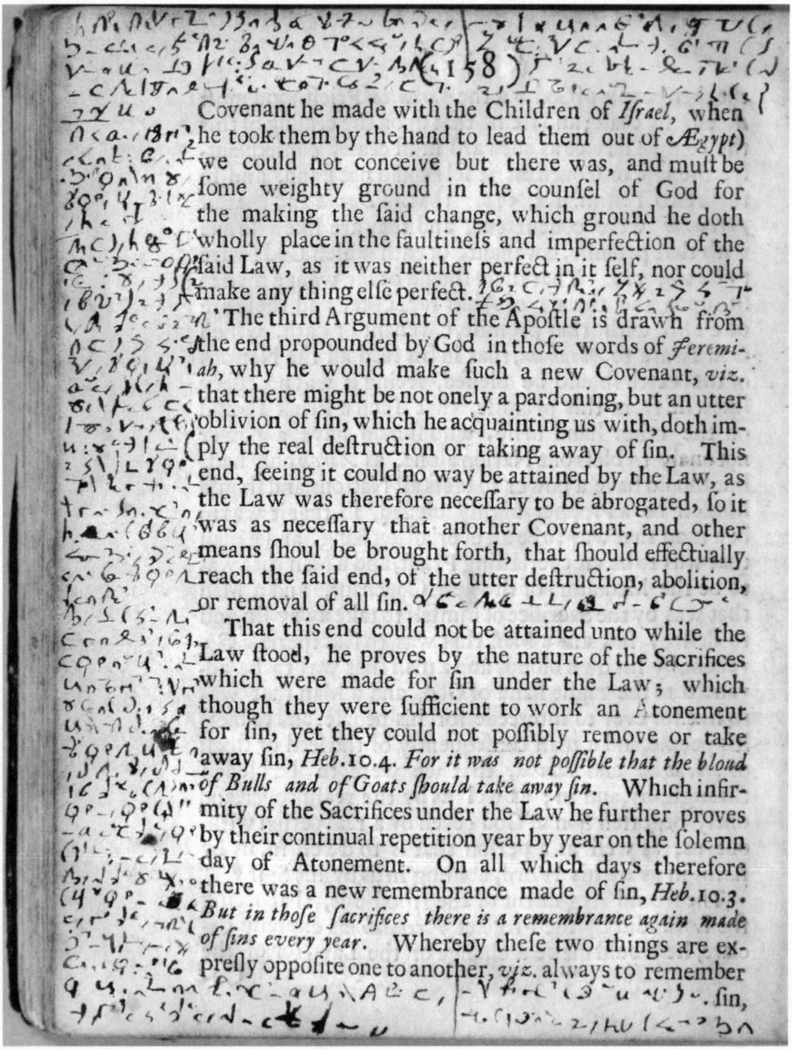

Covenant he made with the Children of *Ifrael*, when he took them by the hand to lead them out of *Ægypt*) we could not conceive but there was, and muſt be ſome weighty ground in the counſel of God for the making the ſaid change, which ground he doth wholly place in the faultineſs and imperfection of the ſaid Law, as it was neither perfect in it ſelf, nor could make any thing elſe perfect. The third Argument of the Apoſtle is drawn from the end propounded by God in thoſe words of *Feremiah*, why he would make ſuch a new Covenant, *viz.* that there might be not onely a pardoning, but an utter oblivion of ſin, which he acquainting us with, doth imply the real deſtruction or taking away of ſin. This end, ſeeing it could no way be attained by the Law, as the Law was therefore neceſſary to be abrogated, ſo it was as neceſſary that another Covenant, and other means ſhoul be brought forth, that ſhould effectually reach the ſaid end, of the utter deſtruction, abolition, or removal of all ſin.

That this end could not be attained unto while the Law ſtood, he proves by the nature of the Sacrifices which were made for ſin under the Law; which though they were ſufficient to work an Atonement for ſin, yet they could not poſſibly remove or take away ſin, *Heb.*10.4. *For it was not poſſible that the bloud of Bulls and of Goats ſhould take away ſin.* Which infirmity of the Sacrifices under the Law he further proves by their continual repetition year by year on the ſolemn day of Atonement. On all which days therefore there was a new remembrance made of ſin, *Heb.*10.3. *But in thoſe ſacrifices there is a remembrance again made of ſins every year.* Whereby theſe two things are expreſly oppoſite one to another, *viz.* always to remember ſin,

FIGURE 39

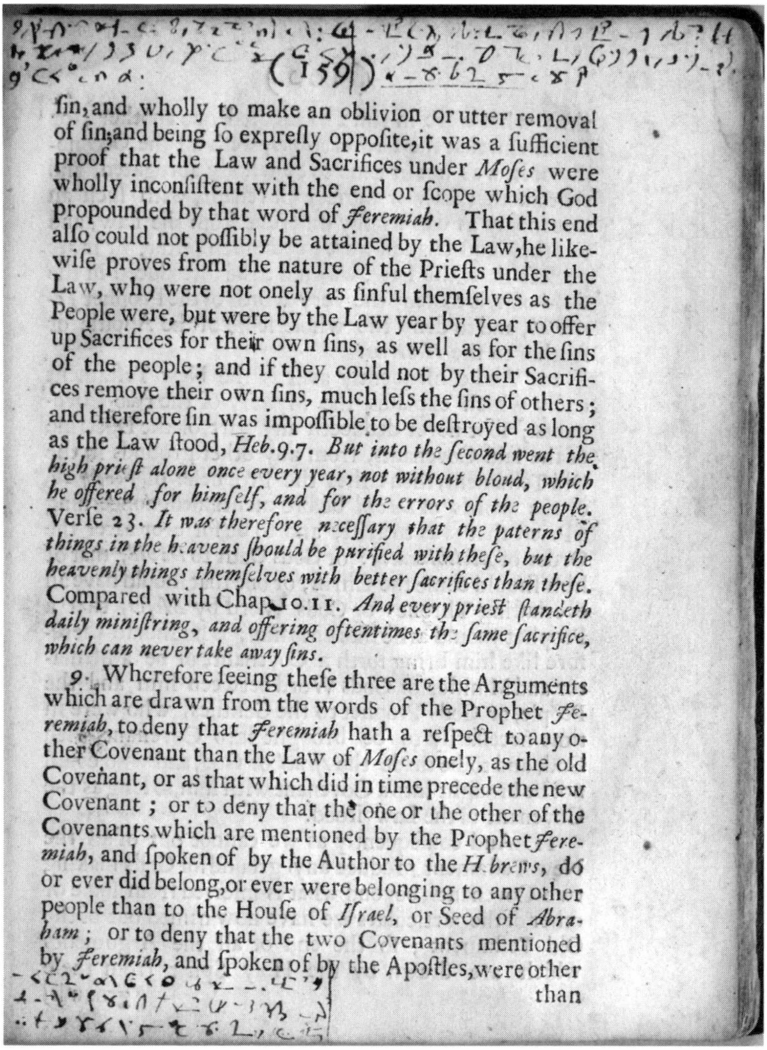

(159)

ſin, and wholly to make an oblivion or utter removal of ſin; and being ſo expreſly oppoſite, it was a ſufficient proof that the Law and Sacrifices under *Moſes* were wholly inconſiſtent with the end or ſcope which God propounded by that word of *Jeremiah*. That this end alſo could not poſſibly be attained by the Law, he likewiſe proves from the nature of the Prieſts under the Law, who were not onely as ſinful themſelves as the People were, but were by the Law year by year to offer up Sacrifices for their own ſins, as well as for the ſins of the people; and if they could not by their Sacrifices remove their own ſins, much leſs the ſins of others; and therefore ſin was impoſſible to be deſtroyed as long as the Law ſtood, Heb. 9. 7. *But into the ſecond went the high prieſt alone once every year, not without bloud, which he offered for himſelf, and for the errors of the people.* Verſe 23. *It was therefore neceſſary that the paterns of things in the heavens ſhould be purified with theſe, but the heavenly things themſelves with better ſacrifices than theſe.* Compared with Chap. 10. 11. *And every prieſt ſtandeth daily miniſtring, and offering oftentimes the ſame ſacrifice, which can never take away ſins.*

9. Wherefore ſeeing theſe three are the Arguments which are drawn from the words of the Prophet *Jeremiah*, to deny that *Jeremiah* hath a reſpect to any other Covenant than the Law of *Moſes* onely, as the old Covenant, or as that which did in time precede the new Covenant; or to deny that the one or the other of the Covenants which are mentioned by the Prophet *Jeremiah*, and ſpoken of by the Author to the *Hebrews*, do or ever did belong, or ever were belonging to any other people than to the Houſe of *Iſrael*, or Seed of *Abraham*; or to deny that the two Covenants mentioned by *Jeremiah*, and ſpoken of by the Apoſtles, were other

than

FIGURE 40

III

JOHN NORCOTT

Baptism Discovered Plainly and Faithfully, According to the Word of God (London, 1675 [1672]*)

When he wrote *Baptism Discovered Plainly* in 1672, John Norcott (?–1676) was the second minister of one of London's oldest Baptist churches on Wapping Lane (a position he held between 1670 and 1676).[1] Outside of this one publication, Norcott has not left an extensive paper trail, but his importance can be gathered from the prominence of his ministerial post, his involvements with his Baptist colleagues, and the popularity of his treatise.[2]

Norcott started his career as a minister in the Church of England. His early service is unclear, but in 1657 he was called to Stanstead Thele parish church (or Stanstead St. Margaret's, often referred to as St. Margaret's) in Hertfordshire, just north of London. His tenure there was short-lived, however, for he was removed from this post along with thousands of other dissenters by the Act of Uniformity in 1662.[3] The restoration of the monarchy in 1660 that brought Charles II to the throne promised religious toleration, but a series of acts known as the Clarendon Code (of which the 1662 Act of Uniformity was a part) made clear that Charles II intended to bring Puritans, Baptists, Catholics, and other dissenters into greater conformity with the Church of England. Norcott's Baptist and "Puritan"

---

* Norcott's book was originally published in 1672, but since original copies of this first edition are extremely rare, we have reproduced the 1675 edition below.

[1] Ernest Frederick Kevan, *London's Oldest Baptist Church* (London: Kingsgate Press, 1933).

[2] Geoffrey F. Nuttall, "Another Baptist Ejection (1662): The Case of John Norcott," in *Pilgrim Pathways: Essays in Baptist History in Honour of B. R. White*, ed. William Brackney and Paul S. Fiddes (Macon, Ga.: Mercer University Press, 1999), 185.

[3] Nuttall, "Another Baptist Ejection (1662)," 186.

convictions prevented him from any oaths of allegiance or conforming to the Book of Common Prayer, so he lost his position. In 1670 he was called to the Baptist church at Wapping Lane.

Norcott was also involved in a controversy between the Baptists and Quakers in 1674. The primary fight was between Baptist minister Thomas Hicks and the notable Quaker and founder of the colony of Pennsylvania William Penn, who argued against each other in print.[4] When Penn accused Hicks of maligning the Quakers, the English Baptists called a meeting to examine Hicks. Norcott served on a panel of Baptist ministers who examined Hicks' claims about Quaker teachings from Quaker publications, and he signed his name to a certificate stating that Hicks' representations of the Quakers were accurate.[5]

John Norcott died on March 24, 1676. His colleague Benjamin Keach preached his funeral sermon, which was published as *A Summons to the Grave*.[6] Keach additionally eulogized Norcott in poem form on a broadside printed that same year, titled *An Elegy on the Death of That Most Laborious and Painful Minister of the Gospel, Mr. John Norcot*.[7]

Before his death, Norcott's 1672 treatise on adult baptism thrust him into an ongoing pamphlet war, started in the 1640s, regarding who should be baptized, when, and how. His clear argumentation in the essay made it a popular and well-used defense of adult baptism. A second edition of the essay came out in 1675, a year before Norcott's death, and subsequent editions and reprintings continued into the twentieth century, even in different languages.

---

[4] Thomas Hicks, *A Dialogue Between a Christian and a Quaker Wherein Is Faithfully Represented, Some of the Cheif [sic] and Most Concerning Opinions of the Quakers, Together with Their Method and Manner of Reasoning in the Defence Thereof* (London: Printed for Henry Hills, 1673); William Penn, *Reason Against Railing, and Truth Against Fiction Being an Answer to Those Two Late Pamphlets Intituled A Dialogue Between a Christian and a Quaker, and the Continuation of the Dialogue &c. by One Thomas Hicks, an Anabaptist Teacher: In Which His Dis-ingenuity Is Represented . . . and Thomas Hicks Proved No Christian . . .* (London, 1673).

[5] Joseph Ivimey, *A History of the English Baptists* (London: Burdett & Morris, 1811), 392.

[6] Benjamin Keach, *A Summons to the Grave, or, The Necessity of a Timely Preparation for Death Demonstrated in a Sermon Preached at the Funeral of That Most Eminent and Faithful Servant of Jesus Christ Mr. John Norcot Who Departed This Life March 24, 1675/6* (London: Printed for Ben Harris, 1676).

[7] Benjamin Keach, *An Elegy on the Death of That Most Laborious and Painful Minister of the Gospel, Mr. John Norcot: Who Fell Asleep in the Lord the 24th Day of This Instant March, 1675/6* (London: Printed for Ben Harris, 1676).

BAPTISM
Discovered plainly and faithfully, according to the WORD of GOD.

by
JOHN NORCOTT

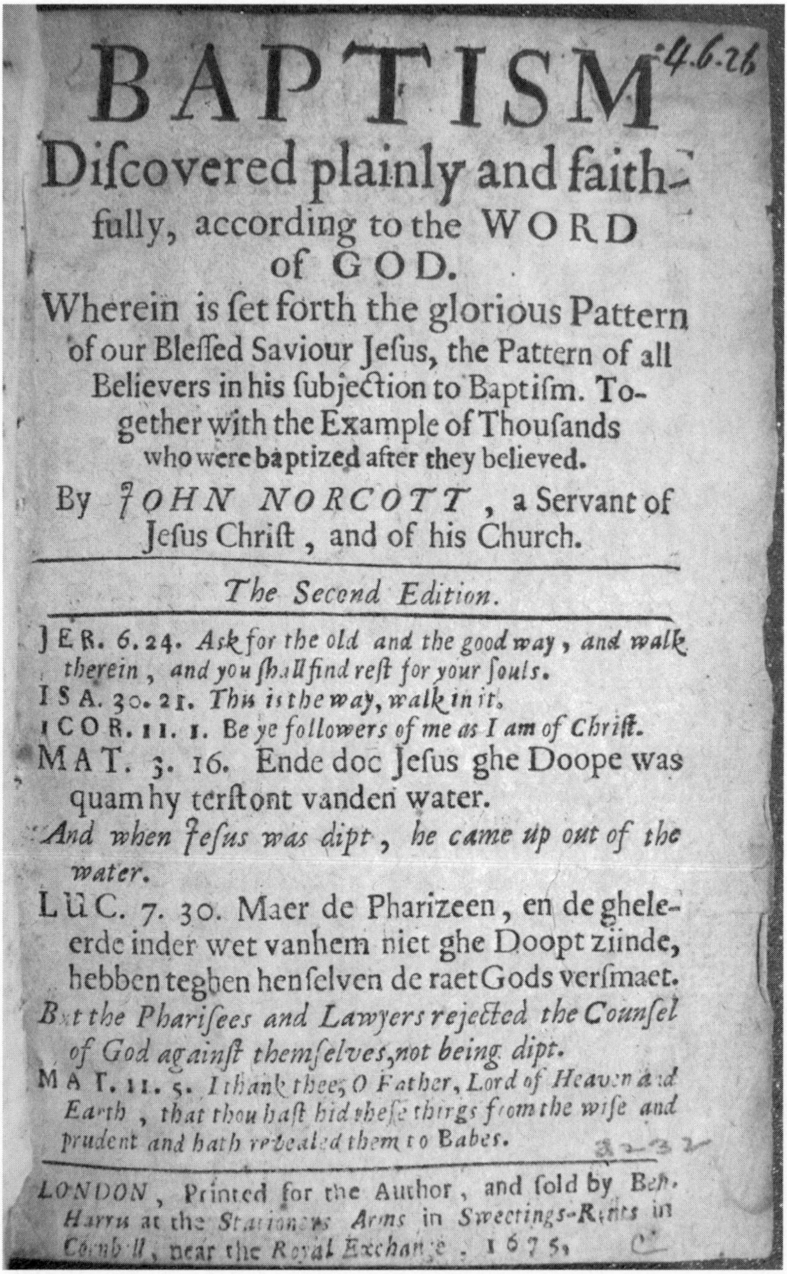

BAPTISM
4.6.26

Diſcovered plainly and faith-
fully, according to the WORD
of GOD.

Wherein is ſet forth the glorious Pattern
of our Bleſſed Saviour Jeſus, the Pattern of all
Believers in his ſubjection to Baptiſm. Together with the Example of Thouſands
who were baptized after they believed.

By *JOHN NORCOTT*, a Servant of
Jeſus Chriſt, and of his Church.

The Second Edition.

JER. 6.24. *Ask for the old and the good way, and walk
therein, and you ſhall find reſt for your ſouls.*
ISA. 30.21. *This is the way, walk in it,*
1COR. 11. 1. *Be ye followers of me as I am of Chriſt.*
MAT. 3. 16. Ende doc Jeſus ghe Doope was
quam hy terſtont vanden water.
*And when Jeſus was dipt, he came up out of the
water.*
LUC. 7. 30. Maer de Pharizeen, en de gheleerde inder wet vanhem niet ghe Doopt ziinde,
hebben teghen henſelven de raet Gods verſmaet.
*But the Phariſees and Lawyers rejected the Counſel
of God againſt themſelves, not being dipt.*
MAT. 11. 5. *I thank thee, O Father, Lord of Heaven and
Earth, that thou haſt hid theſe thirgs from the wiſe and
prudent and hath revealed them to Babes.*

LONDON, Printed for the Author, and ſold by Ben.
Harris at the *Stationers Arms* in *Sweetings-Rents* in
Cornbill, near the *Royal Exchange*. 1675.

FIGURE 41
John Norcott, Baptism Discovered Plainly and Faithfully, According to the Word of God
title page. Photograph by Lucas Mason-Brown.
Courtesy of the Trustees of the Boston Public Library/Rare Books.

BAPTISM
Discovered plainly and faith-
fully, according to the WORD of GOD.

Wherein is set forth the glorious Pattern
of our Blessed Saviour Jesus, the Pattern of all
Believers in his subjection to Baptism. Together with the Example of Thousands
who were baptized after they believed.

By *JOHN NORCOTT*, a Servant of
Jesus Christ, and of his Church.

The Second Edition.[8]

JER. 6.24. *Ask for the old and the good way, and walk therein, and you shall find rest for your souls.*[9]

ISA. 30.21. *This is the way, walk in it.*

I COR. 11.1. *Be ye followers of me as I am of Christ.*

MAT. 3.16. Ende doc Jesus ghe Droope was quam hy terstont vanden water.[10]

And when Jesus was dipt, he came up out of the water.

LUC. 7.30. Maer de Pharizeen, en de gheleerde inder wet vanhem niet ghe Doopt ziinde, hebben teghen henselven de raet Gods versmaet.

But the Pharisees and Lawyers rejected the Counsel of God against themselves, not being dipt.

MAT. 11.5. *I thank thee, O Father, Lord of Heaven and Earth, that thou hast hid these things from the wise and prudent and hath revealed them to Babes.*[11]

LONDON, Printed for the Author, and sold by Ben. Harris at the Stationers Arms in Sweeting-Rents in Cornhill, near the Royal Exchange, 1675.

---

[8] The first edition was printed in 1672, but few, if any, copies have survived. The second (1675) edition is more common, and was the one most likely read by John Eliot.

[9] This verse is a paraphrase of Jeremiah 6:16 not 6:24.

[10] Three of these verses on the title page are given first in Dutch. Although the reasons are not entirely clear, it is possibly due to the ongoing relationship English dissenters like the Baptists had with Dutch Protestants.

[11] This correct reference for this verse is Matthew 11:25 not 11:5, likely the result of a typesetting error.

[A2]¹²

THE
EPISTLE
DEDICATORY.

*To the litile*¹³ *Flock, Heirs of the Kingdom, once as Sheep going astray, but now*
returned to the great Bishop and Shepherd of your souls. Eternal Peace through the
Mercy of Jesus be multiplied.

BELOVED,

WHAT I have presented you with, is what once you have heard, and are
in the Practice of, And what I have written I take the great God for my
Patron and Protector herein, it being but his will: which none can deny
but such as one day will be found to strive with their Maker; and being
satisfied you are such as love the Truth; I am perswaded you will bid this
welcom: because it may conduce to your further confirmation. Let it not
be any trouble to you to be reproached for Christs sake; it is his Authority we contend for, and he will ere long shew himself the only Potentate;
it is possible your lot may be like that of one called *Agrippa*, who was
imprisoned for wishing Caius Emperour, and was laid in an Iron Chain;
but a little after Caius came to be Emperour, and the first preferred was
Agrippa; he took off his Iron Chain, and gave him a gold Chain, link for
link, and weight for weight as heavy as his Iron Chain was: It is but a little
time, and he will come, whom you wish to be Emperour, even the Lord
Jesus: and be sure, if Cups of cold water shall be rewarded, obedience to
his Truth shall; he shall wipe away all your reproaches, he will let it be
seen whether it be his glory or no we aim at: [A3] and if when he puts
Actions in the ballance of the Sanctuary, this be found having weight, and
his own stamp, as undoubtedly it will, then be you cheerful, it is not you
but he that is reproached; it is not you, but his Truth that is slighted. And
the King will be angry when he comes in to see the Guests.
  Therefore as the least Truth is dear to the Children of Truth; so let
not the greatest Truth be rested in, short of a possession of him, who
is Truth it self; It is possible, some may say, why do you begin in your

---

¹² Bracketed numbers throughout are the original page numbers in Norcott, *Baptism*
Discovered Plainly.
¹³ A typesetter error; it should be "little."

publick appearing,[14] to pitch on Baptism, things of greater concernment might have been more useful. But I take the Example of the Lord by the Prophet, who taking notice of that one slighted Ordinance (viz.) The Feast of Tabernacles, *Zach.* 14.16, 17. *And it shall come to pass, that every one that is left of all the Nations that will not come to Jerusalem to worship the King the Lord of Hosts, and to keep the Feast of the Tabernacles, upon them shall be no rain.* The Feast of the Tabernacles being an Ordinance, and not used, on them shall be no rain: a poor thing to cut down boughs and build booths, yet if this is neglected, upon them shall be no rain. Thus I say, this Ordinance of Baptism, it being an Ordinance neglected, and not practiced in Purity, according to the Pattern in the Mount, I thought good to pitch on. When a Ship is to set sail on the vast Ocean, a wise Commander looks not only to have Anchors and good Sails, and brave Galleries, but looks to have every chink stopp'd, for a small leak unstopped, may sink the ship; And shall not we, that ere long must set Sail upon the Ocean of Eternity, look to have every chink stopped. Allow not one known sin, live not in neglect of one Command, it may be that which some call Nothing, God will call Re-[A4]bellion, what will become of them then: Therefore my great Request from the Lord is, that as you have bin buried with Christ by Baptism, so that you would walk in newness of life: Oh let not your Conversations give the lie to your Professions; live as a washed people, and as you see your Calling, that not many wise, not many Noble, after the flesh, are called; but God hath chosen you, who by Nature were vile as any, and hath put you among the Children, live as Children of one Father. And in all your Addresses unto his glorious Throne, think on him who counts it his honour to serve the Lord, and his little Flock, with unfeigned love to the end,

JO. NORCOTT.

To his Truly beloved Friends and Brethren in and about Wapping,[15] who love our Lord Jesus in sincerity, Children of one Father, Partakers of the glorious Spirit of grace.

Beloved Brethren.

 It was Josephs *lot to be seperated from his Brethren, but God meant it for good, though it was not for the present seen, yet in due time it appeared. Josephs dreams were fulfilled; and though the Archers shot sorely at him, and grieved him,*

---

[14] Meaning this was Norcott's first publication.
[15] I.e., Norcott's church at Wapping Lane.

yet his Bowe abode in strength;[16] *Oh how good it is to be upright with the Lord; It is one of the sad evils of the times, Brethren shoot at Brethren: but this will be a Mercy indeed, if all our aim might be more to enjoy and be conformable to Christ; one part of conformity to our Lord Jesus, is obedience to the precious Ordinance of Baptism: Judging you to be such as press after Christ your Head, together with a Testimonial of my unfeigned love to you, I have presented these few thoughts to your serious Consideration. I have read of two loving Friends, who having spent a great part of the day in a matter of difference between them, could not be reconciled and so parted: one of them bethinking himselfe of that Text,* Eph. *4.26. ran to the other, saying,* The Sun is gowing down, *by which they were both immediately reconciled; My brethren, our Sun is going down, Eternity is upon us, and shall we not consider the Works we have to do for the Lord; I beseech you be like the noble* Bereans, *search whether these things be so; and if you find these things not mine, but the Lords, then give him the glory due to his Name, Beloved, as I have, so I shall yet appeal in the Ears of the Lord of Sabbaoth, like* Elijah; Oh Lord, the God of *Abraham, Isaac,* and *of Israel,* let it be seen this day that thou art God, and that I am thy servant, and that I have done these things at thy Word. Now Lord let Fire come down from Heaven on this Sacrifice, that may drink up all the waters of strife: *And that you may all cry,* The Lord he is God, the Lord he is God; *which is the unfeined desire of him who is unworthy to serve you; yet your loving Brother in Jesus Christ,*

JO. NORCOTT.

---

[16] In his dying speech Jacob described Joseph in these terms. See Genesis 49:23–24.

THE CONTENTS.

Chap. I. *Of the Baptism of Christ.*

Chap. II. *Of the great Commission for baptizing Believers.*

Chap. III. *Examples of many thousands baptized after Believing.*

Chap. IV. *That baptizing is dipping.*

Chap. V. *Water Baptism to continue till Christs second coming.*

Chap. VI. *That no Measures of Grace is a sufficient Ground to keep any from Water-Baptism.*

Chap. VII. *Believers Baptism a great Ordinance.*

Chap. VIII. *Answers to the common Objections.*

Chap. IX. *Believers Baptism and Infant-Baptism compared.*

Chap. X. *A Recital of those Scriptures speaking of Baptism.*

Chap. XI. *Consideration of what hath been said by way of Conclusion.*

[1]
BAPTISM
Plainly and faithfully
Discovered.

When thou by reading goest to search out the minde of God, let thy Cry be, *Lord anoint my eyes with eye-salve that I may see;*[17] and if it hath been the day of Gods Power with thy soul, I fear not but thou wilt bid Truth welcom, in whatever dress it comes; and more think on what is comprised in the Letter, then be affrighted at the poor Clothing of the Messenger, especially knowing it comes from one whose Name is the great God. Therefore in handling this Truth (*viz.*) Believers Baptism, as it was practised by Christ, and the Primitive Churches, my great Request to thee is, that thou wilt read what is said without prejudice; and what ever you finde according to Truth receive, as that which is more precious then your lives, and judge of it according to the holy Scriptures; for when all is said that can be, that must be Judge in all Controversies of Religion. And as Christ is the Foundation upon which whoever [2] buildeth, shall never

---

[17] Revelation 3:18.

be confounded; so I shall therefore take a few Observations concerning Christ his being baptized; and herein you may take notice how exact the Holy Scriptures are, to set down the circumstances of his Baptism.

CHAP. I.
CHRIST WAS BAPTIZED IN THE RIVER OF JORDAN.

Concerning the Baptism of Jesus Christ, you may read it at large, Mat. 3.13, &c. *Then cometh Jesus from* Galilee to Jordan *unto* John *to be baptized of him.* Every word hath emphasis (*then*) before he entred upon his public Ministry, as you see in Mat. 4.17. *From that time Jesus began to preach, (cometh)* he might have commanded *John* to have attended him; but in token of his subjection he cometh (*from Galilee*) many miles, and 'tis likely on foot; every step we take for God is acceptable, and one day shall have a glorious Reward (*to Jordan*) where there was a River where Thousands had been baptized, and was a suitable place for *John* to dip Christ in, as will be seen hereafter. Now I shall take notice of eight things concerning the Baptism of Christ.

First, concerning his Age, 'tis said, *Luke* [3] 3.21. *Jesus being baptized,* ver. 23. *began to be about thirty years of Age*; here you see that Christ himself was baptized at grown years; if any might be baptized in Infancy, why not Christ? Christians be not ashamed, your Captain is gone before you, he was thirty years old when baptized. Christ is not ashamed to call you Brethren, *Heb.* 2.11.

Secondly, another thing to be observed in the Baptism of Christ, is the Administrator of this holy Ordinance *John*; who confesseth of himself he was not worthy to unloose the latchets of his shoes, *Mark* 1.7. Now if Christ would receive Baptism from such an unworthy Instrument; never slight the Ordinance because of the unworthiness of the Administrators, let your eye be on Christ, your example.

Thirdly, Note the Repulse, John *forbade him,* Mat. 3.14. Difficulty in duty must be no excuse; we must take no denial in following God, *Strive to enter in at the strait gate.*[18]

Fourthly, Note *John's* Argument, *Mat.* 3.14. *I have need to be baptized of thee, and comest thou to me.* Some will not be baptized but of need; their carnal Argument is, May I not go to Heaven though I be not baptized? is it of necessity to salvation? is this like your Lord and Master? was not he a per-[4]fect Saviour; was not the Spirit poured on him without measure; he had no sin to be washed away, wherefore, see your example, he doth it not of need, but of obedience to his fathers will.

[18] Matthew 7:13.

Fifthly, Note the excellent termes he gives to this Ordinance of Baptism; 1. He calls it Righteousness, *Mat.* 3.15. 'Tis righteous and just that I should be about my Fathers business. 2. It is a comely thing, it becomes us: Oh it is a very comely thing in Gods Children, to have respect to all the Commandments of God. 3. The Conjunction (*us*) thee and me, and all my Followers, *John* 12.26. *if any man serve me, let him follow me; and where I am there shall my servants be.* 4. A Completion, it is a fulfilling, 2. *Cor.* 10.4. *The weapons of our Warfare are not carnal, but Spiritual,* ver. 5. *bringing every thought into captivity to the obedience of Christ,* ver. 6. *having in readiness to revenge all disobedience, when your obedience shall be fulfilled.* Obedience must be fulfilled. 5. The universal term (*all*) Baptism is one of the all. Christ reckons it so, thou canst not walk in all the Commands, if this be omitted.

6. Note, concerning Christs Baptisme the form of Administration, *Mat.* 3. *and straitway he went up out of the water,* (*straitway*) [5] because Baptism is once *Dipping* (*up*) had he not been down, 'twould not have bin said he went up, (*he went*) was not carried in Arms as Infants are (*out*) if he went out of the water then he had been in: we never say one goes out of the house when he never was in. So Christ could not be said to come out of the water, had he not been in, (*he went up out*) had a little water been brought to him in a Bason, he had not been said to go up out (*of the water*) this water was the River *Jordan.* Christ stoops to small things because an Ordinance.

7. Note, concerning Christ Baptism, the Father's Acceptance, *Mat.* 3.16, 17. (*the Heavens was*) opened: some of Christs followers have found glorious openings of Heaven in Baptism (*the Spirit descended*) the very same that is promised to Believers in their Baptism *Acts* 2.38. *Repent and be Baptized every one of you, and you shall receive the Holy Ghost.* Obj. *But doth every one receive the Holy Ghost that is baptized? Answ.* The defect lies not in Baptism, But in Repentance and Faith; without which no Ordinance is effectual: (*And loe, a Voice from Heaven, This is my beloved Son*) Christ as Head was sealed, and in Baptism God seals the Sonship of his Members (*in him I am well pleased*) not only in all he hath and doth do, but in this very [6] Act of Baptism, as an Act of obedience to my glorious Will; I am well pleased, and so is the Lord well pleased in the Act of obedience, wherein from the heart we obey the form of doctrine delivered to us. *Rom.* 6.17. The same Voice the blessed Son of God hath in the Mount,[19] *Luke* 9.35. *This is my beloved Son; hear him*: Hear him in his Commands and Appointments; hear him now in his Baptism: Oh, saith Christ, thus it becometh us; you that have my Father for your Father, you that have my God for

---

[19] This refers to the Mount of Transfiguration (Luke 9:28-36).

your God: Thus it becometh us to be baptized, and to fulfil all righteousness; *Oh he is a beloved Son, hear him.*

8. Note, how in Christ Baptism the Trinity doth as it were meet; the Father with a Voice, the Son baptized in Person, the Holy Ghost descends like a Dove: And surely, it is one Reason why Baptism in special is to be administered in the Name of the Father, Son, and Holy Ghost; because he who baptized, and doth sincerely believe, the whole Trinity, the Father, Son, and Spirit is his portion; and that glorious Union of the Trinity in Christs Baptism, is in every Believers Baptism commemorated. [7]

CHAP. II.
OF THE GREAT COMMISSION FOR BELIEVERS BAPTISM.

As you have heard something concerning your great Pattern, the Lord Jesus: so now I shall shew you something concerning his Command, *Mat.* 28.19. And I pray note what is said of our Lord Jesus, *Acts* 1.1. Christ is said both to do and teach; 'tis good for Teachers to imitate their Lord, both to do and teach; and *ver. 2. He was taken up, after that he through the Spirit had given Commandments to his Apostles*; of which Commandments, this of Believers Baptism is certainly one; and as you see in *Mat.* 28.18, 19, 20. The great God gave him to be a Commander and Leader to his people, *Isa.* 55.4. Christ is a gift as a Commander; Oh what Mercy it is to have such a wise Commander, whose Commandments to Believers are not grievous; in keeping his Commandments there is great reward, *Psal.* 19.11. Now in this Command there is eight things very notable.

First, Note whence Christ came, why he came out of the Grave, A Risen Jesus; *And God raised him from the dead, and sent him to* [8] *bless us, Acts* 3.26. Surely this blessed Jesus would not appoint any thing but what is good for his People; he is a blessed Jesus, and he gives blessed Commands; *Blessed are they that do his Commandments, that they may have a right to the Tree of life, and may enter in through the Gates of the City, Rev.* 22.14.

Secondly, Note, Christ appeared and came to them; now should an Angel appear and command men to be baptized, who would stand against it, but here you have the glorious Son of God in his own Person appearing, and saith, *Go teach and baptize.*

Thirdly, Note what Authority he comes with, *Mat.* 28.18. *All power in Heaven and Earth is given to me*; All Power to command both in Heaven and Earth is given to me; all power to dispose of Heaven and Earth, all power to protect. I have Angels and Men at my Command; I am able to protect you, to stand by you, and to be with you, both in the fire and in the water: I have all power, *Go therefore, teach and baptize*; fear no enemies; *Go teach and baptize.*

Fourthly, Note the Command it self, *Mat.* 28.19. saith Christ, *Go therefore teach and baptize.* Christ said but to Legion, *Go,* Mat. 8.32, and they ran violently,[20] and shall not [9] Believers be as willing people in the day of his power. The Centurion did but say Go, to his servants, and they did go; and he did but say, Come, and they came; and he did but say, Do this, and they did it:[21] And shall Christs servants be worse to him then the Centurions servants were: 'tis Christ saith, *Go.*

Go teach and baptize.

Fifthly, Note, what is precedent to Baptism: Go teach, there must be teaching; God is a Spirit, and he seeks such to worship him. that worship him in spirit and truth, *Joh[n]* 4.24. therefore there must go teaching before Baptism, or else they will never worship him in spirit and truth. *Go teach and baptize.* I confess many men do say the word Teach in the Greek is, Make disciples, and I dare not say against it; for I finde it the very practice of Jesus Christ, he did first make Disciples, and then baptized them, *John* 4.1 *Jesus made and baptized more disciples then* John; here was first a making Disciples, and then a baptizing them; but how many poor souls ignorantly baptize those who never were made Disciples, but Christ saith, *teach and baptize them.*

Sixthly, Note the Extent of the Command, *Teach all Nations and baptize them.* Go into all Nations, whether it be a hot or a [10] cold Climat, Jews and Gentiles, Male and Female; when you have taught them, then baptize them. Now the middle wall of Partition is broken down.[22] Now God is no Respecter of Persons, now let none think to boast that they have *Abraham* for their Father;[23] No, no, go into all Nations, publish the glad tidings of the Gospel to every creature, *Mark* 16.15, 16. *He that believeth and is baptized, shall be saved; Go teach all Nations, baptizing them*: when you have taught them, then baptize them.

Seventhly, Note the words of Institution, *Mat.* 28.19. baptizing them in the Name of the Father, such as receive the Lord Jesus on Gospel-terms, God will be a Father to them, 2 *Cor.* 6.17. Go give them a Call; come out

---

[20] Norcott mixed the two accounts of the Gadarene demoniac found in Mark 5:7-13 and Matthew 8:28-32. Mark has only one madman, who replies that his name is "Legion," being possessed by so many demons. Matthew's account has two men, and in this version Jesus commands the evil spirits, "Go," and they enter a herd of pigs, who wildly run off a cliff into the sea.

[21] Norcott here refers to the story in Matthew 8:5-13 of the Roman centurion who came to Jesus asking for him to heal his gravely ill slave.

[22] In the Jerusalem temple, walls separated the various categories of people, with only the high priest being allowed into the Holy of Holies.

[23] Referring to Jesus' rebuke to those who boasted that they were the children of Abraham (John 8:39).

from amongst Unbelievers, &c. and be separate, and I will be a Father to you, and you shall be my sons and daughters; stand a while, and wonder here, you that make nothing of the blessed Ordinance of Baptism; here below things done in the Kings name carries Power; but here's the great God's Name; yea, here's the Name of the Mysterious Trinity, Father, Son and Holy Ghost; and do'st thou think Baptism hath nothing in it, that hath that glorious Name to be adored and admired, Go, baptize them in the glorious Name of the Father, Son, and Holy Ghost. [11]

Eightly, Note the glorious Promise annexed, *Go baptize, and I will be with you*; Christ is a good Companion, you that love his Company seek it where he promiseth it; *Ask for the old and the good way, and walk therein, and you shall finde rest for your souls*; Is there any Soul-rest short of Christ? No, no, *in his Presence is fulness of joy*; would you have his Presence, do like *Zaccheus*, Get into the way;[24] Believe and be baptized, for he comes this way (*baptize*) and I will be with you always to the end of the world. *Amen*, an *Amen* follows, they are the farewel words of the best Friend, *Baptize, I will be with you*. Amen.

CHAP. III.
EXAMPLES.

Of many thousands who were baptized in Rivers, all of them persons who professed Repentance and Faith, and were of years able to answer for themselves.

First example: Those that Christ is said to baptize, *John* 4.1, 2. it is said *He made them disciples, and baptized them*; first, they are Disciples, then baptized; they are made Disciples, not born Disciples (that is) they are made Disciples by the preaching of Gods Word, and then they were baptized. [12]

Second Example, you have an Example, *Acts* 2.41. *Then they who gladly received his word were baptized*: the occasion of this you have. *ver.* 37. *They were prickt at the heart, they knew not what to do*; the sense of sin lay heavy upon them. The Apostle tells them, *That they should repent and be baptized, then they should receive the Holy Ghost; then they who gladly received the Word were baptized*. Mercy is sweet to a wounded soul, and such a soul sticks at no duty, now he can be plunged in water at Christs Command. *ver.* 41. *And the same day there was added unto them about three thousand souls.*

Third Example; another Example you have, *Acts* 8.12. *But when they believed* Philip, *preaching the things concerning the Kingdom of God, and the Name of Jesus, they were baptized Men and Women*: When they believed, *ver.* 5. They of *Samaria*, and for ought we know, some of those whom

---

[24] Zacchaeus was the tax collector who climbed a tree to see Jesus (Luke 19:2-8).

the Disciples would a little while ago have called for fire from Heaven upon, *Luke* 9.52, 54. yet when these believed, they were baptized Men and Women. Oh, if never so near Hell, yet believe and be baptized, there's Mercy for thee.

Fourth Example, You have another Example of the baptizing of believers, in *Acts* 8.5.[25] *Philip preached unto the Eunuch, Jesus, ver.* 36. *They came to a certain water, and the* [13] *Eunuch said, see, here is water, what doth hinder me to be baptized*; and *ver.* 37. *And* Philip *said, if thou believest with all thy heart, thou mayest*; This If is the If we stand upon, be never so poor, so vile, if God once make thee to believe, then thou may'st be baptized; 'twas not his godly Parents, 'twas not his reading, 'twas not his coming to *Jerusalem* to worship, 'twas not his willingness to be baptized; *but if thou believest thou may'st*; saith the Greek, it is lawful: it is according to Christs Law, *ver.* 38. *They went both down into the water, both* Philip *and the Eunuch, and he baptized him*: Oh behold a Man, the great Treasurer of the Queen of *Ethiopia*, a rich man, an honourable man, a religious man; a man, 'tis like, having many Attendants at his Chariot, he stops all, commands all to stand still, till he yields obedience to his Lord and Master in Water-Baptism; he can now go down into the water for him, who had come down from Heaven for him; he counts it no disgrace to obey Christ by his poor servant *Philip*: Oh the condescension of truly gracious souls: No Arguments works like love, *therefore if you love me keep my Commandments*; here's going down, and coming up, like the glorious ways of Christ, he first casts down, then he raiseth up; first brings to the Grave, and [14] then saith, *Return ye sons of men*, ver. 39. *And he went on his way rejoicing*; Oh what triumph is in Christs ways in keeping aswell as for keeping his Commands; there is, as well as shall be great reward (*he went on his way*) the Righteous shall hold on in his way, and he that hath clean hands shall be stronger and stronger;[26] how many have stuck in their way, wept in their way, droopt in their way, but when baptized have gone on their way rejoicing; he might have a sad heart, though a rich Treasurer: Riches will not do, *being baptized, he went on his way rejoicing. The Jaylor being baptized, rejoyced, believing in God with all his house.*[27]

Fifth Example. The next Example we come to, is the baptizing of the famous Apostle *Paul*, *Acts* 22.16. *And now why tarriest thou, arise and be baptized, and wash away thy sins*; wouldest thou have thy soul filled with

---

[25] Norcott's citation is erroneous. The verses cited are Acts 8:35-37.

[26] "The righteous also shall hold on his way, and he that hath clean hands shall be stronger and stronger" (Job 17:9).

[27] The jailer was about to kill himself because he thought that the earthquake had freed his prisoners, but Paul stopped him, saying, "Do yourself no harm: for we are all here" (Acts 16:25-34). The jailer was then converted and baptized. Norcott also discusses this passage on p. 15 of his treatise (see above).

joy? wilt thou take Christ for thy Lord? Then arise, why tarriest thou, and be baptized: *He that appeared to thee in the way when thou wast a Persecutor, and stopt thee from going to Hell, when thou wast running, hath sent me, saith* Annanias, Act. 9.15. *And now why tarriest thou? arise, and be baptized,* Acts 22.16. *Thou hast been a Persecutor,* and now I must shew thee that thou must be a Preacher, and a [15] Sufferer; as *Acts* 9.15, 16. And therefore Arise, why tarriest thou? and be baptized; oh accept of the termes and tenders of Mercy: bid Mercy welcome, but do not put it off a day; why dost thou tarry? dost think thy self unworthy, and therefore tarriest? do not let that hinder, I tell thee from the Lord, thou art a chosen vessel, *Acts* 9.15. Therefore arise, why tarriest thou and be baptized; The Lord is willing to forgive all thy former sins, and to accept of thee on Gospel-terms, and now why tarriest thou, arise and be baptized, and wash away thy sins.

6. Example; Another Example of Believer's Baptism, is the Baptism of the Jaylor, *Acts* 16.30, 31, 32. He went to bed in his sins, and might have awaked in Hell; but preventing Mercy meets him when his sword was drawing; and by a glorious Instrument God cries, do thy self no harm, there is hope for thee, And he trembling cries, What must I do? that soul that trembles before the Almightly God, will not only cry out what shall I have but what shall I do. *Believe,* saith *Paul, believe on the Lord Jesus*; And to demonstrate his willingness to yield obedience to the Lord Jesus, and accept of him on Gospel terms, he is baptized the same hour of the night, *ver.* 33. And if you note, *ver.* 34. all his believed and were baptized. [16]

7. Another Example you have of *Lydia,*[28] Acts 16.14. a godly woman, a praying woman, God opened her heart to attend his Word by *Paul,* and being at the River she was baptized, When the heart is shut, how backward are souls to obey Christ; one draw from Christ makes the soul run, *Son.* 1.4.[29] The Lord opened her heart and she was baptized.

8. Example, you have Acts 18.8. *Crispus* the chief Ruler of the Synagogue[30] believed on the Lord with all his house; and many of the *Corinthians* hearing, believed and were baptized; Crispus believed, his House believed, all runs in their believing, and then they were baptized. Thus you have Pattern and Precept: if Command or Example be any force, here's both.

---

[28] Lydia was "a seller of purple" in Thyatira, which meant that she was a fairly wealthy woman. "Purple" or "imperial purple" was an expensive dye used for textiles, and sumptuary laws restricted who was allowed to possess such cloth. The dye was said to be worth its weight in silver.

[29] This reference is to the Song of Solomon 1:4, "Draw me, we will run after thee."

[30] Crispus was the head of the synagogue in Corinth.

CHAP. IV.
BAPTISM IS DIPPING OR COVERING UNDER WATER

1. The Greek Βαπτίξο, *to plunge, to overwhelm*. Thus Christ was plunged in water, *Mat.* 16.[31] Thus he was plunged and overwhelmed in his suffering, *Luke* 17.50.[32]

2. The *Dutch* Translation reads *Mat.* 3. *In those days came* John *the Dipper,* John 3.23. *John was dipping in* Aenon, *where there* [17] *was much water*; what need much water were it not dipping.

3. They did baptize in Rivers, *Mat.* 3.6. *They came to* John, *and were baptized in the River of* Jordan, John 3.23. John *was baptizing in* Aenon, *where there was much water*; What need it be in a River, and where there was much water, would not a little in a Bason serve to sprinkle the face?

4. Baptism signifies the Burial of Christ, *Rom.* 6.3. *Therefore we are buried with him in Baptism, Colos.* 2.12. *buried with him in Baptism.* Now we do not reckon a man buried, when a little earth is sprinkled on his face: but he is buried when covered, thus you are buried in Baptism.

5. Christs sufferings are called a Baptism, *Luke* 15.50. *I have a Baptism to be baptized with, and how am I straitned till it be accomplished*; when Christ suffered he was plunged into pains; did his sufferings lie only on his head or on his forehead; no, no, there was not one part free; he was from head to foot in pain; his Head was crowned with piercing Thornes, his hands and feet nailed to the Cross; so stretched out on the Cross, that a man might have told all his bones, *Ps.* 22.17. There was not one part free, the man hath sinned, body, soul and spirit. Christ was baptized into pains, plunged into sorrow, not [18] any part free, this he calls his Baptism. Thus, one baptized is plunged under water, to shew how Christ was plunged into sorrow for our sakes.

6. Baptism is putting on Christ, *Rom.* 13.14.[33] *As many of you as are baptized into Christ have put on Christ.* So *Gal.* 3.27. that as a servant wears his Lords livery, a Garment which demonstrates him to be the Servant of such a Lord. Thus in Baptism we put on our Lords livery, the cloths from head to foot; so we by Baptism put on Christ.

7. *When Christ was baptized he came up out of the water,* Mat. 5.16.[34] Was it only a little water thrown of the face? then he had not been in the water; but because he was baptized in the water, therefore being baptized

---

[31] Matthew 3:16.

[32] This is likely a typesetter error since Luke 17 does not have a verse 50. Norcott probably intended Luke 12:50.

[33] "But ye put on the Lord Jesus Christ, and make not provision for the flesh to *fulfil* the lusts *thereof*" (Rom 13:14).

[34] Another probable typesetter error; it should be Matthew 3:16.

he came up out of the water, *Acts* 8.38. *They*[35] *went both down into the water (and being there in the water) he baptized him, and when he was baptized, he came up out of the water.*

8. The Ark was a type that shewed forth Baptism, I Pet. 3.21.[36] Surely the Ark, on which it rained forty days and forty nights, was well wet all over, 'twas under the water, under clouds of water.

9. *Israel* in the Red Sea, I *Cor.* 10.1, 2.[37] When the Sea, and under the Cloud, are said to be baptized, under the Cloud. Thus persons baptized are under water. [19]

Thus you see the place where they were Baptized, was a River; their Action, they went down into the Water; then being in the Water, they were baptized; this was where [there] was much water. The end was to shew forth Christs Burial. Now if there be not a Burial under water to shew Christs Burial, the great end of Ordinance is lost, but we are Buried by Baptism.

Quest. *But why may not sprinkling with water serve, as well as covering under water; is there any more vertue in a great deal of water to wash away sin, than there is in a little water?*

Answ.

Sprinkling may not serve as well as Dipping under Water.

1. Because God is a jealous God, and stands upon small things in matters of Worship; 'tis likely *Nadab* and *Abihu* thought, if they put fire in the Censor, it might serve, though it were not fire from the Altar; but God calls it strange fire, and therefore he burns them with strange fire, *Lev.* 10.2, 3.[38] and *Moses* adds *ver.* 3. *This it is that the Lord hath said, I will be sanctified in them that draw nigh unto me, and before all the people I will be glorified.* God bid *Moses* speak to the Rock, and *Moses* smote the Rock, and therefore must die short of *Canaan.* Num. 20.11, 12.[39] [20]

---

[35] This refers to Philip and the eunuch.

[36] The common typology of the Puritan-Separatist-Baptist movement interpreted Old Testament events as a "type" that prefigured New Testament events. Norcott here cites 1 Peter 3:20-21, which says, "[w]hen once the longsuffering of God waited in the days of Noah, while the ark a preparing, wherein few, that is, eight souls were saved by water. The like figure whereunto *even* baptism doth also now save us."

[37] This is another example of typology. "Moreover, brethren, I would not that ye should be ignorant, how that all our fathers were under the cloud, and all passed through the sea; And all were baptized unto Moses in the cloud and in the sea" (1 Cor 10:1-2).

[38] Nadab and Abihu were sons of Aaron who failed to make a proper offering, and "there went out fire from the LORD, and devoured them, and they died before the LORD" (Lev 10:2-3).

[39] The Israelites were dying of thirst in the wilderness and demanded that Moses do something about it. Moses received a command from the Lord to speak to the rock. Instead

2. Sprinkling may not serve, because thereby the end of the Ordinance is lost, which is to shew the Death, Burial, and Resurrection of Christ, *Rom.* 6.4. *You are buried with him by Baptism, that like as he was raised*, &c.

3. Sprinkling will not serve, because it is not that God hath appointed. *Naaman* the Leper[40] did think the waters of *Damascus* to be of the same vertue with (or better then) the waters of *Israel*, 2 Kings 5.12, *May I not wash in them and be clean.* God had appointed him to dip in Jordan, not that there was more virtue in that water; but God did appoint him to dip in *Jordan*, and he did, and was clean. Dipping is Gods Appointment.

4. Sprinkling will not serve, because it is not according to the Pattern. Christ went down into the water. *Philip* and the *Eunuch* went down into the water, *Acts* 8.38. *Exod.* 25.40. *See thou do all things according to the Pattern.*[41]

5. Sprinkling will not serve, because we must keep the Ordinances as they were delivered to us, I *Cor.* 11.2.[42] Now Baptism was delivered to us in the first Pattern of Dipping and not by Sprinkling, they went down into the water.

6. Sprinkling will not serve, because it is high presumption to change Gods Ordinan-[21]ces; Is not God wise enough to appoint his own Worship how it shall be performed. *Isa.* 24.5. *The Earth is defiled, because they have changed my Ordinances.*

7. Sprinkling will not serve, because Sprinkling is not Baptism; it is not the thing intended by God; Baptism is *Dipping* or *Plunging*. Sprinkling is not Baptism, therefore Sprinkling will not serve, *Luke* 7.29, 30.[43] Gods Councel is *Baptism* or *Dipping*.

---

he "smote the rock twice," and water poured out. However, because Moses failed to follow the Lord's exact command only to speak to the rock, the Lord condemned Moses and Aaron: "Because ye believed me not . . . therefore ye shall not bring this congregation into the land which I have given them" (Num 20:2-12).

[40] Naaman was "captain of the host of the king of Syria." An Israelite slave of his wife told Naaman about a prophet in Samaria who could cure his leprosy, so he went to see Elisha in Samaria. Elisha told Naaman to dip himself seven times in the Jordan, and he was cured (2 Kgs 5:1-14).

[41] This quote is nearer to Hebrews 8:5: "See, saith he, *that* thou make all things according to the pattern shewed to thee in the mount." The Hebrews verse was based on Exodus 25:40, which says, "And look that thou make *them* [gold objects for the Ark of the Tabernacle] after their pattern, which was shewed thee in the mount."

[42] "Now I praise you, brethren, that ye remember me in all things, and keep the ordinances, as I delivered *them* to you" (1 Cor 11:2).

[43] "And all the people that heard *him*, and the publicans, justified God, being baptized with the baptism of John. But the Pharisees and lawyers rejected the counsel of God against themselves, being not baptized of him" (Luke 7:29-30).

CHAP. V.
PROVING WATER-BAPTISM, TO CONTINUE TILL THE SECOND COMING OF JESUS CHRIST.

That this may appear that Water-Baptism is to continue, and to be practiced by Believers; Take these six considerations:

1. Consider that Water-Baptism was once commanded, and never yet repealed, and no power can repeal a Command of Christ, but the same Power of Christ, by which it was given forth, *Jude ver.* 3. *Contend for the faith which once was delivered to the Saints.*

2. Consider, that Water-Baptism was practiced before, and since the Resurrection of [22] Jesus Christ; That Water-Baptism was practiced since the Resurrection of Christ, read Acts 8.38. *They went both down into the water, both* Philip *and the* Eunuch, *and there he baptized him,* Acts 10.47. *Can any man forbid water that these should not be baptized, who have received the Holy Ghost as well as we; then commanded he them to be baptized.* Here is water, and here it is commanded by an Apostle sent by Christ. Acts 16.13, 14. *Lydia* was by a River-side, in which River she was baptized.

3. Consider that Water-Baptism was commanded after Christs Resurrection, *Mat.* 28.19. *Go teach all Nations, baptizing them.* Had Water-Baptism ceased with Christs death, it had not been commanded and practiced after his Resurrection.

4. Consider that the end of the Ordinance remains as at the Lords Supper; the end of it is to shew forth the Lords death till he come; and to do this in remembrance of Christ; as long as we are to remember Christs death, it is to be done in remembrance of Christ, even till his second coming; so Baptism is to shew the Death, Burial, and Resurrection of Christ, *Rom.* 6.3, 4, 5. the End remaining, the Ordinance remains till his second coming.

5. Consider, it hath been continued by [23] Christians in all Ages, since Jesus Christ left his Command with the Saints.

6. Consider whether the same Argument that throws down Water-Baptism, if granted, will not throw down all Ordinances; for if you grant that when the Spirit is come Baptism ceaseth; may you not as well say, when the Spirit is come Preaching ceaseth, Prayer ceaseth; but this by reason of mans corrupt heart: Christ saith, *Teach them to observe all things which I have commanded you;* Mat. 28.19, 20. *And I will be with you to the end of the world.*

CHAP. VI.
THAT NO MEASURES OF GRACE OR OF THE SPIRIT IS A SUFFICIENT GROUND TO KEEP ANY FROM WATER-BAPTISM.

That no Measures of Grace or of the Spirit is a sufficient Ground to keep from Baptism, may plainly appear, if you

1. Consider, that baptism is from Heaven, as you see, *Mat.* 21.25.[44] Now what should keep from a Heavenly Command.

2. Consider the Lord Jesus has all grace, and the Spirit without Measure; as *John* 3.34.[45] and yet he was baptized in the River [24] of *Jordan*, as you may see, *Mat.* 3.13, 14, 15. Is not Christ a good Pattern for Believers to follow.

3. Consider, where hath God thus limited Baptism to Persons, having little Grace, or little of the Spirit. Nay, on the contrary hath not God promised his Spirit, that you may keep my Ordinances and do them? *Ezek.* 11.19, 20.

4. Consider, the Apostle makes receiving the Spirit, an Argument to encourage to Baptism, *Acts* 10.47. *Can any man forbid water, that these should not be baptized who have received the Holy Ghost as well as we.* Now if you mind, these were so baptized with the Spirit, that they spake with Tongues and prophesied; a strange work to prophesie and speak with Tongues;[46] such a Measure of the Spirit is not in our days, yet he commanded them to be baptized *ver.* 48.

CHAP. VII.
BELIEVERS BAPTISM A GREAT ORDINANCE.

The greatness of the Ordinance of Believers Baptism may appear if you consider these eight Considerations,

1. Consider that Baptism is an Ordinance [25] which hath the great Pattern, the Captain of our Salvation himself did practice it; as you see, *Mat.* 3.13. *Then cometh Jesus to be baptized: If any man serve me,* saith Christ, *let him follow me; And where I am, there shall my servant be,* John 12.26. Christ is the great Example.

---

[44] Jesus said, "The baptism of John, whence was it? from heaven, or of men? And they reasoned with themselves, saying, If we shall say, From heaven; he will say unto us, Why did ye not then believe him?" (Matt 21:25).

[45] "For he whom Goth hath sent speaketh the words of God; for God giveth not the Spirit by measure unto him" (John 3:34).

[46] "For they heard them speak with tongues, and magnify God" (Acts 10:46). Speaking in tongues was regarded as one of the "gifts" of the Holy Spirit. "And they were all filled with the Holy Ghost, and began to speak with other tongues, as the Spirit gave them utterance" (Acts 2:4). See also 1 Corinthians 12:4-11.

2. Consider the great Name in which Baptism is Administered, *Mat.* 28.19, 20. *Baptize them in the Name of the Father, Son, and Holy Ghost*; this Name must not be slighted; it is a great Name.

3. Consider the great Seal that Baptism had. How was the Lord Jesus sealed when he was baptized, *Mat.* 3.17. *The Heavens were opened, and a Voice heard, saying, This is my beloved Son in whom I am well pleased*; The Trinity meets in Christs Baptism.

4. Consider Baptism's great Business, it is called Righteousness: Righteousness is a great thing. Christ calls it a comely thing, *Mat.* 3.15. *Thus it becometh us to fulfill all Righteousness*; it is a fulfilling all Righteousness.

5. Consider Baptism's great Commission; it is one of the last Commands of our blessed Saviour after his Resurrection, a little before his Ascension, as appears *Mat.* 28.19,20, *Go teach and baptize.*

6. Consider Baptism's great promises, [26] *Mat.* 28.19, 20. *Go teach and baptize, and I will be with you*; here's the Promise of the glorions[47] presence of Christ. Then you have the promise of the Holy Ghost, *Repent and be baptized, and you shall receive the Holy Ghost*: Act. 2.38.

Then you have the Promise or Assurance of washing away your sins, *Acts* 22.16. *Arise and be baptized and wash away thy sins.*

Then you shall find the promise of Salvation annexed to Baptism, *Mark* 16.16. *He that believeth and is baptized, shall be saved*; Christs Presence, the Holy Ghost, Pardon of sin, and Salvation; all these are great promises.

7. Consider the Eminencie of Baptism; every word of God is pure, but baptism is called the Councel of God, *Luke* 7.29, 30. *They rejected the Councel of God against themselves, not being baptized*; is not the Councel of God a great thing.

8. Consider, since Christ hath been gone to Heaven, he hath commanded Baptism, *Acts* 8.29. the Spirit bid *Philip* joyn himself to the Chariot, which clearly appears was, that he might preach Christ, and baptize the Eunuch, *And when he was baptized he went away rejoycing*; Here's one call from Heaven. [27]

Another Command from Heaven to baptize, even after Christs Ascension; you have in the Lord Jesus' sending *Ananias* to *Paul*, *Acts* 9.19.[48] *The Lord called* Ananias *in a vision, and sends him to* Paul; *and when he comes, he saith,* Acts 22.16, *and now why tarriest thou arise and be baptized, and wash away thy sins.* This *Paul* tells us were the words of *Ananias*; here you have another Call from Heaven to baptize.

---

[47] A typesetter error; it should be "glorious."

[48] Ananias was a disciple in Damascus who Jesus called to minister to Saul/Paul after his conversion on the road to Damascus, after which Paul was baptized (Acts 9:10-18; 22:6-16).

Then again, you shall finde, *Acts* 10.4, 5. *Cornelius*[49] hath a Call from Heaven to send for *Peter,* who should tell him words whereby he should be saved. *Peter* hath a call from Heaven to go to *Cornelius,* ver. 19, 20. *Go therefore, nothing doubting*; here *Peter* is sent from Heaven, and to speak words whereby *Cornelius* might be saved; and when he came to *Cornelius,* you shall find *ver.* 48. *He commanded them to be baptized.* Thus you see Baptism was commanded after Christs Ascension; all which may shew Baptism to be a great Ordinance.

CHAP. VIII.
ANSWERS TO THE COMMON OBJECTIONS.

Such is the corruption of Mans heart, as he will make Objections against the [28] clearest Truth in the blessed Word of God; and which of the Truths of God, yea hath not God himself been objected against; but I may say of Baptism as once he said, *These things were not done in a Corner:*[50] I only give this Scripture caution, *They have closed their Eyes lest they should see and be converted, and I should heal them;*[51] take heed of closing the eyes, and then I am sure thou wilt be willing in the day of Gods power; but if in conscience thou desirest satisfaction, consider the answers to the following Objections.

Objeɑ. 1.

Some object where it is said, *Mat.* 28.19, 20. *To the end of the World,* that is, *to the end of that Age.*

Answ. I

To which I answer, this cannot be the sense of the Text; First, because Christ bids the Apostles teach them *to observe all things whatsoever I have commanded you, Mat.* 28.20. Now do you think that all things the Apostles

---

[49] Cornelius was a pious Roman centurion living in Caesarea, the Roman administrative center of Judaea. He sent for Peter, but Peter believed that it was "an unlawful thing for a man that is a Jew to keep company, or come unto one of another nation." Before Cornelius' messengers arrived, Peter had a vision from God that "hath shewed me that I should not call any man common or unclean. . . . Of a truth I perceive that God is no respecter of persons: But in every nation he that feareth him, and worketh righteousness, is accepted with him" (Acts 10:1-35).

[50] Defending himself before Herod Agrippa, the Roman puppet king of Judea, on a charge of causing a riot, Paul denied the charges and declared, "For the king knoweth of these things, before whom also I speak freely: for I am persuaded that none of these things are hidden from him; for this thing was not done in a corner" (Acts 26:26).

[51] Acts 28:27.

were to teach them to observe, was only to the end of that Age: Christ commands them to repent, to believe, to be holy, to be baptized; and are we to repent, believe, and be holy, to be baptized; and are we to repent, believe, and be holy, no longer then to the end of that Age. Secondly, Christ promises his Presence to the end of the World, [29] *Mat.* 28.20. *I will be with you to the end of the World.* Now hath Christ promised his Presence but to the end of that Age, this would be a dreadful Doctrine, *Josh.* 1.5. *He hath said, I will never leave thee, nor forsake thee*; so that the Promise of his Presence is to last in all Ages, as the word may be rendered. *I will be with you in Ages,* or, *to the end of the World*; therefore observe, *all things to the end of the World.*

Objeꝗ. 2.

2. *But Water-Baptism was* John's *Baptism.*

I Answer.

Was the Baptism of John from Heaven or of men? *John's* Baptism was from Heaven, *Mat.* 21.25. Then further, *John* was but to prepare Christs way before him, *Luk.* 1.16. *Thou shalt go before the face of the Lord, to prepare his ways*; so that *John* did but prepare Christs way: This therefore was Christs way, not *Johns* way: But further, hath not Christ commanded, and the Churches practised Baptism after *John's* death, and Christs Resurrection? did not Christ say, *Go Teach and Baptize*; and wilt thou say this is *John's* Baptism.

Objeꝗ. 3.

3. *But Circumcision and uncircumsion availeth nothing, but a new Creature.* [30]

I Answer.

Once Circumcision was something, when the Lord would have killed *Moses* because of the Circumcision; as *Exod.* 4.19[52] and when the Lord said, *That whoever was not circumcised, he should be cut off from the people*, Gen. 17.14. Now in the Gospel it is nothing, because abolished, *Gal.* 5.1. *If you be circumcised, Christ shall profit you nothing*; But wilt thou say the Councel of God is nothing? Baptism is the Councel of God, *Luke* 7.29. And is this

---

[52] This reference is off by a few verses. The account of the Lord's seeking to kill Moses because he had not circumcised his son Gershom is found in Exodus 4:24-26. Moses' wife Zipporah cut off Gershom's foreskin and threw it at the feet of Moses. The Lord then let Moses go.

nothing? Baptism is a Command of the Lord Jesus, *Mat.* 28.19, And is his Command nothing?

Objeft. 4.

4. *I am baptised with the Spirit, which is the substance; Water-baptism is but the shaddow.*

I Answer.

Thou mayst as well say so of all other Ordinances, they are but shaddows; the Supper is but a shadow: Prayer, Hearing and Preaching are but shaddows; And then whether wilt thou run? Then further, the Question is not whether it be a shaddow; Is it not a Command? If a Command, dispute not Christs Authority lest he be angry. But further, call Water-Baptism a shaddow, yet consider Christ subjected to it, and who art thou, wilt thou be wiser than Christ? And [31] further, *Acts,* 10.47. *They were Baptized with the Spirit and spake with Tongues,* and yet were Baptized in water. *Remember, he that is faithful in the least, is faithful in much.*

Objeft. 5.

5. *Doth not Baptism come in the room of*[53] *Circumcision?*

I Answer.

No surely, for there's not any Word of God for such a thing, and thou must not be wise above what it written, I. *Cor.* 4.6.[54] And then consider, Circumcision concerned only the Males; but *Acts* 8.12. *When they believed, they were Baptized, Men and Women.*

Objeft. 6.

6. *But are not very learned men for Infant-Baptism?*

I Answer.

Luke 7.29, 30. The Pharisees and Lawyers (the learned men) of the times rejected the Councel of God against themselves, not being Baptized. Do not say as they said, which of the Rulers have believed in him; Hearken to Christs Answer, *Mat.* 11.25. *Jesus answered, I thank thee, O Father, Lord of*

---

[53] I.e., "in the place of."

[54] Paul admonished the church in Corinth "that ye might learn in us not to think *of men* above that which is written, that no one of you be puffed up for one against another."

Heaven and Earth, that thou hast hid these things from the Wise and Prudent, and hast revealed them to Babes. And further, [32] If Learning were an Argument in this case, Are there not many Cardinals and Jesuits Learned men?[55]

Objeἀ. 7.

7. But are there not very Godly men, Pastors of Churches, that hold Infant-Baptism?

I Answer.

You are not to follow an Apostle further than he followeth Christ, I *Cor.* 11.1. *Follow me as I follow Christ.* Again, bring no Examples of good Men against an express word. You have an express word, *Acts* 8.12. *When they believed they were baptized, Men and Women. Elias* was a good man, he called fire from Heaven, but we must not do so.[56] *Jehosaphat* was a good King,[57] but the high places were not removed; follow no Example against a word, I *Kings* 22.42, 43. *Thou shalt not follow a multitude to do evil,* Exod. 23.2.

Objeἀ. 8.

8. But there's not a word against baptizing Infants?

I Answer.

Nadab and *Abihu* were burned with fire, because they did that the Lord commanded not, *Lev.* 10.2, 3. Again, if you mean by a word, an express word, then where have you a word, *Thou shalt not baptize Bells,*[58] as you [33] read in the Book of Martyrs[59] they did: Where have you a word saying,

---

[55] The implication here is that Cardinals and Jesuits (Catholics) were highly educated and yet, from a Protestant point of view, still misguided.

[56] Elias, also known as Elijah, called down fire from heaven in his challenge to the 450 prophets of Baal to show who the real Lord was. Then the prophets of Baal were killed. See 1 Kings 18:17-40.

[57] Jehosaphat (ca. 873–849 B.C.E.) reigned as king of Judah for about twenty-five years. "And he walked in all the ways of Asa his father; he turned not aside from it, doing *that which was* right in the eyes of the LORD: nevertheless the high places were not taken away; *for* the people offered and burnt incense yet in the high places" (1 Kgs 22:43). The "high places" were altars and poles on the tops of hills and mountains where people worshipped the gods Baal and El.

[58] Protestants, beginning with Martin Luther, denounced what they regarded as the "baptizing of bells" by Roman Catholics. The ritual was one of consecrating or dedicating bells before their use, but it never received an official sanction by the papacy.

[59] The Book of Martyrs was second only to the Bible in the English Puritan movement. Begun in 1552 by John Foxe and published first in 1563 as *Actes and Monuments of these Latter and Perillous Days, Touching Matters of the Church,* it particularly focused on Protestant martyrs, especially those executed during the reign of "Bloody" Mary, Queen of England

Thou shalt not use spittle, cream or salt in Baptism, as the *Roman* Catholicks do: But you must know, it is enough against Infant-Baptism, it is not commanded.

Objeĉt. 9.

9. *But were there not whole Families baptized?*

I Answer.

That it is expressly said, *They all believed,* Acts 16.33.[60] *He was baptized and all his.* And *ver.* 34. *They rejoyced, believing in God with all his house,* Acts 18.8. Crispus the *chief Ruler, believed in God with all his house; and many of the* Corinthians *believed and were baptized.* Lydia *and all her house were baptized:*[61] Here's no mention of Husband or Children, whether she was a Maid or a Widdow; only they are called Brethren, *ver.* 40.[62]

Objeĉt. 10.

10. *Infants were once Church-Members, and we do not find they were cut off?*

I Answer.

That the natural Branches were broken off by their unbelief; and if they come to believe, they may be graffed in again, but till then they are broken off, *Rom.* 11.20, 21. Again now in the Gospel, the Ax is laid to the root of the Tree; and every tree that [34] brings not forth good fruit, is cut down and cast into the fire, *Mat.* 3.9, 10. *Therefore you must not think to say you have* Abraham, *or a Believer, for your Father;* This is the sure Word of God. And thus you may see that the *Sadduces* were rejected when they came for Baptism, thinking to say, *They had Abraham for their Father,* Mat. 3.7, 8. And further, Infants were Members of the National Church of the Jews: But where were they ever Members of a particular Church under the Gospel: When Infants were Members, then servants that were bought with Money all were Members, *Gen.* 17.12. *Which is not of thy seed*: God

---

(1553–1558). The first edition had eighteen hundred pages, and the book grew in size in subsequent editions. It had a profound influence upon Protestant thinking about Roman Catholics for at least two centuries, and the book was added to and reprinted at least fifty-five times through to the nineteenth century.

[60] This quote comes from verse 34, not 33.

[61] Acts 16:15.

[62] Acts 16:40. Speaking of Paul's release from prison in Thyatira: "And they went out of the prison and entered into *the house of* Lydia: and when they had seen the brethren, they comforted them, and departed."

now in the Gospel seeks such to Worship him, who Worship him in Spirit and in Truth, *John* 4.23. And further, there was then a middle Wall of Partition; but this middle Wall of Partition is broken down, *Eph.* 2.14, And now God is no Respecter of Persons, but in every Nation such as fear him and work Righteousness, are accepted of him, *Acts* 10.38.[63]

Objeâ. 11.

11. *But is the Priviledge of Believers Children, less under the Gospel than it was under the Law?*

I Answer.

What dost thou mean by Priviledge? [35] was it a priviledge to be under the Law, or is it now a priviledge to be under the Gospel? or do'st thou mean by priviledge to have the Promises which the Apostle tell you of, *Rom.* 9.8. *They which are the Children of flesh, are not the Children of Promise*; or do'st thou mean by Priviledge to partake of the Visible Ordinance of Circumcision; And is this such a Priviledge which the Apostle, *Acts* 15.10. calls a yoke, that neither we nor our Fathers were able to bear, is this the Priviledge thou meanest?

Objeâ. 12.

12. *But the Seed was in Covenant? God made a Covenant with Abraham and his Seed.*

I answer

What dost thou mean by Covenant?[64] dost thou mean the Covenant that was made on Mount *Sinai*? a Covenant of Works;[65] dost thou mean the Covenant of grace,[66] wherein God promiseth to be their God? and dost

---

[63] This is probably a typesetter error; the correct citation is Acts 10:34.

[64] Covenant theology—the idea that God had always dealt with his people through various kinds of contracts and covenants that involved reciprocal obligations—was a central feature of Calvinist theology. John Norcott, John Eliot, and Roger Williams were all Calvinists and shared a belief in covenant theology.

[65] Calvinists held that the Covenant of Works was made between God and Adam in the Garden of Eden. If Adam obeyed the covenant, the reward was life. If he disobeyed, the punishment was death. He disobeyed, and all of humanity was cursed by the Fall of Adam. Nevertheless, the Covenant of Works remained as the moral law (especially as expressed in the Ten Commandments), and redemption from the effects of Adam's sin would come when someone lived a life of perfect obedience. Christ was sent to fulfill that role.

[66] The Covenant of Grace promised salvation and eternal life to those who were forgiven their sins by Christ.

thou make this Covenant of grace to be conditional? and dost thou judge, that *Ishmael*,[67] *Saul*,[68] and *Jeroboam* the son of *Nebat*,[69] and *Ahaz*,[70] and all they, were in the Covenant of grace? or dost thou judge they lost their interest in the Covenant of grace, and so indeed made it a Covenant of works. Therefore consider God did make a Cove-[36]nant with *Abraham* and his Seed, to give them the Land of *Canaan*. Gen. 17.7, 8. but as to the Promise of life and salvation, this was made to *Abraham* and his Seed, Gal. 3.16. *Now to* Abraham *and his Seed were the Promises made; he saith, not unto Seeds, as of many; but as of one, to they Seed, which is Christ.* if you will believe this Text, there's little difficulty in the Objection, *Rom.* 9.8. *The Children of Promise are counted for seed.*

Objeĉt. 13.

13. *But they were so far in the Covenant, as to give them a right to the Ordinance.*

I answer,

Circumcision was entailed on *Abraham* and his Seed, and his Servants; but where is Baptism entailed, upon Believers natural seed?

The Priesthood by a Covenant was entailed on the Tribe of *Levi* and their seed, as you may read, *Josh.* 1.8, 7.[71] *Num.* 25.13. will you now entail the Ministry on Preachers and their natural seed? But as to the point of Baptism, were there not many that came to be baptized; and *John* said,

---

[67] Ishmael was the son of Abraham by Sarah's handmaiden Hagar. Driven out by Sarah, Hagar and Ishmael fled into the desert and were told by an angel to return to Sarah and be submissive. The reward was "I would multiply thy seed exceedingly." However, when Isaac was born, Sarah demanded that Hagar and Ishmael be sent away again. Abraham agreed when the Lord told him, "And also of the son of the bondwoman will I make a nation, because he is thy seed." See Genesis 16:1-17; 21:9-21. The Arabs claim descent from Ishmael and the prophet Mohammed from the second son of Ishmael.

[68] Saul was the first king of Israel, but he disobeyed the Lord, who cursed him and said that he would lose his kingdom. Saul later killed himself after losing a battle against the Philistines. He was succeeded by David, whom Saul had sought to kill.

[69] Jeroboam, son of Nebat, had been in charge of slave labor for Solomon. After the death of Solomon, Jeroboam became king of the northern kingdom of Israel when Solomon's kingdom was split into Israel and Judah. Jeroboam set up golden calves to worship and forbade his subjects to worship in Jerusalem in the temple of Solomon. See 1 Kings 11:26-44; 12:1-3, 18, 27-30.

[70] Ahaz was a king of Judah who was described as exceedingly wicked and who aided in the destruction of the northern kingdom of Israel by calling for aid from and paying tribute to the Assyrian King Tiglath-Pileser III. See 2 Kings 15:9; 16:5; 2 Chronicles 28:19-21. When Ahaz died, "they brought him not into the sepulchers of the kings of Israel" (2 Chr 28:27).

[71] This is a typesetter error: it should be Joshua 18:7.

Think not to say you have Abraham *for your Father,* Mat. 3.9. clearly shewing, that their carnal right was cut off by the Gospel. Now [37] *the Axe is laid to the Root of the Tree, every Tree that bringeth not forth good fruit, is hewn down and cast into the fire.* And note further, Abraham had a word for to warrant his circumcising his seed; but where is there a word for Baptizing Infants.

Objeꝗ. 14

14. *But Christ said, suffer little Children to come to me, for of such is the Kingdom of Heaven.*

I answer,

The Text tells you plainly, they were not brought to be baptized, but that Christ might lay his hands on them, and pray for them, *Mat.* 19.13. *Mark* 10.16. Here's nothing of Baptism.

Objeꝗ. 15.

15. *But 'tis said,* Acts 2.39. *The Promise is to you and to your Children.*

I answer.

Do so much justice to thy own soul as to read the whole Text; and you shall finde, that it is said, *The Promises is to you and to your Children, and to all that are afar off, even so many as the Lord our God shall call*: Here you see it is to such as are called. Now if you say this word *Call* relates not to the Children, but to them that are afar off. I Answer, it must needs relate to the Children and their Parents, and all that afar off, be-[38]cause it is the Promise, *ver.* 16, 17. this is that which is spoken of by *Joel* the Prophet, *I will poure out of my Spirit on all flesh, on your sons and daughters,* Joel 1.28[72] *on the remnant whom the Lord shall call,* ver. 32.[73] Now if the Promise of the Spirit be to Children, though not called; then either the Promise doth fail; and that's a fearful thing to think; or else all the Children of Believers do partake of this glorious Spirit; but the contrary daily experience shews, that many of Believers Children are carnal, not having the Spirit; and it is fulfilled only to such whom the Lord our God shall call.

16. Objeꝗ.

16. *But I have been baptized in my Infancy, therefore what need I be baptized again?*

---

[72] Another possible typesetter error; it should be Joel 2:28.
[73] Joel 2:32.

I answer.

As one saith of Marriage, It is not the Bed that makes Marriage, for then Fornication is Marriage, but a lawful consent by Covenant, that makes Marriage. So I say of Baptism, it is not Water thrown on the face that makes Baptism; but it is a free consent and subjection to Christ according to the Rule, that makes Baptism; Now when thou wast an Infant thou gaveth no consent, thou canst not tell of any such thing but by report; thou knowest not when it was, thou hadst no Faith in the Act? *And whatever* [39] *is not of Faith is sin*, so that thou art not yet baptized. Again we finde, *Acts 19. begin.* there being a defect in their Baptism, they were baptized again; *They were baptized, saying, they should believe in one to come*; as *ver.* 4. whereas Christ was come, therefore they were baptized again, *ver.* 5 But what defects hath there been in they Infant-Baptism. First, there was no Rule to baptize thee while an Infant. Then thou wast not a right subject, for thou ought'st to believe and be baptized: then thou wast only sprinkled, not buried in Baptism, as Christ was and hath commanded; Now wilt thou call that Baptism which was only a Tradition received from thy fore-fathers, when the Lord Jesus did shed his most precious blood to redeem thee from the Tradition of thy forefathers, I *Pet.* 1.18, 19.

17. Object.

17. *But many lay so much stress on Baptism, as makes us more backward to it.*

I answer.

Is there more stress laid by any then by Christ, who said they rejected the Councel of God against themselves, not being baptized, *Luke* 7.29, 30. And is it not our duty *to contend for the faith once delivered to the Saints.* [40]

18. Object.

18. *But the Children of Believers are holy, therefore they ought to be baptized.*

I answer,

As it is said the Children are holy, so it is said the unbelieving Husband is holy, or sanctified by the believing Wife. This Holiness is wholly to the use of Marriage, for the Apostle is in that place, I *Cor.* 7. speaking of Marriage, and whether those who have believed should live with unbelieving Husbands, or put them away, as I. *Cor.* 7.13. So that the Holiness here spoken of, it is wholly to their use; it is said, *Zach.* 14.20. *There shall be Holiness on the Horses Bells, and every Pot in the Lords House shall be holy.*

Now do you think this was a sufficient warrant to baptize Bells, as you may read they did in the Book of Martyrs. But there is a being holy for the use of the Believer, as every creature is sanctified by the Word of God and Prayer; *And to the clean, all things are clean*,[74] that is, to their use: Thus Children are holy, and unbelieving Husbands are sanctified to their use; But if you think, Believers Children are inherently holy; doth not your experience tell you the contrary; do we not see good men have ungodly Children, and bad men have holy Children, so that they are only holy for their use, they [41] are not born in uncleanness.

19. Object.

19. *When they were formerly circumcised, Men of years were circumcised; but afterwards Infants were circumcised; so in the Gospel, when Baptism was first administred Men and Women were baptized, but afterwards Infants were baptized.*

I answer,

When God first commanded Circumcision he commanded that it should be administred to children, *Gen.* 17.10. *every Man-childe*; but when Christ commanded Baptism, he commanded that persons should be taught, and that they should believe and be baptized; and never gave a Command to baptize Children. Then consider we have the Lives and Acts of the Apostles and primitive Churches for divers years, and not one Infant baptized. *Paul* was converted some time after Christs Ascension, and was fourteen years in Christ, 2 *Cor.* 12.2. in these fourteen years surely some Children were born, yet not one baptized.

20. Object.

20. *These were Heathens that were baptized in the Apostle days.*

I answer.

Was the Lord Jesus a Heathen? he was baptized. The Eunuch a Worshipper to the [42] true God, *Cornelius*, a man whose Prayers and Alms came to God for a Memorial, were these Heathens: Nay, do not those who baptize Infants baptize Heathens, *Eph.* 2.3. *We are the children of wrath by Nature*: it is you that plead for the baptizing Heathens, we plead for the baptizing Believers.

---

[74] Titus 1:15 reads, "Unto the pure all things are pure."

21. Object.

21. But Paul *saith*, I Cor. 1.17. *Christ sent me not to baptize but to preach.*

I answer,

That *Paul* did baptize, I *Cor.* 1.14, 15. He baptized *Crispus* and *Gaius*, and the Household of *Stephanus*, and divers others. Now what he did, he did by Commission or Presumption; but he did it not by Presumption, therefore he did by Commission; he was sent to preach. Baptism fell in as part of his Preaching Office; *Philip* was chosen a Deacon, yet he baptized the Eunuch, Baptism fell in as part of his work, *Acts* 8. so that he that is called to be Preacher, needs no call to baptize, the other falls in as his work.

22. Object.

But there were three thousand baptized in one day, how could all these be dipped in one day, they might be sprinkled, but not dipped? [43]

I answer,

They might well be dipped, for there were twelve Apostles, and seventy Disciples, as *Luke* 10.1. that is eighty two; these might well baptize three thousand in a day. [44]

CHAP. IX.
BELIEVERS BAPTISM AND INFANT-BAPTISM COMPARED

1. Believers Baptism hath a Command, *Matt.* 28.19, 20.	1. *Infant-Baptism hath not a Command.*
2. Believers Baptism hath many Examples, *Acts* 8.12. *cap.*[75] 2.37, 41, 42; &c.	2. *Infant-Baptism hath no Example.*
3. Believers Baptism is from Heaven, *Mat.* 21.25.	3. *Infant-Baptism is from Men.*
4. Believers Baptism is the Councel of God, *Luke* 7.29, 30.	4. *Infant-Baptism hath the Councel of Men.*
5. Believers Baptism hath been gloriously sealed, *Mat.* 3.	5. *Infant-Baptism never was sealed by God.*

---

[75] Latin abbreviation for *capitulus*, "chapter."

6. In Believers baptism the person bap-[45]tized acts faith.

6. *But in Infant-Baptism, the Infant acts no faith.*

7. In Believers Baptism the Person subjects in acts of obedience.

7. *But in Infant-Baptism the Infant puts forth no Acts of Obedience.*

8. In Believers baptism the Person knows when he is baptized.

8. *But Infants know not any thing of their baptism.*

9. Believers remember when they were baptized.

9. *Infants remember not their baptism.*

10. Believers are buried with Christ by baptism, *Rom.* 6.3.

10. *Infants are not buried, they are only sprinkled.*

11. All believers that are baptized, are in the Covenant of grace.

11. *All Infants baptized are not in a Covenant of grace.*

12. All believers baptized receive remission of sins, *Acts* 2.37, 38.

12. *But all Infants baptized do not receive the remission of sins.*

[46]

13. God hath promised that all that believe and are baptized shall be saved, *Mark* 16.16.

13. *God hath not promised that all Infants that are baptized shall be saved.*

14. Believers rejoyce when they are baptized, *Acts* 8.16.

14. *Infants do not rejoyce, but usually weep when they aresprinkled.*

15. Believers baptism hath the plain Word of God, *Mat.* 11.19.

15. *Infant-baptism hath humane consequences only.*

16. All the world may undeniably affirm that believers were baptized by the Apostles, *Acts* 8.12.

16. *But all the world cannot affirm that any Infant was baptized by the Apostles.*

17. All those who baptize Infants, do confess Believers were baptized.

17. *But all that baptized believers do deny that Infants were baptized.*

18. Believers baptized do lawfully partake of the Lords Supper.

18. *Infants baptized do not lawfully partake of the Lords Supper.*

[47]

19. All believers baptized, are believing stones fit for Gods House, I *Pet.* 2.5.

19. *But all Infants baptized are not living stones fit for Gods House.*

20. Believers baptized, build on Christ by their own faith.

20. *But such as baptize Infants build on anothers faith.*

21. Such as are baptized on their own faith, shall never perish, *John* 10.28.

21. *But such as are baptized on anothers faith may perish.*

22. Believers baptized are converted, and shall never come into condemnation. *John* 5.24.

22. *But Infants baptized are not converted, and may come into condemnation.*

23. Believers baptized are not the Children of wrath, *John* 3.36.

23. *But Infants baptized,* John *3.36 may be yet under wrath.*

24. Believers baptized do know Christ to be precious, I *Pet.* 2.7.

24. *But Infants baptized, do not know Christ to be precious.*

[48]

25. Believers love Christ, and keep his Commandments *John* 14.15.

25. *But Infants baptized do not love Christ and keep his Commandments.*

26. Believers baptized, worship God in spirit and in truth, and such God seeks to worship him, *John* 4.23, 24.

26. *But Infants do not know what to worship.*

27. Believers Baptism must stand as long as Gods Word doth stand, *Mat* 5.18.

27. *Infant-Baptism must fall, because it hath not the Word of God.*

28. Believers baptized may repel Satan as Christ did, saying it is written, *They believed and were baptized.*

28. *But you cannot repel Satan, saying, It is written, Infants were baptized; for it is not written.*

CHAP. X.
PLAIN SCRIPTURES CONCERNING BAPTISM, WITHOUT ANY HUMANE CONSEQUENCE FROM MANS WISDOM.

Mat. 3.13. Then cometh Jesus to *John* to be baptized, *ver.* 15. And [49] Jesus said, Suffer it to be so now, for thus it becometh us to fulfill all Righteousness, *ver.* 16. And Jesus when he was baptized went up straitway out of the water.

Mat. 21.25. The Baptism of *John*, whence was it, from Heaven or of Men; if we say from Heaven, he will say why did ye not believe in him?

Luke 20.6. But if we say of men, the people will stone us.

Luke 7.29. The Publicans justified God being baptized.

Ver. 30. But the Pharisees and Lawyers rejected the Councel of God against themselves, not being baptized.

Mat. 28.19. Go teach all Nations, baptizing them in the Name of the Father, and of the Son, and of the Holy Ghost.

Acts 2.38. Repent and be baptized every one of you in the Name of Jesus Christ.

Acts 2.41. Then they that gladly received his Word were baptized.

Mark 16.16. He that believeth and is baptized shall be saved.

Acts 8.12. And when they believed they were baptized, both men and women.

Acts 8.36. And the Eunuch said, here is water, what doth hinder me to be baptized

Acts 8.37. And *Philip* said, if thou believest thou mayst. [50]

Acts 8.38. And they went both down into the water, both *Philip* and the Eunuch, and he baptized him.

Acts 9.18. *Saul* arose and was baptized.

John 3.22. After these things came Jesus and his disciples into the Land of *Judea,* and there he tarried and baptized.

John 4.1. Jesus made and baptized more disciples than *John.*

Acts 10.47. Can any man forbid water that these should not be baptized, that have received the Holy Ghost as well as we.

Acts 10.48. And he commanded them to be baptized in the Name of the Lord.

Acts 18.8. And *Crispus* the chief Ruler of the Synagogue believed on the Lord, with all his house, and many of the *Corinthians* hearing, believed and were baptized.

Acts 22.16. And now why tarriest thou, arise and be baptized, and wash away thy sins, calling on the Name of the Lord.

Rom. 6.4. We are buried with him by Baptism.

Gal. [3.]27. As many as have been baptized into Christ, have put on Christ.

I *Pet.* 3.21. The like Figure whereunto Baptism doth save us.

I *Cor.* 12.13. By one spirit we are all baptized into one body.

Acts 16.33. And he took them the same [51] hour of the night, and washed their stripes, and was baptized, he and all his straitway.

Ver. 34. He believing in God with all his House.

Luke 3.21. Jesus being baptized, the Heavens were opened.

Luke 3.23. And Jesus himself being about thirty years of Age.

John 3.23. *John* was baptizing in *Aenon,* near *Salem,* because there was much water.

CHAP. XI.
CONSIDERATIONS BY WAY OF CONCLUSION.

1. Consider that when souls are ashamed, then God will shew them the Ordinances and formes of his House, *Ezek.* 43.11. The Gospel-Church hath its formes.

2. Consider when God gives any soul a new heart, it is to fit him for Gods Ordinances, *Ezek.* 11.19, 20. *I will give them a new spirit, and I will take away the heart of stone, and give them a heart of flesh, that they may walk in my Statutes, and keep my Ordinances, and do them.* [52]

3. Consider what danger it is to resist an Ordinance of God; read *Rom.* 13.2. *Luke* 7.29, 30. they rejected the Councel of God, not being baptized.

4. Consider what Judgments have attended the changing of Gods Ordinances, *Isa.* 24.1. *Behold, the Lord maketh the Earth empty, and turneth it upside down*; there's a change, but why, *ver.* 5. *They have changed the Ordinance*; when Christ commands *Believe and be baptized*; and men baptize Infants who do not believe, whether this be a change of the Ordinance, judge ye.

5. Consider, what fell on *Nadab* and *Abihu* the sons of *Aaron.* Lev. 10.1, 2. They offered what the Lord commanded not: it was not forbidden; but that's not enough, 'twas not commanded; Infant-Baptism is not forbidden, but it is what the Lord commanded not.

6. Consider, That where was an Error in Baptism, there you shall find persons baptized again: Consult *Acts* 19.1, 2, 3, 4, 5, 6. Now if in thy Infant-Baptism thou wast not a right subject, nor was in the right form, then thou oughtest to be baptized again. [53]

7. Consider if what thou didst receive in thy Infancy was no Baptism, and thou hast not been baptized since, then thou livest in the neglect of a great Gospel-Ordinance: wilt thou call that Obedience which was not thy Act, and had not thy consent, nor thou knowest not of, nor canst remember when it was done, and thou hadst no faith in; and wilt thou call that Baptism that was not of thy obedience, but thy Parents will.

8. Consider that the Ordinances must be kept as they were delivered, I. *Cor.* 11.2, But Baptism was delivered to Believers and not to Infants. God did indeed deliver Circumcision to Infants but never did deliver Baptism to Infants.

9. Consider, that many who have not been baptized since they believed, do deny Baptism to their children: Let me ask such, if their own Infant-Baptism was sufficient to them, if they do deny it to their children, why do they reckon their own Infant-Baptism sufficient.—*How long halt ye between two opinions.*

10. Consider, that it is without all doubt Believers were baptized, *Acts* 8.12. The baptizing of Infants at the best is but a doubt; Infant Baptism hath been often disputed, but when was Believers Baptism disputed. It is in very words exprest, *They believed and* [54] *were baptized.* Now is it not better to go in an undoubted way, then in a dark way.

11. Consider, there are multitudes of Examples of Believers Baptism; see page 11 of this Book; but there's not one Example of Infant-baptism.

12. Consider if the salvation of thy soul did lie upon this question, Whether were believers baptized, or were Infants baptized? wouldest thou not say, surely believers.

13. Consider, as Birth-right gave a right to Circumcision under the Law, so Birth-right gave right to the Priesthood. .

Now you would entail Baptism without a word to the believes seed, why then will you not entail the Ministry unto the seed of Ministers— Would it not be strange Logick, to say, the Preachers seed under the Gospel, have less priviledge then the Priests under the Law.

13.[76] Consider, that we are not to think of any above what is written, 1 *Cor.* 4.6. Now if Infant-Baptism be not written as an Ordinance, do not judge it to be an Ordinance.

15. Consider that Christ was faithful in all his House, *Heb.* 3.5, 9.[77] If it had been his Fathers Will that Infants should have been baptized; surely he would have been so faithful as to have left us one word in his blessed Scriptures. [55]

16. Consider, *Moses* the servant of the Lord did all according to the Pattern shewed in the Mount, *Exod.* 25. *ver. last*[78] and shall not the servants of the Lord do all according to the Pattern he hath shewed us in the New Testament; the Pattern left on record is, *They believed and were baptized,* Acts 8.12.

17. Consider, whether those who do so depend on their consequences without a plain Text, will grant Papists[79] and others the same consequences, for Altars, Surplices, &c. seeing all is to be done decently; And they say, Surplices are decent; Railes about the Tables are decent, &c.[80]

---

[76] This item is misnumbered; it should be 14.

[77] Typesetter error; the correct citation is Hebrews 3:5, 6.

[78] The last verse in Exodus 25 is verse 40. The "Mount" referred to in this verse is Mount Sinai, where Moses received the Ten Commandments and the Law.

[79] Roman Catholics.

[80] The Puritans had sought to eliminate altars and altar rails, genuflecting and crossing oneself, surplices and other vestments, crosses, candles, icons and images, the veneration of the Virgin Mary, praying to saints, observation of saints' days, the liturgical calendar (including Christmas, Easter, and Whitsuntide [Pentecost]), the sacramental system, the use of the Common Book of Prayer, or anything else that they could find no "plain Text"

18. Consider, that seeing the Scripture is so exact, in setting down the several circumstances of persons baptized, *Acts* 16.13,14. the time, *the Sabbath*, the place, *by a River-side*; the Custom, *Prayer was wont to be made*; the Company, *Women*; the Name, *Lydia*; the Trade, *a Seller of Purple*; place of abode, *at the city of* Thyatira; her Religion, *a Worshipper of God*; her Action, *She heard Gods Word; the Lord opened her heart*; the Instrument, *words spoken by* Paul. So *Acts* 16.27, 28, 29, 30. so many circumstances, but not one word in any place expressed, that ever any Infant was baptized; why should it be left out, were it Gods Will it should be done. [58][81]

19. Consider, *there is but one Lawgiver who is able to save and to destroy*, James 4.12. *The Lord is our Judge, the Lord is our Lawgiver*, Isa. 33.22. Now where hath this Lord given a Law for baptizing Infants? This one Lawgiver hath not given one Law for the baptizing Infants.

20. Consider, whether baptizing Infants, Godfathers and Godmothers, the Cross in Baptism, the Promises and Vows made for Children, were not all brought in by human Inventions, at the same time or on the same Reasons?

21. Consider, whether it be safe to admit of Consequences against an express Rule, *Mat.* 28.19. *Teach and baptize.*

22. Consider, whether those who baptize Infants, will not have it said to them by the Lord one day, as in *Isa* 1.12. *Who hath required these things at your hands.*

23. Consider, whether any of the Gospel Ordinances hath so many plain words as Believers Baptism.

24. Consider, whether being baptized be not a justifying God, and on thy part thou not being baptized, dost not reject the Council of God, *Luke* 7.29, 30.

25. Consider, whether such as hold Infant-baptism do not preach Baptism to be a Sign of Regeneration, and whether all or any Infants baptized are regenerated. [59]

26. Consider, whether those who have not respect to all Gods Commands will not one day be ashamed, *Psal.* 119.6.

27. Consider, whether Abraham durst circumcise his child without a word of Command, then how durst thou baptize a child without a word.

28. Consider, whether we are not to press after the purity of Ordinances, and whether those Ordinances which have the expresse Rule, are not most pure.

---

in the Bible requiring or suggesting them. See Patrick Collinson, *The Elizabethan Puritan Movement* (London: Jonathan Cape, 1967), 36.

[81] The last two pages are misnumbered and should be pp. 56 and 57.

29. Consider, whether they and only they shall not have the Well-done at Christs coming, who have done what he hath commanded, and as he hath commanded.

Now I beseech thee to consider what hath bin said in this matter; And the glorious God of Truth give thee the Spirit of Truth, which may lead thee into all Truth, and may build thee up, and give thee an Inheritance among them that are sanctified; and as in sincerity, with unfeigned love to God and thy soul, these things have been written. So the very God and Father of our Lord Jesus, sanctifie thee throughout, in body, soul and spirit, and give thee a heart to search whether these things be so.

FINIS

IV

JOHN ELIOT

A Brief Answer to a Small Book Written by John Norcot Against Infant-Baptisme (1679)

John Eliot (1604-1690) was born in Widford, Hertfordshire, England, one year after James I came to the throne. Eliot received his B.A. from Jesus College, Cambridge, in 1622. After a brief stint as the assistant of a school run by the Puritan minister Thomas Hooker in Little Baddow in the late 1620s, he emigrated to Boston in New England in 1631, following an increasingly steady flow of ministers and parishioners who sought to escape pressure to conform to the Church of England. In New England, Eliot first served as the minister of the First Church in Boston in the absence of Rev. John Wilson (a position Roger Williams had declined), but when Wilson returned the following year, Eliot accepted a call to serve as the teaching elder at the Roxbury Congregational Church, a position he held for the rest of his life. Eliot also became involved in the civic and ecclesiastical affairs of the colony, participating in the trial and banishment of Anne Hutchinson and writing a defense of the Massachusetts Bay Colony's actions in the banishment of Roger Williams.[1]

Starting in the 1640s, Eliot began to learn the Massachusett language in order to preach to local Native groups, which he did in the late summer and fall of 1646. These early, feeble attempts quickly grew, along with evangelistic efforts on Martha's Vineyard by Thomas Mayhew Jr. and Sr. at the same time, into a much-publicized and well-financed missionary enterprise by the early 1650s. In 1649 Parliament created the Society for the Propagation of the Gospel in New England, which was rechartered in

---

[1] On Eliot's written defense of Williams' banishment, see Richard W. Cogley, *John Eliot's Mission to the Indians Before King Philip's War* (Cambridge, Mass.: Harvard University Press, 1999), 47.

1662 as the Company for the Propagation of the Gospel in New England and Parts Adjacent (usually referred to as the New England Company, or NEC). This missionary organization, which was based in London and received most of its funding from humanitarians in Old England, served as the primary source of support for Eliot and other New England missionaries to Natives throughout the colonial period.[2] Between the 1640s and his death in 1690, Eliot devoted substantial time to growing a widespread missionary enterprise to New England's Natives.[3] Working in conjunction with regional ministers, magistrates, and lay volunteers, along with Native sachems, students, and laypersons, Eliot helped to craft an enterprise that sought to civilize and christianize Natives by encouraging them to live in separate "praying towns" and adopt various elements of Anglo-European culture, such as living in wood frame houses, wearing English clothing, adopting European gender work norms, and (for men) cutting their hair short. The praying town of Natick, Massachusetts, was founded in 1651 with these goals in mind; by 1674, an additional thirteen such towns were also scattered across eastern Massachusetts and northeastern Connecticut.[4]

The progress of Indian evangelization was broadcast widely through a series of promotional treatises known to historians as the "Eliot tracts." These eleven publications between 1643 and 1671 reported the progress of Indian evangelization to an interested audience in England, often with a combination of optimism and surprising candor. Starting in the early 1650s, Eliot also worked with several Native servants and students to produce a phoneticized written version of the Massachusett language. In addition to publishing several works of devotional piety and catechisms, Eliot's crowning achievement was the publication of the entire Bible in the Massachusett language in 1663.[5]

---

[2] For more on the founding of the New England Company, see Cogley, *John Eliot's Mission*, 70-71. For the activity of the NEC in the eighteenth century, see Linford D. Fisher, *The Indian Great Awakening: Religion and the Shaping of Indian Cultures in Early America* (New York: Oxford University Press, 2012), chap. 2; William Kellaway, *The New England Company, 1649–1776: Missionary Society to the American Indians* (London: Longmans, 1961).

[3] The most authoritative history of Eliot's mission is Cogley, *John Eliot's Mission*. For a more recent interpretation and contextualization in the larger missionary enterprise of the colonial period, see Julius H. Rubin, *Tears of Repentance: Christian Indian Identity and Community in Colonial Southern New England* (Lincoln: University of Nebraska Press, 2013).

[4] For a long-term study of Natick, see Jean M. O'Brien, *Dispossession by Degrees: Indian Land and Identity in Natick, Massachusetts, 1650–1790* (New York: Cambridge University Press, 1997).

[5] John Eliot, *Mamusse Wunneetupanatamwe Up-Biblum God Naneeswe Nukkone Testament Kah Wonk Wusku Testament* (Cambridge [Mass.], 1663). For a full listing of the Indian-language

Although thousands of New England Natives associated themselves in some way with Eliot's missionary program (through education or church membership), the civilization and evangelization of Natives was resented and doubted by English and Indians alike. Missionary efforts among the Wampanoags (and the cultural changes that ensued) were partly responsible for the massive conflict between many Indian groups and the New England colonists in King Philip's War (1675–1676). The war hampered the evangelization process, but under Eliot's guidance and with ongoing funding from the NEC, the evangelization and education of New England Natives continued through Eliot's lifetime and, indeed, throughout the entire eighteenth century as well.

Eliot composed his response to John Norcott regarding baptism late in his energetic and prolific life. Aside from materials related to Indian evangelization, Eliot published only a few more works, including the ill-timed antimonarchy text *The Christian Commonwealth* (1659), *The Communion of Churches* (1665), and *The Harmony of the Gospels* (1678). Despite the relative popularity of his missionary tracts, Eliot's response to Norcott was only published once and subsequent references to it were rare.[6] Historians have known about the text, despite its rather thin readership over time. Many biographers and historians chose to focus on his missionary program, starting with the famed Boston minister Cotton Mather, whose biography of Eliot titled *The Life and Death of the Renown'd Mr. John Eliot* started a long hagiographical tradition that was only seriously challenged in the twentieth century.[7]

---

books and tracts, see "Books and Tracts in the Indian Language or Designed for the Use of Indians, Printed at Cambridge and Boston, 1653–1721," *Proceedings of the American Antiquarian Society* 61 (1873): 45–62.

[6] John Wilson, *The Life of John Eliot, the Apostle of the Indians: Including Notices of the Principal Attempts to Propagate Christianity in North America, During the Seventeenth Century* (Edinburgh, 1828), 224.

[7] Cotton Mather, *The Life and Death of the Renown'd Mr. John Eliot, Who Was the First Preacher of the Gospel to the Indians in America with an Account of the Wonderful Success Which the Gospel Has Had Amongst the Heathen in That Part of the World, and of the Many Strange Customs of the Pagan Indians in New-England* (London: Printed for John Dunton, 1691).

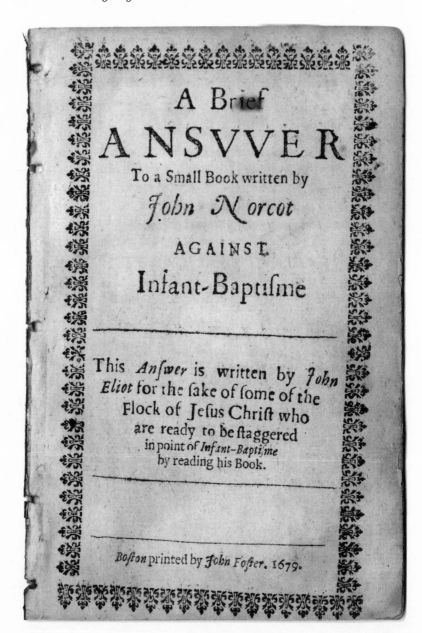

FIGURE 42

John Eliot, A Brief Answer to a Small Book Written by John Norcot Against Infant-Baptisme *title page. Courtesy of The Lilly Library, Indiana University, Bloomington, Ind.*

A Brief

ANSWER

To a Small Book written by

JOHN NORCOT[8]

AGAINST

Infant-Baptisme

This *Answer* is written by *John
Eliot* for the sake of some of the
Flock of Jesus Christ who
are ready to be staggered
in point of *Infant-Baptisme*
by reading his Book.

Boston printed by *John Foster.* 1679.

[8] John Norcott, *Baptism Discovered Plainly and Faithfully, According to the Word of God* (London, 1672).

[1]⁹

A brief Answer to a small Book written by John Norcot, against Infant Baptism.

This Answer is written by John Eliot for
the sake of some of the flock of Jesus
Christ, who were ready to be staggered in the point of Infant Baptism, by reading that Book.

The Book speaketh with the voice of a Lamb, and I think the Author is a godly though erring Brother; but he acteth the cause of the roaring Lyon, who will by all crafty wayes seeketh to devour the poor Lambs of the flock of Christ.¹⁰ The chief hinge that the whole discourse hangeth upon is, that there is no place of Scripture for baptizing Infants.

I will therefore begin there, to stop the gain-saying mouth of this Book.

The baptizing of Believers and their Infants was one of the first Gospel Apostolical Institutions commanded in the Gospel politie, *Acts* 2.37, 38, 39. when those heart pricked penitent Jews solemnly asked touching the great change of Church Polity that was now in motion, *what shall we do?* or how shall we engage our selves into this new Polity? this is one part of their question, as it appeareth by the Answer. The Apostle answered them, *ver.* 38, 39.¹¹ the substance and sense of which words in respect of our question is thus formed.

Every one of you to whom the promise belongeth, we do order and appoint you to be baptized.

But the promise belongeth to all you penitent believers and to your Children. [2]

Therefore we order and appoint all you penitent Believers and your Children to be baptized, consider the words.

Some Gentile Believers, or the Apostle himself on their behalf, further promoteth the same question, touching them that were afar off, *viz.* in respect of Church state, and Interest in the promise. What shall they do that have no Interest in the promise? being afar off, in respect of the Covenant, and afar off in place also, as the Gentile Nations were.

---

⁹ Bracketed numbers throughout are the original page numbers in Eliot, *A Brief Answer.*

¹⁰ Alluding to I Peter 5:8: "Be sober, be vigilant; because your adversary the devil, as a roaring lion, walketh about, seeking whom he may devour."

¹¹ "Then Peter said unto them, Repent, and be baptized every one of you. . . . For the promise is unto you, and to your children, and to all that are afar off, even as many as the Lord our God shall call" (Acts 2:38-39).

The Apostle answereth, that we order the same Law and Institution to all, *viz. whom the Lord our God shall call*;[12] when the Lord our God shall call any of the Gentiles to be penitent Believers, as now you Jews be, then the promise doth belong unto them, and unto rheir[13] Infants; and we do order, that they and their Infants shall be baptized, and marked for the Lambs of Christ, that do belong to his Fold.

Behold here a clear Gospel Institution of baptizing Believers and their Infants, in all the Gospel Churches be they Jews or Gentiles. All endeavours of an Answer to this Text do only mud the waters to hinder a clear sight of the Truth that shineth in the words.

As we see a clear precept for Infant Baptism, so I shall shew a clear practice and example of it, *Act.* 2.41. *then they that gladly received his Word were baptized*, viz they and their Children were baptized. For I ask, did they receive the whole Word of Apostolical Institution? or only a part of the Word? sure you will say, they received the whole Word of Institution, therefore these Believers and their Children first or at last were baptized. Had the believing parents only been baptized, and left out their Children, then they had received but part of the Word of Institution. So then, here we behold a famous example, according to which all the Gospel Churches have walked ever since unto this day, and [3] that without interruption, saving that sometime some small interruption hath been made by the Anabaptists[14] that deny or have questioned Infant Baptisme.

Baptisme is the seal of the Covenant, whomsoever God doth receive into Covenant with him, they have a fundamental right in due order to receive the Seal, the Seal is so annexed to the Covenant, that it is called the Covenant, *Gen.* 17.13.[15] now God doth receive the Children of Believers into Covenant, *Acts* 2.38, 39, the *promise doth belong to you and to your Children*, and therefore the Seal doth belong unto them.

Math. 3.15. *So it becometh us to fulfil all Righteousness*, saith Christ, who are meant by (*us*) of whom Christ speaketh? *Answ.* He speaketh firstly of himself, and *John*, then of all his Church and members thereof. Therefore as it was meet and righteous for Christ the Head to fulfil that Law and

---

[12] Acts 2:38-39.

[13] Typesetter error: should be "their."

[14] Eliot refers to Baptists such as Norcott as "Anabaptists," a term intended to discredit the Baptists by tying them to the radicalism of some branches of sixteenth-century Anabaptism in continental Europe. Baptists themselves strenuously rejected the label.

[15] God, speaking to Abraham and ordering him to keep the covenant, commanded in this verse, "He that is born in thy house, and he that is bought with thy money, must needs be circumcised; and my covenant shall be in your flesh for an everlasting covenant." Eliot argued that just as circumcision was the seal of the covenant with Jews, baptism was the seal of the covenant for Christians.

Institution of God in being baptized; so it is meet that every member of the Church of Christ should in due order do the same, it is righteous that it should be so. Now Infants of Believers are members of the Church of Christ, the Covenant comprehends them, the promise belongeth unto them, and therefore they ought in due order to be baptized.

Mark. 10.14. But when Jesus saw it, he was much displeased, and said unto them, *suffer the little Children to come unto me, and forbid them not, for of such is the Kingdome of God*, Christ saith that the Kingdome of God both Militant & Triumphant doth consist of many such members, how come they into the Church?

Answ. God doth admit them by his Institution into his Covenant, *Ge.* 17.7. *a God unto thee and to thy Seed after thee* and the Church doth solemnly receive them by Baptism.

Quest. How can the Church receive them, when they do not know them to be fit matter for the Church?

Answ. The Church may lawfully admit unto Communion in all the Ordinances upon sufficient Testimony, [4] as *Acts* 9 26, 27, 28. The Primitive Church admitted *Saul* upon the Testimony of *Barnabas*.[16] Now for the admitting of Infants we have the best and greatest Testimony in the World, that they are fit matter for the Church, and that they are duly and acceptibly qualified: for we have the Testimony of God, the Father, and of the Son, and of the Holy Ghost. I have more boldness of Faith in receiving Infants into the Communion of the Church, then up-grown persons, whom we have most accurately tryed, because our Infants are received upon divine Testimony, others though we admit them according to divine Institution, yet upon more inferior Testimony.

Rom. 11.16. *If the first fruits be holy, the lump is also holy, if the Root be holy, so are the branches also.* A Believer and his Children are but one lump, in his Church station, the believing Parents sanctifie the whole household, who are under the Parents tuition, a Believer and his Children are but one Tree in the Church or Vineyard of the Lord, and when the Root is holy, the whole Tree, all the branches are holy, this is the Ecclesiastical state of all believers. Hence therefore we ought to receive all the Infants of believers unto Communion in the Church, according to their Capacities. Now Infants are capable of Communion with the Church in Baptisme: which doth most evidently appear in the Church of the Jews, where they were

---

[16] When Saul/Paul returned to Jerusalem after his Damascus-road conversion, those in Jerusalem "were all afraid of him and believed not that he was a disciple. But Barnabas took him, and brought *him* to the apostles, and declared unto them how he had seen the Lord in the way, and that he had spoken to him, and how he had preached boldly at Damascus in the name of Jesus" (Acts 9:26b-27).

capable of Circumcision, and were admitted into the Communion of the Church therein, and the Apostles were wont to baptize all the Houshold, when the Parents believed. The Lord doth account them visible Believers that are branches of a believing Root, and giveth that Testimony of them. And God who appointed it, best knoweth what is acceptable to himself. The present administration of Baptisme to Infants is a present exercise of Faith, love and duty in all the Church, and especially in the Parents, and [5] it is an after exercise of Faith, love, and duty in the Child, when he is grown up to years of capacity, and as long as he liveth his Baptismal Covenant christianly improved upon him, doth very powerfully by the assistance of the Spirit oblige him to walk as becometh a child of the Lord, and prepareth him for confirmation, in laying hold on the Covenant of God by his own choice, consent, and act. There is a passive reception of Christ and his Kingdome, which Infants are capable of: in which act of grace adult up grown persons must humble themselves to become like Infants, *Mark.* 10.15. *whosoever shall not receive the Kingdome of God as a little child shall not enter thereinto.* If then God knoweth how to have, and exercise such spiritual Communion with Infants, who are we that we should keep them from him when he calleth for them? and hath instituted an Ordinance for that use and end, *Mark.* 10. 14. I return to this Text where Christ saith, *suffer little Children to come unto me, and forbid them not, for of such is the Kingdome of God.* The instituted ordinary way of little childrens coming to Christ is by Baptisme, there coming at this time, instanced in this Text was for his blessing, that was their end at that time, but on that occasion Christ treateth upon the doctrine of Infants coming to Christ, and Christ commanded that it should be so, and hath instituted an ordinary means whereby they may come unto him, and that is by Baptisme, as in the old Church they did by Circumcision. This command of Christ, for Childrens coming to him is of force to this day, and will be to the worlds end, and therefore it doth not intend only a personal coming to the bodily presence of Christ, as at that time, but Christ intends the visible, external instituted way of Infants coming to Christ, this we are commanded to suffer, the Elders and the Church are commanded by Christ to suffer Infants to come to him, the means of their coming to Christ is by Baptisme[.] [6] Christ is so serious and earnest in this matter, as that he expresseth this precept both affirmatively (*suffer them*) and negatively, *forbid them not.* This word speaketh directly and home unto the opposers of Infant Baptisme, Christ hath forbidden you to be an hindrance to them, by word, speech, writing, power, or any other way, *forbid them not.*

And the Lord is so full in the stream of this Command to suffer them, and of his forbidding us, to forbid or hinder them, that he doth urge it with a great Reason, *viz. of such is the Kingdome of God*; the militant Church consisteth of many such members, half our Churches are Infants, and what? will you not suffer Christ to have Communion with them, nor them to have Communion with Christ by the Ordinance which Christ hath appointed for it? the Kingdome of Heaven hath many Infants in it, and shall Christ have Communion with them in Heaven, and will you not suffer him to have Communion with them on Earth in the visible Church when he requireth it?

Yea, this point is several times instanced and repeated in the Gospel, to shew, how much the heart of Christ is upon this point. Yea, this Text saith that Christ was very much displeased with his Disciples upon this occasion, it is very seldome that Christ expressed himself displeased with them (about twice) and this was one of the times, and the occasion of it.

Joh. 21.15.[17] Christ hath appointed it as one great part of our Ministerial charge to feed the little Lambs, so the word signifieth, the Infants being part of them, how can we feed Infants? surely by administering Baptisme unto them, for Infants are capable of this instituted way of feeding, this Text is a strong evidence, Christ hath made the little Lambs the Subjects of Ecclesiastical Ministerial feeding, therefore no doubt the Lord hath instituted some publick Ordinance, that they are capable to be fed [7] withal, and that is Baptisme, Infants are secondarily fed by feeding their Parents, but they are personally fed by Baptisme, and constantly.

From the first Creation of man God hath transacted with man by a Covenant, and hath always comprehended the Parents and children together in his Covenant, thus it was with *Adam* in innocencey, the children of *Adam* were comprehended with him in the Covenant of works,[18] as we know by woeful Experience. After the fall, God brought Adam under the Covenant of grace in Christ,[19] and in that Covenant he comprehended his Seed with him. When God called *Abraham*, he brought him under a Covenant, and comprehended his Seed with him, *I am thy God, and thy Childrens God*. And that was our Gospel Covenant, touching

[17] "So when they had dined, Jesus saith to Simon Peter, Simon, son of Jonas, lovest thou me more than these? He saith unto him, Yea, Lord; thou knowest that I love thee. He saith unto him, Feed my lambs" (John 21:15).

[18] The Covenant of Works was made between God and Adam in the Garden of Eden. If Adam obeyed the covenant, the reward was life. If he disobeyed, the punishment was death. He disobeyed, and all of humanity was cursed by the Fall of Adam. Nevertheless, the Covenant of Works remained as the moral law, especially as expressed in the Ten Commandments.

[19] The Covenant of Grace promised salvation and eternal life to those who were forgiven their sins by Christ.

which the Apostle saith, *the promise belongeth to you and to your Children,*[20] and thus it is with all the Gospel Churches, both Jews and Gentiles, even with all Believers, *whom the Lord our God shall call.* And it is the Infinite mercy of God to bind himself to us by Covenant, both to strengthen our weak Faith, and that his Covenant mercy might bind and stay the revenging hand of Justice from destroying us for our iniquities. God remembreth his Covenant and therefore spareth us and our children, as we may see, *Psal.* 105. 8, 9, 10.[21] and *ver.* 40, 41, 42.[22] and *Psal.* 106. 43, 44, 45.[23] and *Psal.* 89.30, 31, 32, 33, 34.[24] be thankful therefore to God for his Covenant with us, and with our children, exclude them not from this great mercy.

I *Cor.* 7.14.[25] It seemeth some in *Corinth* doubted whether the children of such Parents were in Covenant with God, and to be received by the Church, when only one of the Parents was a believer, the other wicked, a Pagan, and it is like it was a frequent case, sometimes the husband was converted and not the wife, sometimes the wife was converted, and not the husband: and this case might well come into question, by reason of that ancient fam-[8]ous practice of *Ezra,* and the Jewish Church.[26]

---

[20] These were not quotations, but were Eliot's summary of God's covenant with Abraham. See Genesis 12:2, 7; Genesis 13:15-18; Genesis 15:7, 18; and especially Genesis 17:7.

[21] "He hath remembered his covenant for ever, the word *which* he commanded to a thousand generations. Which *covenant* he made with Abraham, and his oath unto Isaac; And confirmed the same unto Jacob for a law, *and* to Israel *for* an everlasting covenant" (Ps 105:8-10).

[22] "*The people* asked, and be brought quails, and satisfied them with the bread of heaven. He opened the rock, and the waters gushed out; they ran in the dry places *like* a river. For he remembered his holy promises, *and* Abraham his servant" (Ps 105:40-42).

[23] "Many times did he deliver them; but they provoked *him* with their counsel, and were brought low for their iniquity. Nevertheless he regarded their affliction, when he heard their cry: And he remembered for them his covenant, and repented according to the multitude of his mercies" (Ps 106:43-45).

[24] "If his children forsake my law, and walk not in my judgments; If they break my statutes, and keep not my commandments; Then will I visit their transgressions with the rod, and their iniquity with stripes. Nevertheless my lovingkindness will I not utterly take from him, nor suffer my faithfulness to fail. My covenant will I not break, nor alter the thing that is gone out of my lips" (Ps 89:30-34).

[25] "For the unbelieving husband is sanctified by the wife, and the unbelieving wife is sanctified by the husband: else were your children unclean; but now they are holy" (I Cor 7:14).

[26] See Ezra 9-10. When the Babylonian Captivity ended and the Hebrews returned to Palestine, they found that the people who had not been carried into captivity had intermarried with non-Hebrew people (Canaanites, Hittites, Jebusites, Moabites, Egyptians, etc.), committing an "abomination." "And when I heard this thing, I rent my garment and my mantle, and plucked off the hair of my head and of my beard, and sat down astonished" (Ezra 9:3). The men confessed, "We have trespassed against our God, and have taken strange wives of the people of the and. . . . Now make a covenant with our God to put away all the wives and such as are born of them" (Ezra 10:2-3).

To the question the Apostle answereth, that if either of the Parents be a believer, their children are accepted by God into the Gospel Covenant, and the Church ought to receive them, because in such a case the unbelieving husband or wife is sanctified by God unto the believing, to bring forth an holy Seed. If they were not so, then all such children of a believing Parent should be unholy, but saith the Apostle, that is not so, for all the children of a believer are holy, though their yoke-fellow were unholy. God received such children into his Gospel Covenant, with the believing Parent and all the Churches did receive such children, and now the question is stated and setled by divine Authority, *viz.* that all such children that had but one Parent a believer, were received by the Church as an holy Seed.

One Rule of judging of the soundness of a Doctrine is by its tendency to holiness, charity, and unity among the Saints. The opinion of the Anabaptists hath not such a tendency, it is a most uncharitable opinion, and therefore contrary to the Spirit of the Gospel of Christ, love and charity is a peculiar character of a disciple of Christ, *Joh.* 13.35.[27] *by this shall all men know that ye are my Disciples,* censoriousness of others, especially when better then themselves is exceeding contrary to the Spirit of the Gospel, and such doth their opinion expose them to be, what their inward state is, I do not meddle with it, but if they follow their opinion, as this book of *John Norcot* doth thoroughly, it leadeth them to the highest excess of censorious uncharitableness, (to say no worse,) and that against men much better then themselves.

Though there be so clear an Instance of circumcision of Infants, and Christ himself was circumcised when he was an Infant. *Luk.* 2.21. though there be so clear an institution of Baptisme to seal the Covenant, as circumcision did unto believers and their Seed, and though there [9] be so clear a Testimony that the primitive Church did so practice, and all the Gospel Churches ever since have so walked: yet because they do not see these things to be so, they do think that the primitive Church had not so much light as to practice so, and whereas all the Gospel Churches in the world have ever since so practiced, they judge they have walked in sin, and their Baptisme is null, all the world are unbaptized persons, saving themselves, and hey now call themselves Baptists, and all the rest of the christian world baptized in their Infancy are unbaptized persons, Churches, Ministry, Sacraments, all are nullified, &c.

What an horrible degree of uncharitableness is this, to say no worse of it.

[27] "By this shall all *men* know that ye are my disciples, if ye have love one to another" (John 13:35).

Again, because if they grant infants of believers to be comprehended in the Covenant, they cannot deny them the Seal of Baptisme. Therefore they do rather exclude (in their opinion) all the world of Infants of believers from the Covenant of God and the Church, then to grant them subjects to be baptized. They rob the Lambs of their interest in the Church, in the communion of Saints, and in the Covenant of God, which is a wicked injury done against the Lambs of Christ, who are not able to help themselves, therefore Christ will help them, and wo to those that do them this injury.

Math. 18.5, 6,10. *Who so shall receive one such little child in my Name receiveth me, but who so shall offend one of these little ones which believe in me, it were better for him that a Mill-stone were hanged about his neck, and that he were drowned in the depth of the Sea.* Christ doth account the children of believers to be believers, the Root and branches make but one Tree, *ver.* 10. *Take heed that ye despise not one of these little ones, for I say unto you* (and Christ doth know it perfectly) *that in Heaven there Angels do always behold the face of my Father which is in Heaven.*

Again, the uncharitableness of this opinion doth sadly [10] appear in this, that they teach men to be without natural affection, which is one of the gross sins of these latter & perilous times, 2 *Tim.* 3.3.[28] & this they do, in one of the highest points in the world, *viz.* that Parents should exclude their own children from sharing with them in Christ, & from Church Interest with Christ, yea, to put them away, & say, you have no portion with me in this great matter.

Christ was displeased with his Disciples when upon occasion of much business in teaching people, they forbad Parents to bring their children to Christ to have his blessing. What think you, he will say to the Anabaptists, who teach and cause their very Parents themselves to put away their children from Christ? not only to bring them, but to exclude them, never since the world began was there more unnatural affection then this is. Parents always endeavour to interest their children with themselves in their Religion, and in the God, as being the best thing they have in the world.

Again, it is great uncharitableness in respect of such Infants of believers, as dye in their Infancy, to judge them to dye without interest in the Covenant of God, thereby depriving both Parents and the Church of the comfort of that hope, that they dyed in Gods Covenant.

---

[28] Eliot used elements of verses from II Timothy 3:1-3: "This know also, that in the last days perilous times shall come. For men shall be lovers of their own selves, covetous, boasters, proud, blasphemers, disobedient to parents, unthankful, unholy, without natural affection, truce-breakers, false accusers, incontinent, fierce, despisers of those that are good."

Again, it is great uncharitableness to hinder (as much as in them lyeth) the Church from opportunity of eminent exercise of Faith in communion with the Father & with the Son, for when we receive little children into communion with the Church, we have communion with Christ, and with the Father, *Math.* 18.5 *who so shall receive one such little child in my Name receiveth me,* Mark. 9.36, 37. *and he took a child and set in the midst of them, and when he had taken him in his arms, he said unto them, whosoever shall receive one of such children in my Name, receiveth me, and whoso shall receive me, receiveth not me, but him that sent me,* Luk. 9.47, 48. *Jesus took a child, and set him by him, and said unto them, whosoever shall receive this child in my* [11] *Name, receiveth me, and whosoever shall receive me, receiveth him that sent me.* We see here is eminent communion with the Father and with the Son, in receiving Infants into our communion, and how do we receive Infants into our communion? the instituted way is, by owning them to be comprehended in the Covenant of God, with the Church, and visibly receiving them into the communion of the Church by Baptisme, if there be any other way of receiving Infants in the Name of Christ, Instance in it: this way is clear in the Scripture our receiving them in Baptism, our communion with the Lambs of Christ, in the Name of Christ which is very well pleasing to him. Never to do this, yea, to refuse to do it, is a sinful and offensive gap in our communion with Christ, to reject Infants from this communion is an offence against Christ of a provoking nature, and especially to glory in our so doing.

Psal. 127.3.[29] children are *the heritage of the Lord,* and how come they to be so interested? it is by virtue of their parental Covenant: our Covenant Interest is our spiritual Patrimony, our Estate in Religion which our Parents conveigh unto to us, it an Estate of good use unto us all the dayes of our life, especially at some difficult times a Christian hath two stocks to live and spend upon.

1. His Patrimony, or Covenant Interest which his Parents left him, 2*dly.* His acquired state in grace which he hath got and gained, by the good improvement of his Patrimony, a Christian liveth and spendeth upon both these stocks, and we need them both, and all little enough sometimes, as we shall see anon.

The Anabaptists deny this spiritual Patrimony, the Covenant Interest by Parents, and live only upon an acquired state of grace, which they have gained without improvement of their parental Covenant, if we may believe them, but they are deceived.

---

[29] "Lo, children *are* an heritage of the LORD: and the fruit of the womb *is his* reward" (Ps 127:3).

For our parental Interest in the Covenant, our spiri-[12]tual Patrimony is a great & sanctified means of conversion, though not the only means, for strangers (as our Indians)[30] are converted by the Gospel without that means, so far as we know. But in the Churches of Christ all our converts are converted by their improvement of their Patrimony, their parental Interest in the Covenant as one means which doth plainly appear in their confessions, when they come into the full communion of the Church, and therefore in this respect they deal very uncharitably, (to say no worse of it) with their children, to deny them their Patrimony of Covenant Interest.

Prov. 13.22. *A good man leaveth an inheritance to his Childrens Children,* that is, by bringing up his children so well, that he seeth his Patrimony secured to his second Generation. So it is in our spiritual Estate, a good man will (through grace) so improve the Patrimony, the Covenant Interest which he doth conveigh to his children, as to bring them to take hold on the Covenant themselves, by their own act, and free consent willingly, *Deut.* 29.10[31] &c. *Nehem.* 10.28.[32] and hereby is the progress of their Covenant Interest secured and conveighed over to his second Generation. Sometimes Parents are put so hard to it in pleading with God for their children, (or for some of them at least) as that they have nothing to plead on their behalf but the Covenant Interest, their Patrimony, they may be so profligate that they have nothing else to plead upon, and blessed be God, that will hold to the last, this was *Davids* case and so he pleadeth, *2 Sam.* 23.5. *although my house be not so with God, yet he hath made with me an everlasting Covenant ordered in all things and sure, for this is all my salvation and all my desire although he make it not to grow.* Now the Anabaptists

---

[30] Eliot has been called the "Apostle to the Indians" and sought to convert the Indians. This single aside was the opening that Roger Williams used in his rebuttal to attack Eliot's conversion efforts.

[31] This reference is somewhat obscure, except that it dealt with covenant and family. In verses 10 and 11, it was commanded that all men, their wives and children, strangers in the camp, hewers of wood, and drawers of water (servants or slaves) stand "before the LORD." Verses 12 and 13 continue, "That thou shouldest enter into covenant with the LORD thy God, and into his oath, which the LORD thy God maketh with thee this day: that he may establish thee to day for a people unto himself" (Deut 29:10-13).

[32] This reference also dealt with the sealing a covenant which included everyone (men, wives, sons, and daughters). The context for this covenant, however, was the purification of the Hebrew people at the return from the Babylonian Exile. "And the seed of Israel separated themselves from all strangers" (Neh 9:2). Having done this, "we make a sure covenant, and write it; and our princes, Levites, and priests, seal unto it" (Neh 9:38). Nehemiah 10:28-30 goes on to say that the rest "clave to their brethren, their nobles, and entered into a curse, and into an oath, to walk in God's law. . . . And that we would not give our daughters unto the people of the land, nor take their daughters for our sons."

cut themselves and their children off from this plea, by denying them their Patrimony, Covenant Interest in God. Sometimes a Christian may be so low brought by desertion and distress of Soul, as that they may be [13] glad to fly to their Patrimony and Covenant Interest to help their Faith. Sometimes *David* was so hard beset, that he was caused to plead and spend upon his Patrimony, *Psal.* 86.16. *O turn unto me, and have mercy upon me, give thy strength unto thy Servants, &c save the Son of thy Handmaid.* And sometimes in his Thanksgiving, he doth acknowledg that his Covenant Interest, his parental Patrimony was one spring of his mercyes which he has received, *Psal.* 116.16. *Truly I am thy Servant, I am thy Servant, the Son of thy Handmaid, thou hast loosed my Bonds.* Sometimes Gods Children may be sunk so low, as that they can see no acquisite grace or Interest to plead, nothing to plead or improve for themselves but their Patrimony, their Covenant Interest, *Isai.* 93.17.[33] *Why hast thou made us to erre from thy wayes, and hardened our hearts from thy fear, return for thy Servants sake the Tribes of thine Inheritance.* How ill do the Anabaptists provide for their own comforts, when they cut off (so far as in them lyeth, if an opinion could do it,) themselves and their children from this plea and succour of Faith. God in his wisdome and mercy saw that we are weak, and have need of a Patrimony, a Covenant Interest by our Parents, and sometimes to live upon a Talent of his providing, when our own good Husbandry would fail us; and when it is so he directeth and commandeth us to improve our Covenant Interest, our Patrimony, *Isai.* 51.2. *look unto* Abraham *your father, and* Sarah *that bare you,* I *Chron.* 16.12, 13. *Remember his marvellous works that he had done, his wonders, and the Judgements of his mouth, O Seed of Israel his Servant, ye Children of* Jacob *his chosen.* but such as reject their own Patrimony, and refuse to provide one for their children, must live only upon their own Trade and gains. What are they so strong in grace as that they need not to improve that Patrimony which God hath provided for our relief? Sometimes Gods people are fallen so low that God hath no ground [14] of shewing them mercy, but only because of their Patrimony, their Parental Covenant, 2 *King.* 13.22, 23, *Hazael*[34] *oppressed Israel and the Lord was gracious to them and had compassion on them; and had respect unto them, because of his Covenant with* Abraham, Isaac, *and* Jacob, *and would not destroy them, neither cast he them from his presence as yet.* And God hath promised thus to deal with his children and people, *Psal.* 89.28, *ad* 35. *My Covenant shall stand fast with him,*[35] *if his Children forsake my Law, and walk not in my Judgements, if they break my statutes, and keep not my Commandments, then will*

---

[33] Typesetter error; it should be Isaiah 63:17.
[34] Hazael was king of Syria (*Aram* in Hebrew). See II Kings 13:3.
[35] Psalm 89:28.

I visit their transgressions with the Rod, and their iniquity with stripes, neverthe-less my loving kindess will I not utterly take from him, nor suffer my Faithfulness to fail, my Covenant I will not break, &c.[36] and what a blessed Patrimony is Gods Covenant, yet the Anabaptists cut off their Children from this blessed privilege. Sometimes Gods people may be so apostate that they have nothing acquired left for their recovery, only their Patrimony, only the Covenant, as it is at this day in that dreadful Apostacy of *Israel* and *Judah,*[37] yet we have Faith for their recovery by their Patrimony, their Interest in the Covenant of *Abraham, for the gifts and calling of God are with-out Repentance,*[38] and the riches of Gods Covenant! how contrary to the Spirit and charity of the Gospel is that opinion, that cutteth off the chil-dren of the Church from this blessed Patrimony! the more I experience the charity of the Gospel, (which God knoweth is but a little) the more doth my Soul loath that uncharitable opinion of the Anabaptists.

Furthermore, this opinion is pernicious and destructive unto the Churches of Jesus Christ, it killeth the Church in the bud, it robbeth them of their Lambs, and will soon make the Churches and Kingdome of Jesus Christ thin and poor, but the world and Satans Kingdome will be full and rich, if this opinion should prevail, which God forbid! when *Laban* hired *Jacob* to serve him for wa-[15]ges, *Jacob* bargained for no other wages but Lambs, and though *Laban* like it well at first, yet he soon found that *Jacob* grew rich, and he grew poor,[39] the same issue will all the Churches find, that the excluding of the Lambs as the Anabaptists do, or the neglecting them as other Churches do, will in a few years make the Churches thin and poor, there is an hurtful bird in some countryes, that spoyleth Orchards, and maketh them barren, by feeding upon, and devouring the buds in the spring time, it is very needful to keep a diligent watch against such evil birds, least our Churches become barren Vineyards, and empty Vines.

It may be some will say, that notwithstanding all that is here said, I do not yet see that there is either precept, institution or Example of baptiz-ing Infants. Ans. what? is it not so, because you see it not? if you be dark, blind, ignorant in so great a point as this is, are all the Churches in the world mistaken, who do see both precept, Institution, and Example for it?

---

[36] Psalm 89:30-34.

[37] This reference is obscure, but it points to the kingdoms of Israel and Judah which both apostatized themselves in the worship of Baal and other gods.

[38] Romans 11:29.

[39] Jacob first asked for the hand of Rachel but was tricked by Laban into working fourteen years to get her. Genesis 29:15-29. Then he asked for any striped, speckled, or spotted sheep and goats from Laban's flocks, connived to cause most newborn to be marred in those ways, and became rich (Gen 30:28-43).

are your dark minds and blind eyes the standard by which every bodies light and understanding must be regulated? Must all men light their candles by your dim light? what bottom doth that flag grow in? consider this, that all they that oppose Infant Baptisme, they do not bring any positive evidence against it, only a negative, and that negative is grounded in their own darkness; and ignorance it is not so, say they, because *I* see it not.

We agree with the Anabaptists in the general proposition which is this, nothing is to be received in Divine worship, but that which hath a Divine *I*nstitution.

We agree to it, but the parcicular[40] proposition, the *minor*, the assumption; there we differ, which is this.

But the baptizing of believers and their *I*nfants hath a Divine *I*nstitution, this we affirm, and prove, and therefore we conclude that believers and their *I*nfants ought to be baptized. [16] They deny this proposition, and what proof bring they? Nothing at all that *I* know off, but this, *I* do not see it, therefore *I* do not believe it, therefore *I* oppose it. Their chief discourses are cavillations against our proofs, whereby Satan doth effectually keep their eyes shut, so that they cannot see the Truth, but are puffed up with their own ignorance.

I shall now take a brief consideration of the Book And *I* will give one direction to such as read it, which being observed it will quite enervate the whole Book, *viz.* when the Book mentioneth baptizing of believers, do you add in your mind (and their Seed) which if you hold unto, the Book hath nothing in it, that I remember, that will hurt you in that point. Nor is this a begging of the question, because I have proved, that when Baptisme of Believers was first instituted in the Gospel Churches by the Apostles, the baptizing of their Infants was also instituted. And I have proved that God doth account the Children of believers to be believers, they may be (for ought we know) actual believers as *John Baptist* was, and if they dye in their Infancy (as many do) we ought to believe that they are saved by the power and grace of Gods Covenant, under which they are comprehended, if they are not actual believers, and live to shew it, yet they are under Gods instituted means and Ordinances, to be trained up to become believers, and therefore all such God doth account (as to Ecclesiastical respects) to be believers, and Subjects capable to be baptized. The believing Parent the Root, and his Infants the branches, make but one Tree in Gods Vineyard, *therefore those things which God hath put together, let not us put asunder.*[41] And for this Reason I give the Reader this direction,

---

[40] Particular.

[41] "What therefore God hath joined together, let not man put asunder" (Mark 10:9). This admonition was specifically related to marriage. See Mark 10:2-9.

always, when the baptizing of believers is mentioned, add in your mind (and their Infants)[.] [17]

CHAP. I.

THat Jesus being about thirty years old was baptized of *John*, in *Jordan*, is true; But Baptisme was not instituted till about that time, by *John*, had it been instituted when Jesus was an Infant, he would have submitted to it, as he did submit himself to the be circumcised, when he was an Infant, *Luk.* 2.21.

CHAP. II.

Of the great Commission for baptizing believers, I add, and their infants.

Go *teach and baptize,* teaching is first, true, and Infants are taught and made Disciples, in that their Parents are so. And God doth account them believers, as their Parents are, and therefore God hath instituted, that they also as well as their Parents should be baptized.

CHAP. III.

Of Examples.

IOhn.4.1, 2. *Jesus made Disciples and baptized,* they were made Disciples, not born so.

Answ, So it was with the first believers, but their Infants had the priviledge to be born Disciples. And this was at the beginning of the publick Ministry of Christ, the order of the Gospel Churches was not yet instituted and fixed, that was done at the beginning of the Apostles Ministry, *Act.* 2. And what though the *Samaritan* believers both men and women are mentioned to be baptized with mention of their Infants, that is no evidence [18] that it was not done either first or last, seeing it is a divine Apostolical Institution that Infants are comprehended with their Parents. The Eunuch was a stranger, and his home, his Family absent, therefore there is no force in that instance, but on the contrary rather, for he carrying home tydings of the Gospel, it was so effectually received (as Historians report) that it continueth with them unto this day, and Infant Baptisme among other parts of Gods worship. When *Paul* was baptized he had no Children, nor was he ever married that we know of, therefore his Example hath no force to oppose Infant Baptisme.

The Example of the Jaylor affordeth consideration of weight, the Head of the Family being converted, his whole Family are accounted believers, and were baptized. Such as were adult in his Family no doubt manifested their Faith; the Infants of his Family were in Gospel order to be trained up in the Faith of the Gospel, and therefore were accounted believers, and therefore all his houshold were baptized. The same may be said of *Lydia* and *Crispus*.

CHAP. IV.

Here the book proceedeth by digressing into another litigious point, *viz*, whether Baptisme is to be administered by dipping, or as we do by washing, or sprinkling. Which manner of administration, though the holy Scriptures have left it indifferent, either way may be lawful, yet this treatise fixeth a necessity upon dipping, yea such, as to nullifie that Baptisme that is not so administered.

In another place the Book blameth, at least seeketh to invalidate our doctrine of Infant Baptisme, because we take it up & teach it, only upon consequence, though it is not so, for we plead positive Institution and Exam-[19]ple, But this point of dipping is taken up only by consequence, and that but probable consequence at the best, there is no proof that any in the times of Christ were baptized by dipping, nor that *John* nor *Phillip* baptized by dipping. Baptisme is a signe, and a little of the signe is enough to signifie great matters, a little bit of bread a little sip of wine is enough to signifie wonderful great things, *Joh*. 13.9, 10. *when Christ washed his Disciples feet, Peter, said, thou shalt never wash my feet,* but when he understood that it was for spiritual use and instruction, he would have more of the signe, *not my feet only, but my hands and my head, but Christ saith, it is enough that the feet only be washed, he that is so washed is clean every whit.* So it is with our brethren, they knowing that Baptisme is of great signification and use, therefore they desire a great deal of the signe, they would be dipped quite under water, over head and ears[42] in the signe. What needs that be? a little of the signe is enough to lead up Faith unto its glorious Objects in Christ. The face is the most eminent and principal part of a man, if therefore the face be baptized, the whole man is baptized. If the face be a little washed, buryed, sprinkled, covered with water, it is enough to signifie unto our faith all that is signified by Baptisme. Baptisme is sundry times set forth to signifie our death, burying, and rising with Jesus Christ. It is sundry times set forth by sprinkling with the blood of Christ, it is sundry times set forth by washing, once by putting on Christ, if therefore Baptisme be administred either by washing, or by sprinkling, or by dipping, our Faith must be raised unto all these significations of the Baptismal signe, & it is

---

[42] One of the most famous tracts attacking the Baptists in the seventeenth century used these words "over head and ears": Daniel Featley, *The Dippers Dipt, or the Anabaptists Duck'd and Plung'd over Head and Ears: at a Disputation at Southwark* (London, 1645).

indifferent which of these wayes be used, either powring[43] with the hands of the baptizer a convenient quantity of water upon the face, by way of sprinkling or washing, or by dipping the face, there is must exercise of divine knowledge and faith in that part of Gods worship in the administration of, and parti-[20]cipating in the Sacrament of Baptisme more then can be expressed by the signe, though all is signified. And to give a short touch of the indifferency of the manner of its administration. It is but in two places where they went into the water to baptize. *John* alwayes so did, for he preached in the Wilderness, where there was no accommodation to do otherwise, and there the River was broad, and by that means more shallow towards the bank, so that people might come to him, standing in the water, and lifting up their faces to Heaven, he taking up water in his hands sprinkling and powring it on their faces, and so they were baptized, in which action there is death, buryal under water, resurrection, washing, covering, sprinkling, a little of the signe of those great things signified thereby, it is more probable, as I conceive, that this was the manner that *John* and *Phillip* used when they went into the water to baptize. *Phillip* and the Eunuch going into the water to baptize, is the second and last Example that I know off, who were travailing in the Road where they had as little accommodation to do otherwise, as *John* had in the Wilderness.

But that great administration of Baptisme, *Act.* 2.41[44] was performed in the Temple, where there was no River, nor deep waters for dipping the whole body, but there was always plenty of water in the Temple, very much was used about the sacrifices in washing and boyling, and much was drank by the people, who did eat and drink in Gods presence, though there was a little wine brought with the Sacrifice by Institution, yet at all their sacrifice Feasts the people would need water also to drink, and it was readily to be had, for there were many whose office it was to be drawers of water for the Temple Service, and who ever needed water might easily have it. And there belonged unto the Temple all sorts of Vessels needful for the Service of God, Basons, Charges, Platters, &c. Therefore in this famous business of baptizing [21] those Gospel Converts; the water drawers would readily supply all the baptizers with sufficient water, in sitting Vessels, not for dipping, but for washing, sprinkling, and pouring water with their hands upon the faces of the baptized.

Acts 16.33. The same hour of the night the Jaylor was baptized, he and all his straight way, there was no going to a River for dipping. *Paul* was baptized in the room where he lay sick, *Acts* 9.18, 19.

---

[43] Pouring.

[44] "Then they that gladly received his word were baptized: and the same day there were added *unto them* about three thousand souls" (Acts 2:41).

Cornelius and his Family, and Friends were baptized in the place where the Word was preached to them, and prayers were made, and the holy Ghost was poured out upon them, they were baptized with the Holy Ghost, and with water Baptisme in the same place, there is nothing intimated of the Assemblies removing to some River for water Baptisme. Baptisme is a part of Gods worship, which is to be administred in the publick Assembly of the Church, and so do the generality of Gospel Churches walk, in all places of the world, which places of Assemblyes rarely be by River sides.

CHAP. V.

IN this Chapter there is no difference of moment that I see, saving that it is affirmed, that *Lydia* was baptized in the River, which cannot be proved.

Chap. VI. I pass by this Chapter also.

Chap. VII. Believers (I add and their Infants) Baptisme is a great Ordinance.

CHAP. VIII.

This Chapter answereth Objections in *Numb.* 22 but many of them are trivial, of little concernment, and unto others of them, I have already said enough for the present, therefore I shall take up here and there one and pass on.

Object. 5. Doth not Baptisme come in the room[45] of Circumcision? the Book answereth, no surely, there is [22] no Scripture for it. *Answ.* I pray consider, Rom. 4.11, *he*[46] *received Circumcision, the Seal of Righteousness of Faith, which he had yet being uncircumcised, that he might be the Father of all that believe, though they be not circumcised.* And Gal. 3.17.[47] This I say the Covenant which was confirmed before of God in Christ, *&c. viz.* confirmed by Circumcision, we see that Circumcision confirmed their entrance into the Covenant of Faith, and so doth Baptisme confirm their entrance into the Gospel Covenant, *Acts* 2.38, 39. Circumcision was one of the first Ecclesiastical Ordinances, which did engage and oblige them to keep the whole Law, *Gal.* 5.3.[48] So Baptisme is one of the first Ecclesiastical

---

[45] I.e., place.

[46] The "he" in this text referred to Abraham.

[47] "Now this I say, that the covenant, that was confirmed before God in Christ, the law, which was four hundred and thirty years after, cannot disannul, that it should make the promise of none effect" (Gal 3:17). The covenant was the one made with Abraham and the promises to his seed mentioned in verse 16.

[48] This is an odd reference because it came in a section where Paul was telling the

Ordinances which doth engage and oblige us to obey the whole Gospel, *all things whatsoever I command*, Matt. 28.19, 20.

Why they deny Baptisme to come in the room of Circumcision I know not, unless it be for fear of an Argument that it affordeth for Infant Baptisme, which they know not how to evade.

Object. 10. Infants were once Church members, and we do not find them cut off. *Answ.* Touching Infants interest in the Covenant I have said a little already, *I* shall add a word or two more to something that is here said, *Math* 3.9, 10. *think not to say we have* Abraham *a Believer for your Father.* Answ. They made a carnal confident use of their parental Covenant, as also they did, *Joh.* 8. and other places, thought they were of ripe years, and should have improved the Covenant by laying hold on it, unto their sanctification, yet they did not do so, they lived in gross sin, and yet plead their paternal Covenant, alass it profits not in that case. It is now with us in our infancy and minority, our parental Covenant alone is of great Efficacy, but when we are up-grown, we must take hold on the Covenant our selves, and improve both our own, and our parental Covenant, for our mortification and holiness of life, *and think not to say* Abraham *a believer* [23] *is our Father*, upon any other Terms, especially if they cloak over a vile conversation, with *Abraham* is our Father, *Abraham* will not own such Children, and further *John* sheweth them that by reason of their carnal abuse of their parental Covenant, God was about to break them off through their unbelief, to which end, *the Axe is laid to the Root of the Tree*, &c. the Tree is the Nation of the Jews, the Root is their Ecclesiastical state, in the Covenant of *Abraham*, the Axe is the Roman, whom the Jews themselves did whet and sharpen to do thorough Execution upon them, and therefore he exhorts them to be penitent and fruitful believers.

The Book further saith, where were infants ever members of a particular Gospel Church? *Answ.* See it *Act.* 2.36, 37.[49] I *Cor.*7. 14.[50]

Galatians that they are free of the law that required circumcision. "Behold, I Paul say unto you, that if ye be circumcised, Christ shall profit you nothing. For I testify again to every man that is circumcised, that he is a debtor to do the whole law. Christ is become of no effect unto you, whatsoever of you are justified by the law; ye are fallen from grace" (Gal 5:2-4).

[49] It is not evident why Eliot cited this Scripture because it has no mention of children, even by implication. "Therefore let all the house of Israel know assuredly, that God hath made that same Jesus, who you have crucified, both Lord and Christ. Now when they heard this, they were pricked in their heart, and said unto Peter and the rest of the apostles, Men and brethren, what shall we do?" (Acts 2:36-37).

[50] "For the unbelieving husband is sanctified by the wife, and the unbelieving wife is sanctified by the husband: else were your children unclean; but now they are holy" (I Cor 7:14).

Object. 16. *I* was baptized in my infancy, what need *I* be baptized again? you say it is not water thrown in the face that makes Baptisme. *Answ.* Alass, who saith so? nor is this any Scripture Language: if the scope of these words be to disparage the Ordinance, we may see how prone we are to drop words that need a pardon in the blood of Christ. The Parent giveth consent to the Baptismal Covenant, and acteth Faith in the behalf of the Child, and the child is trained up and taught to do it himself, and this is accepted of God. They in *Act.* 19.1, &c. were not rebaptized,[51] but instructed by the Apostle, that they were rightly baptized, if there be an error in the Infant Subject, and in the manner, (in both which you are deceived) yet it seemeth great boldness to nullify Baptisme, and to affirm, that all the Churches and Saints from the Apostles to this day are unbaptized persons, except your inconsiderable selves. O what need have we of humility and charity!

CHAP. IX.

The designe of this Chapter is to set the baptizing of believers and of infants in opposition one against the [24] other, when as God hath conjoyned them together, believers and their infants are to be baptixed;[52] there is more deceipt than weight in this doing, the first and the two last of these touches deny that there is any Scripture for infant Baptisme, and upon that Hinge the rest hang. You know we plead Scripture Authority for infant Baptisme, and therefore *I* will pass by this Chapter as a confused heap of hay and stubble.

CHAP. X.

This Chapter is a gathering together of many Texts of holy Scripture, which *I* read with reverence, and find nothing in them against baptizing believers and their infants.

---

[51] This citation seems to contradict what Eliot asserts. "And it came to pass, that, while Apollos was at Corinth, Paul having passed through the upper coasts came to Ephesus: and finding certain disciples, He said unto them, Have ye received the Holy Ghost since ye believed? And they said unto him, We have not so much as heard whether there be any Holy Ghost. And he said unto them, Unto what then were ye baptized? And they said, Unto John's baptism. Then said Paul, John verily baptized with the baptism of repentance, saying unto the people, that they should believe on him which should come after him, that is, on Christ Jesus. *When they heard this, they were baptized in the name of the Lord Jesus*" [emphasis added] (Acts 19:1-5).

[52] Typesetter error: should be "baptized."

CHAP. XI.

This last is a Chapter of Considerations and Conclusions, which I shall answer unto with my Considerations: wherein I am occasioned to say the same thing many times over, because I make Answer to every Proposal.

1. Infant Baptism is one of the Ordinances of the Gospel Churches. Lord make the Opposers of it ashamed that they may see it to be thine Ordinance.

2. Lord give us all renewed hearrs,[53] that we may walk in thy Statutes and wayes to do them.

3. They reject the Counsel of God that reject the Infants of believers from Baptisme.

4. To exclude infants of believers from the Seal of the Covenant, is to change Gods Ordinance: God hath commanded that believers and their infants should be baptized.

5. God hath commanded to baptize believers and their infants: we therefore offer to God that which he hath commanded, and hath alwayes accepted ever since the institution thereof unto this day.

6. There was no error in their Baptisme, *Acts* 19.1. & nor were they rebaptized, they were so far instruct-[25]ed by the Apostle as to see that they were rightly baptized. There have been many errors and stains in baptisme, by the corruption of Antichrist: but we are not therefore to be rebaptized: an error in the infant-subject, and in the manner of the action, as you suppose in our infant-baptism, is not essential, and therefore neither destroy baptism, nor require a rebaptizing, were the case as you say.

7. My infant baptism is true baptisme according to divine institution. I live in the obedience of that gospel ordinance, my parents believing, covenanting, promising on my behalf are accepted with God, I am brought up by Gods grace, and taught to make them mine by my one[54] voluntary taking hold of the Covenant; and praised be God for this gospel way of propagation of Religion, and the continuation of the Churches.

8. Baptism was delivered to believers and their infants as Circumcision was.

9. I know not who those believers be that deny baptism to their infants, unless some of the Anabaptists approve themselves to be found believers.

10. What Truth hath not been opposed and disputed? Truth cometh forth, not the worse, but the brighter; & I believe so will the issue of the doctrine of baptizing of infants. Letters passing between Mr. *Jesse*[55] and

---

[53] Typesetter error; should be "hearts."

[54] Typesetter error; should be "own."

[55] Henry Jessey (1601–1663) was a prominent Baptist pastor in the 1640s and 1650s. Schooled at Cambridge University, Jessey was ordained in 1627 with episcopal orders, but in

me, *I* proposed that Question to him, Whether when the Jews are converted will they baptize their infants? He answered, He believed that they would, and gave me two Texts of Scripture for it, one was *Jer.* 30.20.[56] the other I have forgotten, I think it was in *Isai.*

11. There is a famous Example of baptizing believers and their infants, *ut supra*,[57] *Acts* 2.41.[58]

12. If the salvation of my Soul lay upon it, I dare with holy boldness of Faith affirm, that believers and their infants were baptized in the Primitive Church.

13. This I pass by as inconsiderable. [26]

14. Baptisme of believers and their infants is a written Ordinance by divine institution.

15. Christ hath in faithfulness to the Church left us many Scripture Testimonies for Infant Baptisme.

16. Christ hath left written in the holy pattern of Gospel institutions, that believers and their infants are to be baptized.

17. The baptizing of believers dependeth not only upon sound Consequence, but also upon the plain written Word. Baptizing by dipping dependeth only upon probable Consequence, and therefore cannot nullify such Baptisme as is done by sprinkling.

1637 he became the pastor of the famous Jacob-Lathrop-Jessey church in Southwark, London. It was a semi-separatist church, founded by Henry Jacob in 1616. After Jacob moved to Virginia in 1622 (where he died in 1624), he was succeeded as pastor at Southwark in 1624 by John Lathrop. The church was troubled by extreme separatism and by "anabaptists." Lathrop left in 1633, and the church went without a pastor until 1637 when Jessey became the pastor. The Southwark church continued as a mixed communion congregation with ongoing disputes about baptism, and by about 1643, Jessey concluded that sprinkling was a recent innovation and that dipping was the biblical way. In 1645 he was baptized (by immersion) by Hanserd Knollys, pastor of the Swan Alley Baptist Church in London. (Knollys himself had come to Boston in 1638 and was quickly denounced as an Antinomian, and moved to New Hampshire, where he remained until about 1641–1642 before returning to England.) In the 1650s, Jessey continued as pastor of the Southwark church, now a fully Particular Baptist church, even when he was elevated by Cromwell to be one of the "Triers" (examiners of candidates for the ministry). He was also appointed rector of St. George's church in Southwark, London. When the Restoration came and the re-establishment of the Church of England, Jessey was one of those "ejected" by the Act of Uniformity. He was then arrested and thrown into prison where he died in September 1663.

[56] It is a stretch to connect this Scripture to the issue of infant baptism. "Their children also shall be as aforetime, and their congregation shall be established before me, and I will punish all that oppress them" (Jer 30:20). The context for that verse was a prediction about the return from captivity and the restoration of the nation of Israel in the promised land. Speaking through Jeremiah, God promised that things would be restored "as aforetime," as before captivity.

[57] Latin, meaning "as above."

[58] "Then they that gladly received his word were baptized: and the same day there were added *unto them* about three thousand souls" (Acts 2:41).

18. Though the infants in *Lidiahs* house be not named, yet the whole houshold is mentioned, and who shall teach the Holy Ghost to speak.

19. Christ our Law-giver hath given us an express institution for baptizing believers and their infants.

20. Baptizing believers and their infants is brought into the Church by express institution and command.

21. It is safe to admit baptizing believers and their infants being expresly commanded; and when the parents are taught, the infants also are taught.

22. We can say with a cleer Faith, Lord thou hast required us that we should baptize believers and their infants, you cannot so answer for excluding infants from the Covenant, and from the Seal thereof.

23. Baptizing believers and their Seed is a Gospel Ordinance in express words and command.

24. We are baptized according to the express command of God, to reject infants from it, is to reject the Counsel of God.

25. We ought to believe that our infants may be regenerated from the womb, if not, yet they are in the way to be regenerated, and are brought under the gale of the Spirit to accomplish it, and this is accepted.

26. We are not ashamed of baptizing believers & their [27] infants they that exclude such infants have cause to be ashamed Lord make them ashamed.

27. We baptize believers and their infants by an express word of command.

28. Baptizing believers and their infants is a pure Ordinance of God by an express Rule.

29. In baptizing believers and their infants, we do what God hath commanded, and we shall have the comfort of *well done my good Servant*,[59] but they that exclude such infants, shall in that point lose the comfort of, *well done my good Servant*, Christ was much displeased with them, for hindring infants to be brought unto him.

When *I* say the same thing over and over, do not nauseate at me, but consider that *I* am led unto it, by the paper that *I* answer, which proposeth all the matter which *I* answer to, *I* confess it is a very confused heap.

Lord lead us into thy Truth, and help us to Truth it in love. Eph. 4.15.[60]

FINIS

[59] Matthew 25:21, 23.

[60] The wording here is incorrect. Ephesians 4:15 reads, "But speaking the truth in love . . ." Eliot probably meant to say, "Lord lead us into thy Truth, and help us to *speak* it in love."

SUGGESTIONS FOR FURTHER READING AND RESEARCH

ROGER WILLIAMS

The study of Roger Williams must begin with his writings and correspondence. *The Publications of the Narragansett Club* issued six volumes of Williams' writings between 1866 and 1874, and these were reprinted in 1963 with a seventh volume of additional material as *The Complete Writings of Roger Williams* (New York: Russell & Russell). This latter project was the work of Perry Miller, who wrote an interpretative essay about Williams for the seventh volume. The most recent significant addition to the scholarship on Williams is the two-volume edition of Williams' letters (with extensive footnotes and annotations), edited by Glenn LaFantasie, *The Correspondence of Roger Williams* (Hanover, N.H.: University Press of New England, 1988).

More books have been written about Roger Williams than any other seventeenth-century American. He has gone from being largely forgotten by the beginning of the eighteenth century and being regarded as a "polemical porcupine"[1] to being elevated recently as the source of half of the "American soul."[2] In 1834 James Davis Knowles wrote the first biography of Williams, *Memoir of Roger Williams: The Founder of the State of Rhode-Island* (Boston: Lincoln, Edmands). Since then many biographies and studies of Williams' thought and writing have appeared, including

---

[1] John Quincy Adams, entry in his diary on May 19, 1843. See *The Diaries of John Quincy Adams: A Digital Collection*, Massachusetts Historical Society, http://www.masshist.org/jqa diaries/index.cfm.

[2] John M. Barry, *Roger Williams and the Creation of the American Soul: Church, State, and the Birth of Liberty* (New York: Viking Adult, 2012).

studies by Oscar S. Straus, James Ernst, Samuel H. Brockunier, Perry Miller, Ola E. Winslow, Edmund Morgan, John Garrett, W. Clark Gilpin, Edwin Gaustad, and, most recently, John Barry.[3]

Baptist scholars first promoted Williams, especially those connected with Brown University in the nineteenth century,[4] but nonreligious historians, such as George Bancroft, fixed upon Williams as a great hero of religious liberty in America.[5] As freedom of religion was increasingly touted as part of the American way of life, Williams was given great credit for his contributions by historians and writers in the nineteenth and twentieth centuries. By the 1920s Williams had come to be identified by the "Progressive historians" as one of the founders of the liberal tradition in America,[6] so much so that by the 1930s and 1940s, historians began to lose sight of Williams' intensely religious character. By 1940, he had become an "irrepressible democrat" and a thoroughly modern man.[7] In the 1950s Perry Miller restored Williams to his own time by emphasizing Williams' religious focus.[8] Since then, writers have sought to place Williams in the Puritan-Separatist tradition of the seventeenth century.[9]

---

[3] Oscar S. Straus, *Roger Williams: Pioneer of Religious Liberty* (New York: Century, 1894); James E. Ernst, *Roger Williams: New England Firebrand* (New York: Macmillan, 1932); Samuel H. Brockunier, *The Irrepressible Democrat: Roger Williams* (New York: Roland Press, 1940); Perry Miller, *Roger Williams: His Contribution to the American Tradition* (New York: Bobbs-Merrill, 1953); Ola E. Winslow, *Master Roger Williams: A Biography* (New York: Macmillan, 1957); Edmund Morgan, *Roger Williams: The Church and the State* (Harcourt, Brace & World, 1967); John Garrett, *Roger Williams: Witness beyond Christendom* (London: Macmillan, 1970); W. Clark Gilpin, *The Millenarian Piety of Roger Williams* (Chicago: University of Chicago Press, 1979); Edwin S. Gaustad, *Liberty of Conscience: Roger Williams in America* (Grand Rapids: Eerdmans, 1991); Edwin S. Gaustad, *Roger Williams* (New York: Oxford University Press, 2005); Barry, *Roger Williams*.

[4] The first major Baptist promoter was Isaac Backus, who wrote *A History of New England with Particular Reference to the Denomination of Christians called Baptists*, 3 vols. (1777–1796); see also David Benedict, *A General History of the Baptist Denomination in America and Other Parts of the World*, 2 vols. (Boston: Manning & Loring, 1813); Romeo Elton, *Life of Roger Williams: The Earliest Legislator and True Champion for a Full and Absolute Liberty of Conscience* (New York: G. W. Putnam, 1852); William Gammell, *Life of Roger Williams: The Founder of the State of Rhode Island* (Boston: Gould & Lincoln, 1854); Francis Wayland, *Notes on Principles and Practices of Baptist Churches* (New York: Sheldon, Blakeman, 1857); and Reuben Guild, *Footprints of Roger Williams* (Providence: Tibbetts & Preston, 1886).

[5] George Bancroft, *History of the United States of America, from the Discovery of the Continent*, 6 vols. (New York: Appleton Century, 1886), vol. 1.

[6] Vernon Parrington, *Main Currents in American Thought: An Interpretation of American Literature from the Beginnings to 1920* (New York: Harcourt, Brace, 1930).

[7] Brockunier, *Roger Williams*.

[8] Miller, *Roger Williams*.

[9] Gilpin, *The Millenarian Piety of Roger Williams*; Garrett, *Roger Williams*; Morgan, *Roger Williams*; Sacvan Bercovitch, "Typology in Puritan New England: The Williams-Cotton Controversy Reassessed," *American Quarterly* 19 (1967): 166–71; H. Leon McBeth, *The*

Since the Supreme Court handed down its first rulings on the issues of church and state in the 1940s, books have continued to roll off the presses that bring Roger Williams into that debate. Virtually every book that deals with the First Amendment, freedom of religion in America, and church-state issues includes Williams in the argument. While William McLoughlin thinks that Williams' and Rhode Island's role in the achievement of religious liberty was overrated,[10] many other writers go back to Williams as a starting point.[11] But Williams' profound Christian biblicism and firm belief in the separation of church and state continue to be a stumbling block to members of the religious Right and the "Christian Reconstructionist" movement, which maintains that the United States was founded as a Christian nation.[12]

To a lesser extent, historians have also long been interested in Williams' relations with Native Americans. The primary interpretive difficulty has been how to understand Williams' early evangelistic optimism regarding Native Americans in light of his essential inaction on the matter, especially when compared to the work of John Eliot in neighboring Massachusetts. W. Clark Gilpin's *The Millenarian Piety of Roger Williams* (Chicago: University of Chicago Press, 1979) still stands as perhaps the most nuanced discussion of Williams' evangelistic views, which Gilpin

---

Baptist Heritage: Four Centuries of Baptist Witness (Nashville: Broadman Press, 1987); Martin Marty, *Pilgrims in Their Own Land: 500 Years of Religion in America* (New York: Penguin Books, 1985); William G. McLoughlin, *New England Dissent, 1630–1833: Baptists and Separation of Church and State*, 2 vols. (Cambridge, Mass.: Harvard University Press, 1971); C. Leonard Allen and Richard T. Hughes, *Illusions of Innocence: Protestant Primitivism in America, 1630–1875* (Chicago: University of Chicago Press, 1988); Hugh Spurgin, *Roger Williams and Puritan Radicalism in the English Separatist Tradition* (Lewiston, N.Y.: Edwin Mellen Press, 1989); Gura, *A Glimpse of Sion's Glory*; James P. Byrd Jr., *The Challenges of Roger Williams* (Macon, Ga.: Mercer University Press, 2002).

[10] William G. McLoughlin, *Soul Liberty: The Baptists' Struggle in New England, 1630–1833* (Hanover, N.H.: University Press of New England, 1991).

[11] Richard E. Morgan, *The Supreme Court and Religion* (New York: Free Press, 1972); Leonard Levy, *The Establishment Clause: Religion and the First Amendment* (New York: Macmillan, 1986); William Lee Miller, *The First Liberty: Religion and the American Republic* (New York: Knopf, 1986); Gerald U. Bradley, *Church-State Relationships in America* (New York: Greenwood Press, 1987); Neal Riemer, "Religious Liberty and Creative Breakthroughs in American Politics: Roger Williams and James Madison," *Journal of Political Science* 16 (1988); Steven Waldman, *Founding Faith: Providence, Politics, and the Birth of Religious Freedom in America* (New York: Random House, 2008); Michael I. Meyerson, *Endowed by Our Creator: The Birth of Religious Freedom in America* (New Haven: Yale University Press, 2012).

[12] Peter Marshall and David Manuel, *The Light and the Glory: Did God Have a Plan for America?* (Old Tappan, N.J.: Fleming H. Revell, 1977). Marshall and Manuel say that God did have a plan for America, but Roger Williams and Thomas Jefferson are to be blamed for derailing it.

places firmly in relation to Williams' particular millennial views (regarding the need for an appropriate apostolic mandate for Native conversions). But some historians and linguists continue to wrestle with Williams' *A Key into the Language of America* (1643), debating his motivations for writing as well as the sincerity of his beliefs.[13]

JOHN ELIOT

John Eliot, the famed "Apostle to the Indians," has commanded far less attention than Williams, although numerous biographies have been written of him over the past three centuries. Almost immediately after Eliot's death, the Boston Puritan minister Cotton Mather published a glowing account of Eliot's labors: *The Triumphs of the Reformed Religion, in America: The Life of the Renowned John Eliot* (Boston: Harris, Benjamin, 1691).[14] Several more Eliot biographies were published in the nineteenth century, most of which continued Mather's clear admiration.[15]

While Samuel Eliot Morrison dealt at length with Eliot in his *Builders of the Bay Colony* (Boston: Houghton Mifflin, 1930), it was not until the 1960s that Eliot again received sustained scholarly treatment. Almost without exception, this renewed interest in Eliot continued the laudatory tone of his nineteenth-century biographers, including Ola E. Winslow, *John Eliot: Apostle to the Indians* (Boston: Houghton Mifflin, 1968) and Sidney H. Rooy, *The Theology of Missions in the Puritan Tradition: A Study of Representative Puritans: Richard Sibbes, Richard Baxter, John Eliot, Cotton*

---

[13] See especially Jennifer Reid, "Roger Williams' *Key*: Ethnography or Mythology?" *Rhode Island History* 56, no. 3 (1998): 77; Patricia E. Rubertone, *Grave Undertakings: An Archaeology of Roger Williams and the Narragansett Indians* (Washington, D.C.: Smithsonian Institution Press, 2001); William S. Simmons, "Cultural Bias in the New England Puritans' Perception of Indians," *William and Mary Quarterly* 38, no. 1 (1981): 63; J. Patrick Cesarini, "The Ambivalent Uses of Roger Williams's *A Key Into the Language of America*," *Early American Literature* 38, no. 3 (2003): 469–94; Jonathan Beecher Field, *Errands into the Metropolis: New England Dissidents in Revolutionary London* (Dartmouth, N.H.: University Press of New England, 2009).

[14] A subsequent version was published a few years later as *The Life and Death of the Reverend Mr. John Eliot, who was the first Preacher of the Gospel to the Indians* (London: John Dunton, 1694).

[15] See Martin Moore, *Memoirs of the Life and Character of Rev. John Eliot: Apostle to the N.A. Indians* (Boston: T. Bedlington, 1822); John Wilson, *The Life of John Eliot* (Edinburgh: Wm. Oliphant, 1828); Convers Francis, *Life of John Eliot, the Apostle to the Indians* (London: R. J. Kennett, 1834; New York: Harper & Brothers, 1844); Nehemiah Adams, *The Life of John Eliot, with an account of the early missionary efforts among the Indians of New England* (Boston: Massachusetts Sabbath School Society, 1847); and Robert Boodey Caverly, *Life and Labors of John Eliot, the Apostle Among the Indian Nations of New England, Together with an Account of the Eliots in England* (Lowell, Mass.: George M. Elliott, 1881).

Mather, and Jonathan Edwards (Delft: W. D. Meinema, 1965). The pinnacle of this optimism was Alden T. Vaughan, *New England Frontier: Puritans and Indians, 1620–1675* (Boston: Little, 1965). Vaughan emphasized the good intentions of the Puritans, despite the obvious disastrous consequences for Native populations.

With the advent of the new social history and the burgeoning American Indian Movement, however, such rosy-glassed views could not possibly last long. Vine DeLoria Jr. was one Native writer whose scathing critiques eventually hit the mainstream of discourse about the treatment of Natives in American history. His groundbreaking book *Custer Died for Your Sins: An Indian Manifesto* (London: Macmillan, 1969) set a tone that was for many Americans difficult to read, but the time was exactly right for such a revision. The field took a decisive turn with Francis Jennings' *The Invasion of America: Indians, Colonialism, and the Cant of Conquest* (Chapel Hill: University of North Carolina Press, 1975), which used language of conquest and invasion to demonstrate the willing participation of Puritans in the destruction of Native populations. Jennings' work was and remains somewhat controversial, but it started—along with Deloria's writings—an entire generation of revisionism with regard to the history of Native-European interactions. James Axtell built on Jennings' critiques and focused more on the missionary enterprise in his book *The Invasion Within: The Contest of Cultures in Colonial North America* (New York: Oxford University Press, 1985). Native scholars continued to provide their own critiques, often resonating with the new critical turn in the field, including the Osage theologian George E. Tinker's *Missionary Conquest: The Gospel and Native American Cultural Genocide* (Minneapolis: Fortress, 1993). By the 1990s, a more moderate and nuanced interpretative tone prevailed among most scholars; while serious criticisms of Puritan evangelization remained, the focus shifted to Natives themselves. Dozens of books and articles have attempted to understand the responses of Natives to these missionary attempts, along with investigating the exact nature of the missionary project itself.

Richard W. Cogley's *John Eliot's Mission to the Indians before King Philip's War* (Cambridge, Mass.: Harvard University Press, 1999) is still the most comprehensive survey of Eliot's evangelistic work; Cogley additionally helpfully highlights the importance of Eliot's millennial thinking for understanding his evangelistic efforts. For an analysis of Eliot's interest in and use of the Native languages in conversion, see Kathryn N. Gray, *John Eliot and the Praying Indians of Massachusetts Bay: Communities and Connections in Puritan New England* (Lewisburg, Pa.: Bucknell University Press, 2013). Most histories of Native-Indian relations in New England emphasize King Philip's War as the end of an early missionary era, such as Jill Lepore's *The Name of War: King Philip's War and the Origins of American Identity* (New York: Knopf, 1998). Other historians highlight the long-term appropriations by Natives of Christian ideas and rituals that emerged from these seventeenth-century missionary efforts, including David Silverman, *Faith and Boundaries: Colonists, Christianity, and Community among the Wampanoag Indians of Martha's Vineyard, 1600–1871* (New York: Cambridge University Press, 2005) and Linford D. Fisher, *The Indian Great Awakening: Religion and the Shaping of Indian Cultures in Early America* (New York: Oxford University Press, 2012).

Recent scholars of international Protestant missions have also begun to recognize the ways in which Eliot's seventeenth-century missionary projects influenced later generations of missionary activity. This included the forming of the American Board of Commissioners for Foreign Missions in 1812, which explicitly leaned on Eliot's example as it sent missionaries to the Cherokees in the American southeast, to the indigenous populations of Hawaii, and to Muslims in the Middle East, as Ussama Makdisi has shown in *Artillery of Heaven: American Missionaries and the Failed Conversion of the Middle East* (Ithaca, N.Y.: Cornell University Press, 2008).[16]

BAPTISTS IN THE SEVENTEENTH CENTURY

The Baptists in England in the seventeenth century have been closely studied, but the Baptists in America in the same period have not been treated in a detailed history. One reason for this is that the Baptists in England numbered in the thousands by midcentury, while the Baptists in America numbered only in the hundreds even by 1700. Every general history of Baptists in America races through the founding of Baptist churches in the seventeenth century on its way to the Great Awakening in the eighteenth century, when Baptists began to grow as a significant religious group. The *Baptists in Early North America* series, edited by William H. Brackney, aims at deepening the understanding of Baptist history through approximately thirteen volumes.[17] An excellent recent discussion of New

---

[16] See also Sylvester Johnson, "Religion and Empire in Mississippi, 1790–1833," in *Gods of the Mississippi*, ed. Michael Pasquier (Bloomington: Indiana University Press, 2013), 36–55; Hilary E. Wyss, *English Letters and Indian Literacies: Reading, Writing, and New England Missionary Schools, 1750–1830* (Philadelphia: University of Pennsylvania Press, 2012). Joseph Tracy had already identified such a lineage in the nineteenth century: Joseph Tracy, *History of the American Board of Commissioners for Foreign Missions* (New York: M. W. Dodd, 1842).

[17] The first two volumes appeared in 2013: William H. Brackney and Charles Hartman, *Baptists in Early North America*, vol. 1, *Swansea, Massachusetts* (Macon, Ga.: Mercer

England Baptists can be found in Adrian Chastain Weimer, *Martyrs' Mirror: Persecution and Holiness in Early New England* (New York: Oxford University Press, 2011). Likewise, Philip Gura's study of dissent, *A Glimpse of Sion's Glory: Puritan Radicalism in New England, 1620–1660* (Middletown, Conn.: Wesleyan University Press, 1984), has an illuminating chapter on the Baptists. Other studies of early Baptists in New England include Sidney V. James, *John Clarke and His Legacies: Religion and Law in Colonial Rhode Island, 1638–1750* (University Park: Pennsylvania State University Press, 1999) and Nathan E. Wood, *The History of the First Baptist Church of Boston, 1665–1899* (Philadelphia: American Baptist Publication Society, 1899). Also see Edwin S. Gaudstad, *Baptist Piety: The Last Will and Testimony of Obadiah Holmes* (Grand Rapids: Eerdmans, 1978), and the two books by William McLoughlin mentioned above.[18] Janet M. Lindman's *Bodies of Belief: Baptist Community in Early America* (Philadelphia: University of Pennsylvania Press, 2008) deals mainly with the eighteenth century, but it traces some beliefs and practices back to the seventeenth century.

Many authors have written about the English Baptists, beginning with such filiopietist histories as Thomas Crosby, *The History of the English Baptists*, 4 vols. (London, 1738); Joseph Ivimey, *A History of English Baptists*, 4 vols. (London: T. Smith, 1811); Adam Taylor, *History of the General Baptists of England*, 2 vols. (London: T. Bore, 1818); George H. Orchard, *A Concise History of Foreign Baptists*, ed. James R. Graves (Nashville: Graves & Marks, 1855); and Thomas Armitage, *A History of the Baptists Traced by their Vital Principles and Practices from The Time of Our Lord and Savior Jesus Christ to the Year 1886* (New York: Bryan, Taylor, 1887). By the end of the nineteenth century, a more professional and much less admiring generation of Baptist historians emerged, led by William T. Whitley, *The Witness of History to Baptist Principles* (London: Shepard, 1897) and his *A History of British Baptists* (London: Charles Griffin, 1923).

Until Whitley, the standard Baptist view was that the English Baptists had their origins as a result of Anabaptist, especially Mennonite, influence. Baptist origins have continued to be a matter of debate among historians.[19] Scholars of sixteenth-century Anabaptism continue to argue for

---

University Press, 2013), and J. Stanley Lemons, *Baptists in Early North America*, vol. 2, *First Baptist, Providence* (Macon, Ga.: Mercer University Press, 2013).

[18] McLoughlin, *New England Dissent*; McLoughlin, *Soul Liberty*.

[19] The Landmark Baptists still hold to the successionist idea that Baptists are not Protestants, never having been part of the Roman Catholic Church. They trace a succession outside of the Catholic Church from the original church in Jerusalem to modern-day Baptists. No other Baptist or other professional historians accept this theory.

continental Anabaptist influence, including William R. Estep, *The Ana-baptist Story* (Nashville: Broadman Press, 1996). Many scholars of seven-teenth-century Baptists, however, interpret English Baptists as emerging from the Puritan-Separatist movement. The most influential publications in this school of thought are Barrington R. White, *The English Separatist Tradition: From the Marian Martyrs to the Pilgrim Fathers* (London: Oxford University Press, 1971) and White, *The English Baptists of the Seventeenth Century* (Didcot, Oxfordshire: Baptist Historical Society, 1996). White's conclusion is reinforced by Stephen Wright, *The Early English Baptists, 1603–1649* (Woodbridge, UK: Boydell Press, 2006), and echoed by C. Douglas Weaver, *In Search of the New Testament Church: The Baptist Story* (Macon, Ga.: Mercer University Press, 2008) and David W. Bebbington, *Baptists through the Centuries: A History of a Global People* (Waco, Tex.: Baylor University Press, 2010). See also Michael R. Watts, *The Dissenters,* 2 vols. (Oxford: Clarendon, 1978); Leon McBeth, *The Baptist Heritage: Four Centuries of Baptist Witness* (Nashville: Broadman Press, 1987); and William H. Brackney and Paul S. Fiddes, eds., *Pilgrim Pathways: Essays in Baptist History in Honour of R. B. White* (Macon, Ga.: Mercer University Press, 1999).

The complicated evolution of the English Baptists has been outlined in White, *The English Baptists of the Seventeenth Century*; Wright, *The Early English Baptists*; Murray Tolmie, *The Triumph of the Saints: The Separate Churches of London, 1616–1669* (Cambridge: Cambridge University Press, 1977); Jason Lee, *The Theology of John Smyth: Puritan, Separatist, Baptist, Mennonite* (Macon, Ga.: Mercer University Press, 2003); and William H. Brackney, *A Genetic History of Baptist Thought* (Macon, Ga.: Mercer University Press, 2004).

The English Revolution generated a vast literature, but the most help-ful studies for understanding the Baptists in that context are Christo-pher Hill, *The World Turned Upside Down: Radical Ideas during the English Revolution* (New York: Viking Press, 1972); Ann Hughes, *Gangraena and the Struggle for the English Revolution* (London: Oxford University Press, 2004); and J. M. McGregor and B. Reay, eds., *Radical Religion in the English Revolution* (London: Oxford University Press, 1984). The many pam-phlets and tracts of the seventeenth century are accessible through Early English Books Online.

SHORTHAND AND CRYPTOGRAPHY

The history of shorthand and cryptography is its own vibrant little sub-field. A helpful starting point for an overview of early modern shorthand can be found in Frances Henderson, "'Swifte and Secrete Writing' in Seventeenth-Century England, and Samuel Shelton's Brachygraphy," *British Library Journal*, Article 5 (2008). Older and more detailed summaries include *Shorthand and Typewriting* 1 (1895) and Isaac Pitman, *A History of Shorthand*, 3rd ed. (London: I. Pitman, 1891). The single best overview of the history of cryptography is David Kahn, *The Codebreakers: The Story of Secret Writing*, rev. and updated ed. (New York: Scribner, 1996).

Although reports of shorthand usage circulated in Europe in the 1520s and elsewhere (it was used at Martin Luther's trial at the Diet of Worms in 1521, for example), English medical doctor Timothy Bright claimed to have published the first English shorthand manual in 1588.[20] Bright protected his invention by receiving a patent from Queen Elizabeth that same year and forbidding the republication of the book, titled *Characterie: An Arte of Short, Swifte, and Secrete Writing by Character*, by other printers.[21] In part because Bright's system was cumbersome (it consisted of a core of 536 characters), it was soon replaced by subsequent authors. The clergyman John Willis developed a novel shorthand system, which he published in *The Art of Stenographie* (London, 1602). Because it had a far smaller core of symbols (roughly the same number as the English alphabet), it opened the door for several new derivative systems in the decades that followed.[22] It was Willis' shorthand system that Williams likely learned and adapted for his own use. The most popular early modern English shorthand system was devised by Thomas Shelton in the 1620s. The first manual of his shorthand was published in 1626 as *Short-writing*; from 1636 it appeared as *Tachygraphy: The Most Exact and Compendious Methode of Short and Swift Writing That Hath Ever yet Beene Published by Any*.[23] Well-known examples of early modern English shorthand usage include Roger Morrice, who used Willis' system, and Samuel Pepys, who used Shelton's system.[24] In New England, a fascinating example of the use of shorthand can be found in William G. McLoughlin and Martha Whiting Davidson, "The Baptist Debate of April 14–15, 1668," *Proceedings of the Massachusetts Historical Society* 76 (January 1, 1964): 91–133.

---

[20] *Shorthand and Typewriting* 1 (1895): 79–81.

[21] Timothy Bright, *Characterie: An Arte of Short, Swifte, and Secrete Writing by Character* (London: I. Windet, 1588), title page. For the patent, see *Shorthand and Typewriting* 1 (1895): 81.

[22] Henderson, "'Swifte and Secrete Writing,'" 3–4.

[23] Henderson, "'Swifte and Secrete Writing,'" 4–5.

[24] Mark Goldie et al., eds., *The Entring Book of Roger Morrice, 1677–1691*, 6 vols. (Woodbridge, UK: Boydell & Brewer, 2007); Samuel Pepys, *The Diary of Samuel Pepys* (n.p.: BiblioLife, 2008).

For those interested in attempting a more complete transcription of Williams' "A Brief Reply," the book into which Williams wrote this shorthand essay, *An Essay Towards the Reconciling of Differences Among Christians*, is at the John Carter Brown Library; high-resolution images are also available online.[25]

[25] http://archive.org/details/essaytowardsreco00will.

INDEX

Abraham, 28, 60n136, 73–74, 76, 79, 80n118, 85–86, 120, 125, 125n23, 139, 140, 141–42, 141n67, 151, 159n15, 162, 163n20–22, 168–69, 174n46, 174n47, 175

Act of Uniformity, 27, 58n103, 113, 178n55

Adamites, 25

Adams, John, 21, 55n62

affusion (pouring): *see* baptism

American Indians: *see* Indians

Amsterdam, 21, 73n13

Amsterdam Declaration of 1611, 21; *see also* Baptists

Anabaptists, 20–22, 31, 52n44, 54n59, 55n62, 55n63; Baptists denied association with, 21, 22, 55n63; Baptists identified as, 19, 21, 22, 24, 25, 26, 27, 30–31, 52n41, 52n44, 55n62, 57n85, 57n90, 59n117, 77, 77n76, 77n84, 78, 159, 159n14, 164–70, 172n42, 177, 178n55

Anabaptistry, 19

Anglican: *see* Church of England

Angus Library, Oxford, 48n7

Antichrist/Antichristians, 20, 22, 23, 24, 36, 48n6, 51n38, 54n60, 55n67, 58n107, 177

Antinomians, 20, 52n40, 178n55

antipaedobaptism: *see* baptism, believer's

Apostle to the Indians, 33, 62n181, 155n6, 167n30; *see also* John Eliot

Apostolic Succession, 22, 54n60

Apostolici, 25

Aquidneck Island, 4

Arians, 20

Arminians/Arminianism, 20

Arnold, William, 61n175

Art of Stenographie, The, 8, 49n18, 49n19; *see also* John Willis

Aspinwall, William, 59n108

Baillie, Robert, 24, 25, 57n88, 57n99

baptism, 10, 23, 18, 19; believer's, 1, 10, 18–32, 47, 52n41, 54n59, 54n60, 55–56n71, 60n124, 60n130, 113–53; controversies regarding, 20, 22–23, 25, 27–32, 57n102, 58n107, 60n124, 113–53, 157–79; immersion/dipping, 18, 20, 22, 23, 25, 29, 32, 53–54n53, 55–56n71, 55n64, 55n68, 56n77, 60n149, 83, 83n164, 84, 113–53, 177–78n55, 183n166; infant/sprinkling, 18, 29, 31, 130–31, 55–56n71, 60n124, 60n130, 61n163, 83n166,

157–79; of Natives, 20, 32, 35–36, 37, 39–40, 44, 46, 47, 65n207, 77; pouring/affusion, 18, 21, 29, 83n166, 173, 173n43

Baptism Discovered Plainly and Faithfully, 1, 10, 26, 48n7, 72n3, 78n95, 113–53; *see also* John Norcott

baptistic, 18 19, 21, 27, 32, 46, 52n41

Baptists, 3, 10, 18, 19, 21–23, 24–25, 26–27, 29–32, 51–52n39, 52n40, 52n41, 52n44, 53–54n44, 53n50, 53–54n53, 54n59, 54n60, 55n61, 55n62, 55n63, 55n67, 55n70, 55n71, 57n91, 57n99, 57n102, 58n104, 58n107, 59n115, 61n116, 61n170, 61n172, 61n175, 73n13, 77n76, 78–79n97, 83n166, 87, 87n229, 113–14, 117n10, 159n14, 164, 172n42; Anabaptists, so called, 19, 21, 22, 24, 25, 26, 27, 30–31, 52n41, 52n44, 55n62, 57n85, 57n90, 59n117, 77, 77n76, 77n84, 78, 159, 159n14, 164–70, 172n42, 177, 178n55; General, 22, 24, 31, 55n71; Landmark, 52n40, 53–54n44; numbers and growth of, 57n91, 59n115; origin of, 21–23, 52n41; Particular, 22, 24, 31, 48n8, 55n67, 55n71, 58n104, 61n173, 178n55; persecution of, 26–27, 55n61, 57n93, 58n104, 58n106, 61n173

Barber, Edward, 22, 23, 60n149, 61n154

Bartholin, Thomas, 10, 50n24

Bartholinus Anatomy, 10, 50n24

Bartlett, John Russell, 49n13

Baxter, Richard, 48n6

Billerica (Mass.), 27

Blackwood, Christopher, 48n6

Blake, Thomas, 48n6

Bloody Tenent Yet More Bloody, The, 42, 68n243, 69n263; *see also* Roger Williams

Bloudy Tenent of Persecution, The, 4, 14, 56n83, 57n84, 62n177, 68n243; *see also* Roger Williams

Book of Common Prayer, 114

Book of Martyrs, The, 68n248, 138, 144; *see also* John Foxe

Boston (Mass.), 3, 51n38, 59n117, 153, 155, 177–78n55

Brackney, William H., 22

Bradstreet, Simon, xiii, 42

breaking the code: *see* code breaking

Brief Answer to a Small Book Written by John Norcot Against Infant-Baptisme, A, 3, 10, 37, 48n9, 50n27, 72, 72n2, 153, 158–79; *see also* John Eliot

Brief Reply to a Small Book Written by John Eliot, A, 3, 5, 10, 17, 20, 37, 39, 44, 45, 46, 48n10, 71–88; *see also* Roger Williams

Bright, Timothy, 7, 49n20

Brown Jr., Nicholas, xii, 49n16

Brown University, 1, 47n3, 74n4, 78n5, 50n25, 68n248

Brownists, 20, 25

Bunyan, John, 58n104

Calvinist Baptists: *see* Baptists, Particular

Cambridge (Mass.), 40, 43, 59n119, 59n120

Cambridge University, 3, 7, 59n117, 59n119, 59n120, 60n121, 153, 177n55

Canonicus, 63n184

Carpenter, William, 61n175

Catholics, 20, 21, 22, 26, 38, 44, 54n60, 58n106, 113, 138n55, 138n58, 139, 139n59, 150n79

Charles I, King, 50n23

Charles II, King, 26, 51n37, 58n103, 58n106, 113

Charlestown (Mass.), 27

charter: *see* Rhode Island 1663 charter

Charterhouse School, 7

Christenings Make Not Christians, 11,

20, 35–37, 42, 44, 54n55, 62n179, 64n200; *see also* Roger Williams

Church of England, 3, 19, 21, 22, 23, 26, 33, 55n47, 55n48, 57n88, 58n103, 58n106, 113, 153, 178n55

circumcision, 28–29, 58n107, 81, 85–86, 113, 136–37, 140, 141, 144, 149, 150, 159, 161, 164, 174–75, 174–75n48, 177

Clarendon Code, 26, 58n103, 113

Clarke, John, 20, 26, 52n40, 55n71, 59n108, 60n122, 61n175

Clear Sun-shine of the Gospel, The, 40, 42, 66n232, 66n233, 67n240; *see also* Thomas Shepard

Cobbett, Thomas, 27, 60n122

code breaking, 1, 5–17, 47n3

Coke, Edward, 3, 7, 49n17, 49n18

Cole, Robert, 61n175

communion, 27, 30, 53n47, 55–56n71, 75, 78, 78n91, 160–61, 162, 165, 166, 167, 177–78n55

Communion of Churches, 155; *see also* John Eliot

Connecticut, 4, 45, 59n119, 154

consonantary, 8

conversion of Indians, 20, 34–40, 47, 62n179, 64n195, 64n199, 64n200, 65n215, 66n226, 66n232, 66n235, 66n236, 66n237, 153–55

Cosmographie in Foure Bookes, 6, 9–10, 13, 17, 50n23; *see also* Peter Heylyn

Cotton, John, 5, 27, 42, 59n117, 59n118, 67n237

covenant, 26, 28–30, 37–38, 59n110, 59n120, 60n130, 60n140, 65n218, 74–80, 78n91, 86, 140–41, 140n64, 140n65, 140n66, 141–44, 146, 158–170, 159n15, 162n18, 162n19, 163n20, 163n21, 163n22, 163n23, 163n26, 167n31, 167n32, 174–77, 174n47, 179; church, 54n40, 59n120, 60n130, 65n218; Half-Way Covenant, 26, 59n110, 78n91; new, 29,

60n140, 75, 80, 140n66, 141–44, 146, 162, 162n19, 164–67, 174–76, 174n47; old, 28–30, 37–38, 59n120, 74–80, 140, 140n64, 140n65, 141–44, 146, 158–70, 159n15, 162n18, 163n20, 163n21, 163n22, 163n23, 163n26, 167n31, 167n32, 174n47, 175, 177, 179

Crandall, John, 26, 61n175

Cromwell, Oliver, 26, 58n104, 177–78n55

cryptography, 7, 188–189; *see also* shorthand; code breaking

Danforth, Thomas, 50n30

Declaration of Indulgence (1672), 26, 58n106

Deer Island, 44

Dexter, Henry Martyn, 48n7, 48n8

Dippers, Dipt, 25, 57n58, 172n42; *see also* Daniel Featley

dipping: *see* baptism

Donatists, 25

Dorchester (Mass.), 59n118

Dunster, Henry, 27

Dutch, 33, 49n18, 51n37, 117n10, 129

Eastern Niantic (Indians), 69n264

Edwards, Thomas, 24, 25, 57n88

Eliot, John, 3–4, 10–11, 19, 20, 26–33, 37–47, 48n9, 49n10, 51n38, 60n131, 62n181, 66n232, 67n236, 67n237, 67n239, 68n249, 68n259, 68n260, 69n264, 71, 72, 72n2, 72n11, 72, 73n179, 73n19, 74–88, 117n8, 140n64, 153–55, 157–58, 159n14, 167n30; historiography, 184–86; Roger Williams and, 3, 4, 10, 11, 19, 27–29, 31–33, 37, 38–47, 48n10, 67n237, 67n239, 68n249, 71–88, 78–79n97, 79n100, 84n186, 140n64, 153, 153n1, 167n30; *see also A Brief Answer to a Small Book Written by John Norcot Against Infant-Baptisme*

Eliot Bible: *see* Indian Bible

Eliot tracts, 40, 43, 66n233, 67n240, 154

English Revolution (English Civil War), 23, 24, 55n61

Enthusiasts, 20, 25

Essay Towards the Reconciling of Differences Among Christians, An, 5–7, 47n2, 48n10, 50n33, 51n36, 72; *see also* Mystery Book

excommunication, 19

Experiments in Spiritual Life and Health, 51n38: *see also* Roger Williams

Familists, 20

Featley, Daniel, 24, 25, 57n85, 172n42

Field, Edward, 49n13

Field, Jonathan Beecher, 35, 59n108, 64n200

Fifth Monarchists, 58n103

Fisher, Linford D., xiii, 47n3, 67n236, 69n260, 69n264, 70n266, 154n2, 186

Fisher, Samuel, 22

First Baptist Church in America, 3, 19, 52n40, 53–54n53

First Baptist church in England, 21

First Baptist Church, Newport, 52n40, 55n71

First Great Awakening, 46, 69n265

Fox, George, 65n215

Foxe, John, 68n248, 238n59

frequency analysis, 7–8; *see also* code breaking

Gangraena, 24, 25; *see also* Thomas Edwards

George Fox Digg'd out of his Burrowes, 5, 51n38, 53n47; *see also* Roger Williams

Gilpin, Clark, 53n49, 62n179

Gookin, Daniel, 46, 68n255, 69n264

Gorton, Samuel, 59n108, 59n117

Goths, 15, 17, 51n35

Grantham, Thomas, 48n6

Great Apostasy, 23, 54n60

Great Awakening; *see* First Great Awakening

Half-Way Covenant, 26, 59n110, 78n91

Harris, William, 61n175

Helwys, Thomas, 21, 22, 30, 31, 56n72, 57n93

Heresiography, 24, 57n87; *see also* Ephraim Pagitt

heresiologists/heresiographers, 20, 24, 25, 52–53n46, 52n51, 56n82

heresy/heresies, 20, 21, 24, 25, 56n82

Heylyn, Peter, 6, 9–10, 13, 17, 50n23

Hicks, Thomas, 114

Holifield, E. Brooks, 38

Holliman/Holyman, Ezekiel, 19, 52n42

Holmes, Obadiah, 26–27, 61n175

Hooker, Thomas, 27, 59n118, 59n119, 59n120, 153

Hutchinson, Anne, 19, 42, 52n44, 117n59, 67n239, 153

immersion: *see* baptism

Independents, 23–24, 56n83

Indian Bible, 41, 43, 47n5, 50n25, 68n247, 68n248, 68n260, 154, 154n5

Indian language, 32, 35, 43, 66n230, 68n248, 154n5

Indians, 4, 33, 35, 37, 42, 44, 45, 46, 47, 62n177, 63n182, 63n184, 69n263, 69n264, 155; Pequot War, 34, 62n177, 69n263; King Philip's War, 4, 5, 13, 33, 44–45, 46, 49n11, 49n12, 69n263, 69n264, 155; raid on Providence, 4, 13; *see also* conversion of Indians

Jackson, John, 67n237

Jacob, Henry, 55n67, 58n104, 177–78n55

James I, King, 21, 153

JCB: *see* John Carter Brown Library

Jessey, Henry, 55n67, 58n104, 177–78n55

Jesuits, 25, 138, 138n55

Jews, 14, 17, 125, 139, 158, 159, 160, 163, 175, 178

John Carter Brown Library, xi–xiii, 5, 47n2, 49n15, 190

John Hay Library, 48n5, 50n25, 68n248

Keach, Benjamin, 31, 61n172, 114

Key into the Language of America, A, 3, 32, 34–36, 39, 45, 62n177, 64n195, 64n199, 64n200, 66n232, 68n248; *see also* Roger Williams

King James Bible, 50n27, 73n13

King Philip's War, 4, 5, 13, 33, 44–45, 46, 49n11, 49n12, 69n263, 69n264, 155

Knollys, Hanserd, 56n57, 56n77, 58n104, 58n107, 177–78n55

LaFantasie, Glenn, 39, 65n207

Lambe, Thomas, 48n6

Laud, William, 50n23, 59n117, 59n119

Lemons, J. Stanley, xiii, 47n3, 187n17

Lepore, Jill, 49n12, 68n259

Leverett, John, 50n32

Libertinists, 20

London, 3, 21, 22, 23, 24, 33, 37, 40, 41, 55n67, 57n91, 58n104, 59n108, 59n120, 61n173, 63n184, 64n195, 64n199, 66n232, 113, 154, 177–78n55

London Confession (1644), 22, 56n77

Lucar, Mark, 20

Luther, Samuel, 55–56n71

Lynn (Mass.), 26, 27, 60n122

Mamusse Wunneetupanatamwe Up-Biblum God; *see* Indian Bible

Marcionites, 25

marginalia, 1, 6, 9–10, 13–17

Martha's Vineyard, 66n230, 153

Massachusett (language), 39, 43, 153, 154

Massachusetts Bay Colony, 3, 4, 10, 13, 19, 24, 26, 32, 33, 34, 35, 37, 39, 41, 42, 43, 45, 46, 47, 51n38, 52n40, 59n117, 59n118, 59n119, 59n120, 61n175, 62n179, 64n199, 67n237, 67n239, 69n263, 153, 154

Massachusetts Court of Assistants, 19

Massachusetts General Court, 19, 34, 37, 39, 40, 41, 45, 63n186

Massachusetts Standing Order, 21, 55n62

Massasoit, 34, 63n184

Mason-Brown, Lucas, xii, 47n3, 47n4

Mather, Cotton, 155, 155n7

Mather, Increase, 65n218

Mather, Richard, 27, 59n118

May, John, 49n18

Mayhew Jr./Sr., Thomas, 153

Miantonomi, 63n184

Miller, Perry, 53n52

Millenarianism, 58n103, 62n179

Moors, 15, 17

Münster, 21, 26, 52n44, 55n62

Murton, John, 57n85

Myles, John, 27, 55–56n71

Mystery Book, xi, xiii, 5; *see also An Essay Towards the Reconciling of Differences Among Christians*

Narragansett Bay, 3, 4, 33, 34, 35

Narragansetts (Indians), 4, 33, 35, 37, 42, 45, 46, 62n177, 63n182, 63n184, 69n263, 69n264

Natick (Mass.), 154, 154n4

Native Americans; *see* Indians

New England, 3, 4, 13, 18, 26, 27, 32, 33, 34, 35, 43, 45, 46, 51n38, 52n41, 52–53n46, 53n49, 59n115, 62n181, 644n199, 64n200, 65n218, 66n236, 69n263, 78n91, 153, 154, 155

New England Company, 33, 62n181, 154, 154n2

New England Way, 23
New England's First Fruits, 35, 64n195, 64n198, 64n199, 66n232
New Model Army, 24, 25
Newport (R.I.), 26, 49n14, 52n40, 55
Niles, Samuel, 46
Norcott, John, 1, 3, 10, 26, 27, 28, 29, 30, 31, 32, 48n7, 48n9, 72n3, 73n13, 78–79n97, 82, 86n214, 87n234, 113–14, 125n20, 125n21, 127n27, 130n36, 140n64, 155, 159n14; *see also Baptism Discovered Plainly and Faithfully*

original sin, 31

paedobaptism: *see* baptism, infant
Pagitt, Ephraim, 24
pamphlets and tracts, 5, 22, 23, 25, 27, 37, 40, 48n6, 55n70, 56n79, 56n83, 58n107, 66n230, 154–55n5, 172n42
paper, scarcity of, 1, 13, 50n32
Parker, William, 48n6
patent: *see* Rhode Island 1644 patent
Pelagians, 20
Pembroke College, 3, 7
Penn, William, 114
Pepys, Samuel, 11, 50n28
Pequot War, 34, 62n177, 69n263
persecution, 21, 22, 26, 44, 55n61, 58n103, 58n104, 59n109
Peter, Hugh, 19, 59n108
Phillips, George, 27, 60n121
Plymouth Colony, 4, 20, 26, 33, 34, 45, 55n71, 63n184
Polygamists, 25
Portsmouth Compact, 52n40
pouring: *see* baptism
Praying Indians, 39, 44, 45, 68n259
Praying Towns, 39, 40 (Map 2), 45, 66n230, 154
Presbyterians, 23, 24, 57n90
Providence (R.I.), 3–5, 11, 13, 19, 20, 34, 45, 52n40, 52n46, 53n47, 53n49, 55n71, 61n175

Providence Plantations, 3, 34
Prynne, William, 24, 56n83
Psychopannychists, 25
Punham, 67n237
Puritan Revolution: *see* English Revolution
Puritans, 3, 10, 22, 26, 39, 42, 47, 50n23, 58n103, 69n263, 113, 150n80

Quakers, 5, 26, 51n38, 53n47, 57n99, 61n175, 114

Reform of the Church of England, 3, 23–24, 55n67
Rehoboth (Plymouth Colony; now Mass.), 20
religious liberty/freedom, toleration, 5, 17, 21, 24, 25, 26, 37, 42, 46, 51n37, 52–53n46, 56n83, 57n85, 57n93, 113
Rhode Island, 3–4, 13, 17, 19, 26, 34, 45, 46, 59n115, 61n175, 63n184, 67n237, 67n239, 69n263
Rhode Island 1644 patent, 35
Rhode Island 1663 charter, 51n37
Rhode Island Historical Society, 47n5, 50n25
Ritor, Andrew, 22, 23
Rogers, Horatio, 49n13
Roman Catholic Church: *see* Catholics
Rowlandson, Mary, 45, 68n257, 68n258
Roxbury (Mass.), 3, 4, 33, 42, 153

sachem, 37, 42, 44, 69n264, 154
Sadleir, Ann, 49n17
Salem (Mass.), 19, 33, 63n187
Scott, Catherine, 19, 52n44
Scott, Richard, 19, 52n44, 53n47, 61n175
Seekers/Seekerism, 20, 25, 52n43, 53n49, 53n50, 53n52, 67n237
Separatist/Separatists, 3, 19, 21, 22, 23, 53n48, 55n67, 73n13, 130n36, 177–78n55
Shawmut: *see* Boston

Shepard, Thomas, 27, 42, 59n120
Short Declaration of the Mistery of Iniquity, A, 21, 57n93; *see also* Thomas Helwys
shorthand, 1–2, 7–17, 49n18, 49n19, 49n20, 50n21, 50n25, 50n34, 71, 188–89
slavery/servitude, 5, 45–46, 69n263
Smyth, John, 21, 31, 54n60
Sober Word to a Serious People, A, 67n237
Society for the Propagation of the Gospel in New England, 153, 66n236
Socinians, 20
Southwark Church, 55n67, 57n85, 172n42, 177–78n55
Soveraignty & Goodness of God, The, 45, 68n257; *see also* Mary Rowlandson
Spaniards, 16, 17
spiritual patrimony, 28, 37–39, 65n218, 73n19, 78, 78n90, 79, 79n97, 79n103, 166; *see also* covenant
Spilsbury, John, 22, 31, 54n60, 60n122
Spitalfields, 21
sprinkling: *see* baptism
Spurgeon, Charles H., 48n8
Standard Confession (1660), 22
Star Chamber, 7, 49n17
stenography, 7, 11; *see also The Art of Stenographie*
Swan Alley Baptist Church, 58n104, 177–78n55
Swansea (Plymouth Colony; now Mass.), 20, 27, 55–56n71

Taylor, Jeremy, 48n6
Test Act (1673), 58n106
Thomason, George, 56n79
Throckmorton, John, 61n175
Tillinghast, Pardon, 61n175
Treatise Against Toleration, 25

United Colonies, 4

Venner, Thomas, 58n103, 59n108

Verrazzano, Giovanni da, 33

Wales, 27, 58n104
Wampanoags (Indians), 33, 44, 63n184, 155
Watertown (Mass.), 60n121
Way of the Congregational Churches Cleared, The, 42
Wequash, 35, 36, 64n195
Whitley, William Thomas, 48n7
Whitsitt, William, 53–54n53
Whore of Babylon, 22
Widow Tweedy, xi, 5, 49n14, 49n16
Williams, Providence, 69n263
Williams, Mary, 19
Williams, Roger, 1, 3–5, 7–11, 13, 14–20, 23, 24, 25, 27–30, 31–37, 38–39,40, 41, 42–45, 46, 47n1, 47n2, 47n5, 48n9, 48–49n10, 49n11, 49n16, 49n17, 49n18, 50n25, 50n26, 50n27, 50n32, 50–51n35, 51n36, 51n37, 51n38, 51–52n39, 52n40, 52n41, 52n43, 53n47, 53n48, 53n49, 53n50, 53n52, 53–54n53, 54n60, 55n71, 56n82, 56n83, 57n85, 59n108, 59n117, 61n170, 61n175, 62n177, 62n178, 62n179, 62n180, 63n184, 63n187, 63n192, 64n193, 64n195, 64n199, 64n200, 65n207, 65n215, 65n226, 66n232, 66n234, 67n237, 67n239, 68n243, 68n248, 68n249, 69n261, 69n263, 71, 72n1, 72n3, 73n13, 73n19, 76n57, 78n95, 78–79n97, 79n101, 79n103, 79n106, 84n186, 88, 140n64, 153, 153n1, 167n30; baptism of, 19, 20, 53–54n53, 54n60; baptism, on, 18–20, 27–30, 31–32, 47, 52n40, 65n226; Baptist claims, 18, 51n39, 52n40, 52n41, 53–54n53; biography, 3–5, 7, 19–20, 33–35, 45–46, 52n41, 63n187, 65n207; controversialist, 3, 18–19, 24, 27, 32, 35, 38–39, 42–45, 51n38, 53n47, 53n48, 59n117, 78–79n97, 84n186; conversion of

Indians, 4, 32–37, 38–39, 42–44,
45, 46, 47, 62n179, 63n184, 63n192,
64n195, 64n199, 64n200, 65n207,
65n215, 65n226, 66n232, 66n234,
67n237, 167n30; excommunication, 19; founding the first Baptist
church, 19, 52n40, 54n60, 55n71;
historiography, 17, 19, 32–33, 51n37,
51–52n39, 62n177, 62n178, 62n179,
180–84; Indian relations, 4–5, 19,
32–33, 34–35, 45–46, 63n192,
66n234, 69n261, 69n263; John Eliot
and, 3, 4, 10, 11, 19, 27–29, 31–33,
37, 38–47, 48n10, 67n237, 67n239,
68n249, 71–88, 78–79n97, 79n100,
84n186, 140n64, 153, 153n1,
167n30; King Philip's War, 4–5,
45–46, 69n263; linguistic abilities,
33, 35, 36, 39, 43, 62n179, 64n199;
martyr/witness, 20, 53n49; publications, 4, 5, 32–33, 34, 35, 51n38,
62n177, 62n178, 62n179, 64n193,
64n199, 64n200, 68n243; religious
liberty/freedom, 37, 56n82, 57n85;
Seeker, 20, 25, 52n43, 53n49,
53n50, 53n52, 67n237; shorthand,
1, 5, 7–11, 14–17, 47n5, 48–49n10,
49n17, 49n18, 50n25, 50n26,
50–51n35, 68n248, 71, 72n1; trouble
with Baptists, 61n175
Willis, Edmond, 49n20
Willis, John, 7, 49n18, 49n19, 49n20
Willis, Robert, 49n18
Wilson, Rev. John, 153, 155n6
Winslow, Edward, 34, 66n233
Winslow, Josiah, 50n32
Winthrop, John, Jr., 20
Winthrop, John, Sr., 19, 34, 44n52,
53n47, 53n48, 60n121, 63n187,
67n239
Woburn (Mass.), 27
Wollaston (Mass.; now Quincy, Mass.),
33
Wright, Stephen, 22